Mahaprabhu Aghoreshwar
Baba Bhagwan Ram

The Book of Aghor Wisdom

Translated By Akinchan Ram

Cover illustration: Baba Bhagwan Ram

Published in 2007 by
Indica Books
D 40 / 18 Godowlia
Varanasi - 221 001 (U.P.)
India
email: indicabooks@satyam.net.in

ISBN: 81-86569-66-9

Printed in India by First Impression, Delhi
011-22484048, 09811224048

Table of Contents

Baba,

This book has your thoughts, ideas and blessings. My effort has been simply to translate it. I offer it humbly in your holy hands.

-Akinchan

Acknowledgement

A book like this one, dealing with mystical and social concepts and ideas, some with very culturally nuanced meanings, is always the product of willing cooperation of many people. Baba Bhagwan Ram had asked me to translate this book before he left his body, and I am grateful for his instruction. Baba Harihar Ram at the Sonoma Yoga Ashram, California, was always enthusiastic about the project, and could seek the help of Jaan Haag to edit the manuscript I sent to him. My deep thanks to both of them. Equally important is the interest of Baba Gautam Ram Ji in the project, and the consequent assiduousness with which Shri Anjani Kumar Jha, Librarian of the *Aghor Shodh Evam Seva Sansthan*, set to make it a reality, the enthusiastic support of Shri Arun Kumar Singh and rest of the folks at Baba Kinaram Sthal, too numerous to count, without whose good wishes and blessings this book would not have become a reality. I would like to extend special thanks to Shri Dilip Kumar Jaiswal of Indica Books, as well as *Aghor Shodh Evam Seva Sansthan*, for agreeing to publish the book in its present cover.

Note on the transcription

As Baba Bhagwan Ram would speak in Hindi or Bhojpuri, we have chosen to transcribe Indian words as they are pronounced in these languages (losing the final short *a*), instead of their usual transcription in Sanskrit. In this way, we write *Brahm* instead of *Brahman*, *pran* instead of *prana*, etc.

Preface

This book is a translation of the words of Aghoreshwar Mahaprabhu Baba Bhagwan Ram, as presented in the book *Aghor Vachan Shastra*. Baba would communicate in either Hindi or a dialect of Hindi called Bhojpuri, depending upon with whom he spoke. He would use language in its most cogent and pithy manner. To Baba, language was not just a means of communication, to make the other person understand in the simplest, clearest, most lucid terms the deep import of even the most complex concepts and ideas, but also to express love and other emotions. However, in translating those ideas from Hindi into English, the simplicity of the presentation or the lucidity of expression is sometimes lost. I apologize for that. Also, oftentimes in translating complex ideas it requires an interpretation of the idea by the translator, and the translator thereby becomes the eye, as it were, through which the reader sees the text. That is inevitable, but I have tried to stick as close to the original meaning of Baba's words as possible.

Spoken language was only one of the means of communication used by Baba. There lived in him a much greater communication system, one based entirely on a person's being 'in tune' with him. Baba had a very subtle and refined language of proximity, of body language, of unsaid words and gestures rather than the spoken ones, a language that always spoke to a greater or lesser degree, depending upon how 'in tune' the other person was with Baba at the moment of communication. The raising of an eye, or taking of a step, the placing of his palm on his cheek, an inquisitive look, a word mumbled in passing, a turn while walking, the raising of a hand, the rejection or acceptance of foods and gifts apparently at random; all these may have seemed as so many eccentricities of an enlightened person to many, but to those who knew, they spoke more volumes than spoken words ever could. That language added subtle meanings to all that Baba said overtly, and it made his communication both very contextual and personal. There were numerous occasions when Baba would speak to a large gathering of people, yet his choice of words and narrative examples, together with his gestures, would be such that a single person within that large crowd could properly understand the various levels of meaning being imparted in a single sentence, whether the spoken message was exclusively for him or not. Unfortunately, in a translated text, that complex structure of meaning is possible only with great difficulty.

The limitations of this text are purely the shortcomings of my ability of translation. It is seldom easy to transpose ideas absolutely from one language into another. Also, languages lend themselves more easily to descriptions of certain kinds of concepts than others, with subtleties most easily understandable only within a cultural context. In translating what Baba had to say, some of the flavour of how he said things is lost, and some words or concepts can, at best, be translated only tangentially. But I have made an honest attempt here to present accurately what Baba brought up from the churnings of the depths of his inner ocean of wisdom.

In the process of giving a final shape to the book, several people have looked over my translation and have provided helpful suggestions as well as editing help with the manuscript. I would like to extend my heartfelt thanks to all of them, especially to Jan Haag at the Sri Sarveshwari Samooh ashram, Sonoma, California. Jan's undaunted perseverance turned the sometimes obscure wording of complex concepts in my translation into lucid English understandable to all. I am also indebted to Baba Harihar Ram of the Sonoma ashram, as well as Lisa Wilcox of the Center for Southeast Asian Studies at Northern Illinois University, for looking over the manuscript and giving me very helpful suggestions.

Aghoreshwar Mahaprabhu Baba Bhagwan Ram: A Brief Biography

There is a badly potholed road that starts from the Ara railway station in the Bhojpur district of Bihar and heads Northeast into the countryside, meandering for eight miles through rice fields and fruit orchards. It turns into a dusty bullock cart track halfway along, before it leads into the large village of Gundi. Even today, Gundi is a beautiful village, abundant with groves of mango, guava, *peepal*, *neem* and banyan trees, lush green fields with the distant sounds of water flowing through irrigation channels and a serenity in the atmosphere that seems to still the mind and makes the senses strain to hear the whispers of nature. Walking through the lanes of the village brings into view a temple to Lord Ranganathan, a form of God Vishnu, and an ancient Shiva temple with its tall, sculpted silhouette against a line of trees, its walls crumbling with roots poking through the hallowed stones, reminding the visitor of the classic British lithographs portraying eternal India. But the most famous temple here is known as the Yagyawatar temple, a Vishnu temple where people say many enlightened saints have stayed and worked for the benefit of the community. In fact, residents of this approximately 30,000 strong community believe that their village has been a blessed seeding ground for many spiritual seekers who have started their arduous, and often perilous journey, from the thatched huts set in its fields.

Aghoreshwar Mahaprabhu Baba Bhagwan Ram Ji was born on Sunday, the 12th of September 1937 to Babu Baijnath Singh and his wife Lakhraji Devi. Theirs was a prosperous, land-owning family with enough spare time from work for Babu Baijnath Singh to indulge in his passion for wrestling. The story of his son's birth, as narrated by the villagers, makes fascinating reading. Babu Baijnath Singh always wanted a boy, but even after eighteen years of marriage he did not have one. Given to the rhythms of agricultural life in rural India, he would get up well before the crack of dawn and go for a morning dip in the holy river Ganga, about three miles north of the village. To most Indians, Ganga is a sacred river with wish-granting powers, and he too would pray to her for the blessing of a son. One day, in the dim pre-dawn light on the riverbank, he met a *sadhu* (an ascetic) with matted locks, a long beard, and ashes on his body. The saint blessed him and gave him a fruit to share with his wife with the intention of having a son. Babu Baijnath Singh did as he was instructed and after nine months, a son was indeed born to them. The couple was ecstatic with joy. Since their son had been born after long years of prayers and by the blessing of a saint, they named the child 'Bhagwan', literally, God. But their Bhagwan was an unusual child. Their son had a long lock of hair on his head which led the village children to nickname him 'Jatuli', literally, one with a *yogi*'s matted locks. True to his name, Bhagwan had an overwhelming spiritual quest ever since his infancy. Many believe he was not an ordinary soul because miracles kept happening around him throughout his childhood. He had a definite, perceptible healing ability that sometimes cured a sick villager, sometimes a buffalo having difficulty in birthing its calf. On many occasions baby Bhagwan would disappear from between his mother and grandmother in bed and would be discovered elsewhere, alone. There is an especially interesting story of an event that happened on the sixth day after his birth. In the afternoon at around twelve or one o'clock, a strong dust storm began to blow everything around the family courtyard. Lakhraji Devi, Bhagwan's mother, got up and went out to pick up the clothes that were drying out in the sun lest they be blown away. When she came back with the clothes in her arms she saw that the door to go into her room had slammed shut in the strong wind. She tried to open the door but it did not budge. It seemed as if someone had latched it shut from the inside. She peeked through the crack in the door and saw that her baby was not on the bed. Instead, she saw a boy of about ten or twelve years sitting on the floor in the lotus position, meditating. She panicked with the thought that some one had stolen her baby and began to scream. But no sounds came from her mouth. Suddenly, for no apparent reason, the door opened with a bang and she rushed inside. That meditating boy said to her, "I am the very same, mother; don't worry". She blinked and looked again; she saw he was again her newborn baby.

For those who took care of him, such stories of unusual sightings and visions were common throughout Bhagwan's childhood. Another remarkable story is told of his drowning in the waters of Ganga during a great flood, when he was three years old. Floodwaters came right into the village and children would splash and play in the swollen river. One day, as the children were playing, little Jatuli went under. The children began to scream that Jatuli had drowned when he did not come up. Fruitlessly, for two days the villagers searched of him with divers and nets; on the third day someone spotted his characteristic *jata* in the waters. He was fished out and was found to be still breathing. This was a true miracle for the villagers and they began to have a special respect for Babu Baijnath Singh's little son.

Bhagwan lost his father when he was just five years old. He was raised by his mother and his maternal grand-parents, all of whom began to be neglected by their extended family and the larger community, especially since some members of the family may have had their eye on their landed property. All this made no difference to little Bhagwan, whose spiritual quest not only began to manifest with full force, but also began to break the bounds of acceptable family life. The first evidence of this was his absolute reluctance to study or attend school. He would regularly run away from school and sit in a mango grove to meditate or play at performing rituals. Often, he would gather his little classmates under a huge banyan tree to sing *bhajans*, devotional songs in praise of the gods. The second was his characteristic tendency to not live at home. He would walk out of his family's house and spend the night under a tree in a grove, or in a field on the outskirts of the village, and not return home for days. While other children were afraid of the dark

— and of ghosts — little Bhagwan knew no fear. In this time, he once lived for several days under a huge banyan tree in a grove that the villagers thought to be haunted. It made no difference to Bhagwan, but his mother got very upset and he was forcibly brought back home, only to run away again. During religious festivals, especially during the nine-day long sacred period called *navaratri*, he would fast and seek the company of ascetics and monks who came through the village. Such a regimen of physical abstinence and devotion was not only unusual; it was decidedly difficult for a boy of his age.

This was also the time when the village people began to see more tangible examples of his spiritual prowess. In the Hindu tradition, snakes (and especially cobras) are at once feared and seen to be sacred, being associated with Shiva. A story is mentioned in the Hindi book *Aughar Bhagwan Ram*, published by Shri Sarveshwari Samooh in Banaras (p. 148, 1973), about the time Bhagwan was living in a field on the outskirts of the village. A snake entered his thatched hut while he slept. He woke up in the morning to find the cobra sitting with its hood up, looking at him. Somehow the villagers came to know of it, a crowd gathered around his hut and they wanted to kill the cobra. Bhagwan stopped them from doing so and after a while the snake slithered away. Another story mentions an incident that happened with his mother. In quest for solitude, Bhagwan has made his home in a guava grove, under the aforementioned haunted banyan tree. He began to conduct his worship there without food and water. When his mother heard of this, she found it intolerable. If her son would not eat, then neither would she; but on the third day, when his mother could not stand the pangs of hunger any longer, she made a pot of *halwa* (an Indian sweet made usually with flour, sugar and milk), put it in a plate, covered it with a cloth, and took it to him in the garden. She asked him to eat but Bhagwan refused, insisting instead that she should eat it herself. His mother explained to him that she had not performed her daily worship yet, and that she would eat after she had finished her worship. With that thought, she served out most of the *halwa* for Bhagwan onto another plate, saving a little for herself as *prasad* (holy food) and covered it with the same cloth under which she had brought out the food for her son. He asked her to take her share away, but when she picked up the plate she felt something crawling on her hand; she again removed the cloth from the plate and found a cobra sitting there. These are small incidents with cobras, but later in his life there were other snake-filled incidents which, together with his recognized spiritual powers, made people know Bhagwan to be Shiva incarnate. In the Hindu imagination, Shiva lives as an ascetic, wanders in cremation grounds, and is friendly to every creature, whether poisonous or not. In fact, one would almost certainly expect to see such dangerous creatures in places associated with Shiva, for they are, in a sense, his companions.

Then there is the story of the village barber's wife whose water-buffalo had run into birthing difficulties, and she came to little Bhagwan for help because she had seen him regularly perform meditation. Bhagwan did not know what to do, but since he had been asked to do something, he wrote "Ram, Ram" (the name of the incarnation of Vishnu as the prince of Ayodhya in the epic Ramayana), stuck it on the buffalo, sprinkled water on her, and the buffalo was relieved of its pain to deliver a healthy calf.

The Hindi book *Brahmanishtha Padya* (Ramashankar Pandey, Shri Sarveshwari Samooh, 1965, p. 15) tells another tale. While Bhagwan was searching for solitude to conduct his meditations in peace, the marriage proposal for his elder sister was finalized. As is the custom in rural north India, his mother asked him to visit the groom and his family, but Bhagwan refused to go, insisting that he had already seen the groom. Not only that, he said he could show the groom to his mother if she promised not to discuss it with anyone. His mother agreed. As she stood there, the vision of the groom appeared before her eyes and then faded after a few moments. She recognized the groom at the time of the wedding from the vision Bhagwan had shown her.

Little Bhagwan's spiritual absorption was such that nothing else mattered to him. His mother, understandably, did not approve of his continuous wanderings and his habit of seeking solitude outside the house. Perhaps because his association with the wandering *sadhus* had convinced him that he needed a guru (a spiritual master) to find what he was seeking that the little boy Jatuli took initiation in the *Vaishnav* tradition from the village's holy man and teacher, Shrikant Maharaj. *Vaishnav* initiates are worshippers of God Vishnu, and, true to that tradition, they must maintain a strict vegetarian diet. After initiation his teacher renamed him Bhagwan Das. Shrikant Maharaj, also called Paramhans Ji by most villagers, helped Bhagwan with his ever-growing spiritual thirst. He was barely nine years old when, one day, Bhagwan became totally disenchanted with domesticity and started walking towards the town of Gaya (a distance of about 120 kilometres). It was the winter season, and he did not know the way; he would spend most of his nights in fields of *arhar* lentils. One evening, weary from walking, he reached a village after night had already fallen. He went to the village temple looking for a place to stay for the night. It was late and everyone had already gone to sleep. He managed to rouse someone who gave him a piece of burlap to cover himself for the night, but there was no food for him. Bhagwan spent the night cold and hungry, but set out again in the morning. Although he was used to fasting, the rigors of this journey on foot made him ravenously hungry. When his hunger pangs became intolerable he entered a field and plucked some peas before he was chased away. He felt life and strength return to him for his journey onward.

On reaching Gaya Bhagwan visited all the holy places, but the folk from his village were searching for him; they found him and forcibly brought him back home. A few days later he ran away again, this time on a trip to Jagannath Puri, a holy town in the eastern state of Orissa. Once again people from home went out in search of him and tracked him down to an ashram of Ramanuja Vaishnava *sadhus*. This time when he was brought back he insisted he would not return to his parental home. He came back to the village but lived outside the house in various gardens and temples.

A little while later he heard of a convention organized by the Ramanuja sect in the Maner hamlet of Patna district. Little Bhagwan went to this convention with his guru Shrikant Maharaj. There, he heard the teaching, "unless one achieves the state as that achieved by Ramanuja, no one attains salvation", and loved it. He understood well that to become someone who can liberate himself from the laws of nature — as well as to be helpful to others — it would be necessary to attain this state.

Little Bhagwan Das had become initiated as a *Vaishnav*, but his true path was waiting for him in the holy city of Kashi, also known as Banaras or Varanasi. When he felt his spiritual quest was not being fulfilled in the village of Gundi, Bhagwan decided to go to Kashi on the advice of Shrikrishna Maharaj. At that time his age was 14 years, the year was 1951, the month was *Sawan* (June-July) by the Hindu lunar calendar, and the day was the eighth of the lunar month. Bhagwan left his village alone at night, went to Ara station and jumped onto a train. He alit at the Banaras Chhawani station at one o'clock in the morning. The rest of this trip, which proved to be a turning point in his life, is described very well in the book *Aughar Bhagwan Ram*:

> Coming out of the station, he asked the way to the Vishwanath temple. Leaving the station behind he came to Chetganj. It was a rainy night and street dogs made his journey forward very difficult. So he lay down there on an empty cart by the side of the road and spent rest of the night. In the brahma-muhurta (divine hour of the morning) when people began to go to the river Ganga for their morning ablutions, he also started in the same direction. He followed the straight road to Dashashwamedha Ghat, but stopped near the Derhsi bridge.
>
> While he was standing there in awe of the city, a stately old woman, wearing a silk sari with a red border came to him and asked him with affection, "Where do you want to go?" He said that he wanted to have a darshan (a sacred glimpse) of Shri Vishwanath Ji (God Shiva as he is known in Banaras). The old woman asked him if he had taken his bath.[1]

[1] It is customary in Kashi to perform ablutions in the Ganga before going into the Vishwanath temple.

When he said he had not, she indicated to him to go take his bath in the river Ganga flowing nearby. He went a little ways forward and took his bath at Ghora Ghat. While taking his bath he was wearing his loincloth and dhoti.[2] A thought came into his mind and he let his dhoti float down the river. After his bath he came back wearing only his loincloth, to the old woman.

He found the old woman standing at the place where he had left her, carrying all the puja materials in a plate. The old woman walked forward and he followed her to have a glimpse of Vishwanath Ji. On reaching the Vishwanath temple he felt very happy and amazed, and he felt drawn to the place. If he could stay in Kashi he would come to have a glimpse of Vishwanath Ji every day [he thought]. The old woman helped him perform the puja of Vishwanath Ji with great affection. At that time, he did not ask for anything but that God's glory and its continuous presence should always remain.

After the darshan and worship of Shri Vishwanath Ji he went towards the temple of Goddess Annapurna with the old woman. Even as he watched, the old woman disappeared inside the temple. He waited outside for sometime thinking that this was a rich person's house, and since he was in a very poor condition, it would not be appropriate for him to enter this house. When the woman did not come out for sometime, finally he moved away and came to Derhsi bridge and again he saw the old woman standing there! He was surprised because so far he had been thinking that the old woman was from a prosperous family and had mistaken the Annapurna temple to be her home. On seeing his reaction, the old woman asked him affectionately, "What is your purpose in coming to Kashi?" When he told her his purpose, she advised him to go towards Assi Ghat. "On the way, there is a monastery of Paramhans seekers. Your desire will be fulfilled there." Before he could

[2] Dhoti is a garment that is made of a plain white length of cloth, which can be worn in many different ways. Usually, it is tied around the waist as one would tie a bed-sheet, and then wrapped and tucked in intricate ways.

say anything more, the old woman disappeared! He began to wonder "who was that kind woman?" Before he could think more, the thought came to him that he should walk on the path indicated by the woman.

> Having made this decision he walked towards Harishchandra Ghat. On going a little further he reached Shri Kinaram Temple at Krin-Kund at about 7:30 in the morning. At that time the current abbot of the monastery, Shri Rajeshwar Ram Ji was sleeping. He sat down in the courtyard." (Pages 152-153) [Author's translation]

Bhagwan had reached Krin-Kund monastery, also known as Baba Kinaram's temple, on a Saturday in the Hindu month of *Sawan* (June-July), 1951. The *aghora* practices of this *Vaishnava*-initiated seeker started from here. After Bhagwan was initiated into the Aghora tradition by Baba Rajeshwar Ram, Ashu Baba, the assistant administrator at the temple, gave him rice mixed with fish from the food that had been cooked at the Temple. Since Bhagwan was a *Vaishnava* vegetarian who used to consecrate his vegetarian food with basil leaves at the temple in his village, he hesitated to eat it. With effort he ate a little and put the rest in the *kund* (the in-house pond which gives this temple its name), but then he decided that if he was to become an *aghori*, he would have to stop being disgusted by eating meat. During his initiation ceremony he had tasted wine for the first time in his life. Wine is an important element in *aghora* rituals and he learnt to use it properly. With his initiation into the *aghora* tradition Bhagwan became a tonsured ascetic, a *Sarbhanga*, a monk with a shaved head, a celibate renunciant. At the time of initiation his name was changed to Bhagwan Ram, according to the tradition among the Aghora saints of the Kinaram lineage in Banaras. According to the custom in India, he also began to be addressed simply as Baba, an epithet used for *sadhus* of all traditions in India. Bhagwan Das of Gundi village had now become Baba Aughar Bhagwan Ram.

Baba would get up every day in the divine hour of the morning (an hour and a half before sunrise), and sing *bhajans*, devotional songs. Having become a novice disciple, he began to practice with faith and sincerity the *mantra* given to him by his Aghora guru Baba Rajeshwar Ram, and he also served his guru while sharing the chores around the ashram. This included going to the cremation ground and fetching the wood from there for firewood at the temple. It used to be difficult to carry back the heavy load of wood from the cremation ground and, true to ways of the Aghora tradition, Baba was treated with strictness lest he fall prey to the worldly illusions. Of course, there was no such danger in Baba's mind for his spiritual quest did not allow him to think of anything else. The rigors of a monk's celibacy came to Baba naturally. A story is told of how, while sitting with several people at the pond in the ashram one day, he suddenly called out to a person working in the nearby field to get him a chilli pepper. When the chilli was brought to him Baba crushed it with his own fingers and put it in both his eyes. Those present there couldn't believe their eyes! They rushed to him saying hey what are you doing? Baba's reply was very simple — "Nothing much. My gaze had fallen on something inappropriate for me." People looked around to discover a woman bathing in the pond who Baba had inadvertently gazed upon while carrying on his conversation. Baba was atoning for it by cleansing his eyes with the chilli pepper!

Baba had a powerful spiritual experience in his early days at the Kinaram ashram. This experience further reassured him that he was, indeed, walking on the right path:

> One day he was lying half asleep near the dhuni (sacred fire). He felt as if a divine man wearing wooden sandals came and stood next to him. That divine person put his foot with the wooden sandals he was wearing on his chest and spoke some mantras in a clear voice. Because of an inner inspiration he repeated it and remembered it thereafter. From that day till today, he has been meditating on that mantra. By his guru's grace another incident occurred after a few days, which reinforced his faith in the afore-

> mentioned mantra. He was sweeping the area around Baba Kinaram's samadhi. While doing so when he went to the south of it, he heard the same mantra clearly, and with that the instruction that he should meditate on this very mantra. (Aughar Bhagwan Ram, Page 155, 1973) [Author's translation].

As Baba practiced his *mantra* his talents blossomed out for everyone to see. Although he was a novice disciple hundreds would go to seek the blessings of this new initiate. During his devotions, Baba would take a harmonium or a tabla, both musical instruments, and sing *bhajans* for long periods. The abbot, his guru, did not approve of all this. Or, one could say, in keeping with the *aughar* tradition, he began to treat his disciple severely. One day an incident occurred which made Baba leave the monastery. It was the month of *Sawan*. His guru had gone somewhere putting Baba in charge of the key to the storage room. While completing his chores at the ashram, Baba forgot where he had put the key. When the abbot came back he asked for the key, but Baba could not find it. He said he had forgotten where he put it, but he would find it within the day. The abbot became suspicious. He scolded Baba and said that he wanted the key back immediately. When Baba could not find any way out, he touched the storage room lock in front of everyone. The lock opened by itself. The abbot went in and reassured himself that everything inside was in its right place. But this incident made the abbot very suspicious about whether his disciple had another guru besides him. He asked Baba to leave the ashram.

Although this incident portrays Baba Rajeshwar Ram, Aughar Bhagwan Ram's guru as a harsh and intolerant administrator, there is more to this story than meets the eye. Baba Rajeshwar Ram was himself a spiritually enlightened saint, and he knew very well that for Bhagwan Ram to achieve his full potential he would have to leave the physical confines of the Kinaram monastery and venture out into the world. Since Aughar Bhagwan Ram was very devoted to his guru, this was Baba Rajeshwar Ram's way of setting him free to discover his destiny.

After leaving the ashram Baba remained in Banaras for some time at Ishwargangi, at the place of Chhedi Baba, who was regarded as a good saint in Banaras. Baba began to live in the gymnasium near Ishwargangi, and began his ascetic practice. From Iswargangi he used to go to the Dhumavati temple every day for a vision of deity. However, Baba was like the flowing wind; he never stayed at one place. Three more places within the city of Banaras became his regular 'camping sites' — the garden of Poona Estate near Nati Imli, the garden of Rai Panarudas, and Dhelwariya, which is a beautiful monastery north of the railway station at Chaukaghat. From Rai Panarudas' garden, devotees both faithful and curious began to come to Baba. They would play music and sing folk songs called *chaita* for him, but never anything that would be considered inappropriate. Hidden within that song and dance would be both *bhajan-kirtan* and devotion.

However, to continue on his path in solitude, Baba began to wander alongside the sacred river Ganga, begging for food in the many villages and hamlets that lined its banks. As a part of his Aghora practice he would never stay in a single place for too long, but would go out into the village to ask for food only once a day at noon, and would never beg for food from the same house twice. At about ten or eleven in the morning Baba would go into the village and cry out, "Ma, give me *roti* (bread)". If anyone put *dal* (lentils), *roti* or jaggery in his bowl, he would eat it while he walked, also feeding the group of eight or ten dogs that would follow him through the village. He would often repose during the day in the hot, dry bed of a village pond under the direct hot sun, covered only with a thin cotton sheet, and would perform his rituals in the evening. He would live in cremation grounds, writing his mantra over the ashes of the dead, over and over again. He did not own anything, nor did he owe anything. His practice led him to harsh seclusion where he avoided human company for years, living in the forests and caves around the river, with only the light of the sun and the stars to illuminate his world. He was positively emaciated; all the bones of his skeleton could easily be counted.

This was the period of Baba's most austere ascetic practices. Wandering and meditating in this way, in 1954 Baba walked along the banks of the river Ganga from Banaras to the Kumbh Mela at Prayag (Allahabad), a distance of about 90 miles. The Kumbh Mela is an ideal place to meet with saints and seekers of other variegated spiritual traditions in India. On this journey, he would eat only if someone gave him food; otherwise he would just drink Ganga water. When he reached Prayag sometime later, he hadn't eaten food for many days. He thought of asking for alms and almost immediately an old woman appeared before him, took him affectionately to her hut, fed him and gave him clothes.

He used to spend nights at the Mela sitting around a *dhuni* (sacred fire of the *yogis*). A famous naked *awadhutin* (a female seeker of the Shakta tradition) who used to wear a hibiscus flower in her *yoni* (vagina) began to come and sit around his *dhuni*. Although it was not a distraction to him, it certainly was not a part of his practice. One day she stopped coming to his *dhuni*. Baba felt at that point that he did not have any other emotion in his heart for her but the one that a child has for his mother. As Baba said later, "A child always gains strength from the mother. Those who keep other sentiment, lose their strength." After spending a month at the Mela meeting with *sadhus* from all over India, he returned to Kashi, where his worldly guru was going to have surgery. He spent a few days looking after him. Then, the desire to be alone became very strong in him again.

Baba spent another long period of time just wandering along the banks of Ganga. He would eat the food that shepherds would give him and wore the delicate muslin cloth left in the cremation ground from the shrouds of the corpses. For some time he lived in a cave on the banks of the Ganga near Sherpur village. Then he walked up to the town of Buxar, a distance of 62 miles. Wandering this way he reached his own village Gundi in his full *aughar* regalia on the festival day of *holi*, the festival of colours and gaiety. Baba had decided to free himself from the ties of human bonds, and so entered the village in his true Aghora form. On his body was only a meter-long shroud-cloth. He had the corpse of a dog in one hand and a bottle of liquor in the other. He looked terrifying. He was successful in his attempt; most of his family decided he was no longer fit to be included back into village society. Baba spent the festival day of *holi* at Gundi, and started walking along the bank of the Ganga again in the middle of the night. From there Baba travelled by foot to the Mahraura cremation ground near Banaras.

One day as he was wandering on the bank of the river Ganges at the Mahraura cremation ground, he attained enlightenment. This is how he described that experience:

> One time I remained absorbed in meditation for three days and three nights. I became *achyut,*[3] I became *urdhvareta,* I became *urdhvagami.*[4] Sitting at the bank of the Ganga at Mahraura cremation ground I became one with my mantra. All my senses dissolved unto themselves. A circle arose in front of my eyes. In that circle I saw green, red, yellow, white, purple, blue and orange colours. Those eight coloured concentric circles turned into an eight-petalled lotus. I saw my life force arisen within my consciousness. My voice, all my limbs, my deep vision, they all gained a lot within themselves. People of Mahraura, Kanwar, Manihara began to look at me with respect from that time on; they began to give me all that I needed. I would think of something, and before the thought was finished it would materialize in front of me. I would think I should see a particular thing, and before the thought was finished that thing would become visible to me. I would think something should come out from under the ground. Soon as I would remove the dirt, that thing would emerge. I would

[3] *Meenakshi Hindi Angrezi Kosh* (Meenakshi Prakashan, India, 1990) defines the word *achyut* as '1. Not fallen, not deviating. 2. Infallible'. In yogic terms, however, the word signifies the state when none of the worldly illusions affect the person. In essence, his seed does not fall.

[4] The words *urdhvareta* and *urdhvagami*, again, in yogic terminology refer to the rise of energy from the base of one's spine towards the crown of the head, rather than flowing down, as happens naturally.

> think I should remain standing next to the village people but they should not be able to see me — it used to happen. I would think I should do some good for someone and my spoken words would do so. I would think I should touch tree-leaf-vegetation and give it to someone for his benefit, and it would become beneficial for him. This is the effect of that circle. All this happened when I became urdhvareta. I had heard the stories of the Siddhas, Sudharma; it is not possible to narrate it... At that time my age was fourteen-fifteen years old. (Aghoreshwar Smriti *Vachanamrit,* Shri Sarveshwari Samooh, 1981, p 57). [Author's translation].

Even after achieving enlightenment, true to his Aghora tradition, Baba kept wandering from place to place. Sometimes he would live in a cave in the Vindhyachal mountains (in Uttar Pradesh state) near the temple of the Goddess Ashtabhuja; sometimes he would travel to the state of Madhya Pradesh and live in the hamlets there. Sometimes he would take off, barefoot, for the western state of Gujarat and the Girnar mountain complex there. His life was now as free as the sun and the wind; his actions were unorthodox and unconventional, there was no difference for him between a jungle and a home, and the presence of the divine was always with him like a shadow. Little happenings revealed this presence to those who had the good fortune of spending time with him. There is one story that Chhote Babu of Banaras, a devotee of Baba, tells of the time when Baba took him to the Vindhyachal Mountains for a *darshan* of the Devi, the Goddess.

Baba took the car towards the Durga cave in the Vindhyachal range. At that time one had to leave the car at the foot of the hill and walk for some distance to get to the cave. On doing so, Baba asked Chhote Babu to take the rear seat out of the car and carry it with them. He put the seat on his shoulder and they began to climb up the mountain. All around them was the dense, desolate jungle. Occasionally they would come across small ruins of old structures that were so dilapidated they looked haunted. They crossed an old, weed-choked pond whose boundary walls had crumbled. The jungle spread for miles around them. Far away, on some hill, was a little ruined building. Half of its roof had caved in and the rest looked like it would collapse at any moment. Weeds and vines had taken over the structure completely. Dislodged bricks and stones were strewn all around. On the one side were a few broken stairs which Baba climbed to the rooftop. He asked Chhote Babu to put the car seat down on the floor as a bed, and they went to sleep.

In the morning, Baba took him for a *darshan* of the mother Goddess. Chhote Babu had slung Baba's *kurta* over his shoulder; before doing so he had checked its pockets to make sure there was nothing in them that would fall out. Since there was nothing in them, he felt reassured and began to wander with Baba. They went around the temple complex of the mountain and had a *darshan* of the Mother. After all this walking when they came back to the car and sat down, Baba asked him, "Say, you came for a *darshan* of the Mother, did you not take any *prasad*, sacred food offering, from her?"

Chhote Babu had, of course, been quite oblivious to the *prasad* factor. He said, "Baba, you did not ask me before, so I did not take *prasad*".

Baba said, "Look at him! Anyway, look in the pocket of my *kurta*".

Chhote Babu knew there was nothing in Baba's *kurta* pockets. But since Baba had asked him to, he put his hand inside one pocket. There was freshly made sweet wrapped in a leaf inside that pocket, as if someone had just made it and put it there! He took it out, opened the leaf package, and they had a little *prasad*. Then they returned back to Banaras.

As Baba travelled and continued his practice, more and more people came in contact with him and realized that he was not an ordinary boy of fifteen, wandering like a beggar on the riverbank. Slowly, people of the villages around Varanasi became cognizant of Baba's true nature and his spiritual powers. They began to gather around him in ever-increasing numbers.

In 1953, at the request of devoted people from the villages of Hariharpur and Tajpur near Banaras, Baba established his first ashram there and called it 'Adi Ashram Hariharpur'. But this ashram did not spring up in just one day; first, Baba lived there and practiced very hard *sadhana* (ascetic practices). Then the villagers requested Baba to perform a Vishnu-*yagya*, a grand ceremony for the god Vishnu. That *yagya* was performed with great joy by the villagers and, at its culmination, the owner of the land where the *yagya* had been performed donated the land to Baba. The ashram was built there. People who participated in this *yagya* had many spiritual experiences. Around 1956, Baba had an underground cave built within the ashram. To perform his meditation Baba once closed himself in the absolute darkness of that cave for seven days without food and water and remained there in a state of *samadhi*, spiritual union with the divine. Such meditative practices were very common for him.

Although he kept the habit of constant wandering, the Hariharpur ashram turned into a place where he would spend some time whenever he returned to the Banaras area, and it was here that some amazing incidents occurred. Stories of Baba's severe ascetic penance had begun to circulate in Banaras and its environs. Those in his company used to experience miracles around Baba as if they were natural, everyday events. Although Baba never favoured performing miracles, there are some events where one can clearly see that Baba forcibly changed the laws of nature to help someone.

One such story is that of Upendra Singh. By chance Baba was in Hariharpur at the time that Upendra Singh's family in Hariharpur was celebrating the wedding of his sister. A girl's wedding in an Indian village! It was a very important occasion for the whole family. But, with only a little time before the groom's party was to arrive at the bride's Family house, Upendra Singh died. It seems very odd when said like that, but it was true. Upendra Singh had left his body.

Now the whole house was in an uproar. Everyone in the house was stricken with grief; on hearing the news, his mother fainted. How could the girl be wedded now? A pall of grief hung over the wedding house. Everyone knew how complicated it was to get a girl properly married in India; on this occasion, with the marriage party's arrival so imminent, it seemed impossible to save this wedding, for if they found out that a death had occurred in the house, they would certainly turn back without going through with the ceremony. But the elders of the house had not given up yet: one of them thought of going to Baba.

They got together and brought him all the traditional sweets; Baba welcomed them and asked the purpose of their visit. They joined their palms and told him about the death of the bride's brother. How could she be married now? The boy's mother was already half dead with grief. Baba looked at them with guileless eyes and asked how he could be of help. They requested him to do whatever he could to save the wedding. Baba acquiesced, and told them to return, and to keep the body of the dead youth alone in a room and continue as before with all the duties associated with the wedding. "I will come in a short while", he promised. They listened to Baba and went back. When they reached back they found that the groom's party was already there, curious about the delay in the proceedings. The situation had become very delicate.

Just then, people saw Baba, stick in hand, parting the crowd of the groom's party. Walking briskly and with purpose, Baba went straight to the room where the dead boy's body lay, although he had never been to this house before. The boy had now already been dead for almost four hours. Baba did not say a word as he came to the corpse. Not a word. He went straight to the dead boy's room and — *smack-smack-smack!* — hit him hard three times with his stick, saying "Idiot! Your sister is getting married and you are sleeping here!" Baba said this as he hit the boy's body, and the boy, who had been dead for four hours, sat up. Immediately, Baba turned and left the house. By the time anyone could say anything, Baba had sped away, already far out of the courtyard.

The daughter of the family was properly married; the honour of her family had been saved. Baba came back to his hut and became engrossed in his Self. Upendra Singh is alive even today and lives happily with his wife and children.

Incidents like this — and there were many others — established Baba as a truly realized saint in the consciousness of the people in this region. They knew that, for Baba, nothing was impossible. Baba himself never claimed to perform miracles. Whenever someone would approach him with a plea, he would simply say, "I will pray to the Mother". In fact, all his life he spoke against the pitfalls of performing miracles, as they drew people away from making an honest effort to achieve their goals. But in life and death situations, he had to act for the benefit of his devotees. Sometimes his efforts to remain anonymous and yet help someone with his unorthodox methods produced humorous results. Chaman Munim, a long-time devotee of Baba from his itinerant days in the city of Banaras, tells a funny story about an event that took place at the Haji Suleman's garden in Maruadih.

A washerman who used to work right next to the Maruadih garden had a son who was mute from birth. Someone told him to seek the Baba who lived in the Suleman Sahab's garden. The washerman did not know Baba and so he came to Chaman Munim for help. Chaman Munim informed him, "Baba wears a red loincloth and sits in the chair. Every morning when he washes his face I sit on the ground and pour out water for him. So come and greet him, and tell him whatever you want."

The next day, Baba sat down on the ground, not on the chair. He also put on a *lungi*, as Chaman Munim used to wear. When Munim-ji began to pour water for him Baba said, "The muddy water is splashing onto your feet. Sit in the chair."

Munim-ji sat down on the chair and began to pour water. By then, the washerman had arrived. Now, he could not make out who was Baba, because Baba had reversed the roles. He asked Munim-ji, "Where is Baba?"

Baba gave Munim-ji a stern look and so, instead of replying to the washerman, Munim-ji stared at the washer man, dumbfounded. Baba sent out Munim-ji on the pretext of fetching two eggs and then asked the washer man, "Who are you looking for? What is the matter?"

The washerman narrated that Munim-ji had asked him to come and meet with Baba to find a cure for his son's inability to speak. Baba told him not to trust the Munim, who would (he said) work as an agent for a fee, but also told him an unconventional cure, "I have heard that a mute person was cured by this method once. Go outside and if you find a donkey, put its mouth to your child's, and rub them together. Your son will speak. And don't come here again. If the Baba finds out about this, he will ask you for a lot of money."

The washer man went out and right then rubbed his son's face to that of a donkey, and his son, of course, began to speak. But from that day the washer man stayed angry with Munim-ji for trying to trick him.

People soon realized that Baba was a true Aghora saint. He did not discriminate on the basis of caste, colour or class. He gave no distinction to gender or age in his behaviour. Contrary to the customs of a caste-based society, he observed no restrictions of what he could eat or drink and what he could not. To him, there was no difference between a comfortable house and the open skies of a cremation ground. He had transcended all human limitations; he had become an Aghoreshwar, the highest of all spiritually realized saints in the Aghora tradition, a walking, talking deity, Shiva incarnate. The state of being an Aghoreshwar is the same as being a Paramhans in the *Vaishnava* tradition, or *Kaivalya* in the Shakta tradition, the state of being a free, liberated, unfettered soul. Most importantly, people felt that Baba truly loved everyone who went to him. He was always there for them. He could be approached at every hour of the day or night. His life was no longer for his own self; he lived for those who came to him. It was this feeling that led Baba to be regarded as the Shiva incarnate within the Banaras hinterland. Hundreds of thousands of devotees from far-flung villages would come for a glimpse of him on the occasion of Guru Purnima, a festival where Hindus express their respect for their guru. Over the course of one day he could be seen conversing with poor farmers from some inaccessible village, or with visiting spiritual seekers of various other traditions from different parts of India, or meeting with government officials, politicians, and foreign dignitaries.

To give this amorphous gathering of devotees the force of a social goal, on the 21st of September 1961 Baba laid the foundation of the organization called Shri Sarveshwari Samooh in the holy city of Banaras, an organization with a mandate to fight social evils like leprosy, dowry and illiteracy. Especially with reference to leprosy, it must be mentioned that it is a dreaded disease in India which even the Government of India does not have adequate facilities to adequately treat. People who become afflicted with this disease are often ousted from home and left to fend for themselves in the streets. It is not just a physical disease that rots the body; it is also a social disease where the whole family of the patient is often stigmatized as 'being punished for their sins' by suffering through an occurrence of leprosy in their household. Given the Aghora practice of non-discrimination and treating even the most disfigured, downtrodden and persecuted as an equal, Baba had no difficulty stepping in to make his own those who had been thrown out by their own families. To fulfil the goals of the organization, Baba started an ashram and a leprosy hospital by the name of 'Awadhut Bhagwan Ram Kusht Sewa Ashram' (The Awadhut Bhagwan Ram Leprosy Service Ashram) at Parao, Varanasi. After the society was founded, there were initially no funds to run it, and its members would go out begging for operational resources. Some would go to the villages and beg for food; meals were prepared with whatever they got in charity. Usually, even if there was enough rice, they would not even have any spices to put into it. They would cook the rice, mix the leftover rice-water with salt, and eat it. They would go and ask for bricks for the hospital building, then carry it to the hospital site and put each brick begged atop the other, with Baba helping, to build the wards for the patients. Despite these trials, the society members began to know their special purpose in life, giving them a pure joy that convinced them that this was Baba's way of training them to live a simple, contented life. In the beginning, Society members would go and pick up leprosy patients from the streets of Banaras. Two or three thatched huts were initially constructed to house the residents and to store and prepare the herbs to make medicine. Members would bring bark of the *neem* tree, jasmine leaves and whatever Baba asked them to; they would then grind them on a stone and cooked the resultant balm in mustard oil. When the medicine was ready, the wounds of the patients would be washed, then filled with the balm and tied in with bandage. It worked as a fast antiseptic, also drying their wounds. Those patients who observed discipline in what they ate and drank would heal very quickly.

The programs of the society included serving the leprosy patients and to inculcate a better social consciousness within the greater society. The aims of the society were simple but powerful when practiced in daily life: to consider the whole of humanity as one's kin; to have a respectful sentiment towards women; to encourage little boys and girls towards progress in their lives, and to never behave cruelly manner with them; to donate a little once a year to the Society; to conduct life passage rites according to the methods observed in the ashram without placing strictures on their family members to do the same; to help members of the society in need; to pursue one's respective business honestly; to meditate daily to the best of one's ability on the *mantra* given by the ashram.

Shri Sarveshwari Samooh progressed rapidly under Baba's direction, soon becoming a refuge for hundreds of thousands to get free leprosy treatment. People began to donate resources and land to the ashram. Maharaja Vijaybhushan Singh Ju Dev of Jashpur in Madhya Pradesh donated three villages from his estate, where Baba established several ashrams. Slowly the ashram built a boundary wall and the hospital developed better facilities to produce its own *ayurvedic* medicine, for leprosy as well as for other common ailments. Enough agricultural land was donated to Baba so the ashram could cultivate the fields and harvest enough grains, cereals and vegetables to become self-sufficient. *The Guinness Book of World Records* lists the achievements of the Society in December 15, 1998, under the title "Most Leprosy Patients Treated", as follows:

> The Awadhoot Bhagwan Ram Kusht Sewa Ashram Hospital at Parao, India, has treated more leprosy patients than any other hospital. The total number of registered patients since 1961 has been 99,045 with full Leprosy and 147,503

with partial Leprosy — all of whom were fully cured. The hospital was established in 1961 and receives no government funding — it runs entirely from public donations and gifts. Patients are treated free of charge using Ayurvedic herbal medicines and the Fakiri system, a method invented by the Indian religious saints.
(http://www.guinnessworldrecords.com)

Baba also started a drive to eliminate the curse of dowry from Hindu marriages. All members of the organization who chose to have the marriage of their children performed in the ashram had to do it in a very simple manner, without the expense of dowry. With that, Baba also started a primary school for disadvantaged children and a fight for social equality, with the goal of eliminating the ills of the caste system.

Baba still travelled extensively, sometimes to manage the various ashrams he had established in Uttar Pradesh, Bihar and Madhya Pradesh, and sometimes to visit holy shrines in different parts of India. Baba visited several times the Himalayan shrines of Haridwar, Rishikesh, Badrinath and Kedarnath, the Girnar mountain complex in Gujarat, the numerous shrines and pilgrimage places in the states of West Bengal and Assam, as well as the temples of south India. In 1968 Baba visited Nepal and the temple of Pashupatinath in Kathmandu, as well as holy places in Sikkim and the independent Himalayan kingdom of Bhutan. One year later, in 1969, his devotees in Afghanistan arranged for him to visit Kabul, Kandhar and Heart, and Tehran in Iran. He was also invited for a visit by his devotees then living in Mexico. In 1972 Baba visited Mexico and toured through Mexico City, Acapulco, and Iguala City.

As the Shri Sarveshwari Samooh developed, so did the number of Baba's devotees increase exponentially. This led to further expansions of the various ashrams and more responsibilities to fulfil. Those who came in contact with Baba soon realized that, even while doing the most mundane activities, Baba was actually trying to do something good for whomever was with him. He would, through his spiritual powers, take on some of their problems upon himself, and expiate them in his own body. As a result, later in his life, Baba became sick with a number of ailments; most prominent amongst these was that his kidneys stopped functioning. His doctors in India advised him to visit the United States for a kidney transplant operation in 1986. He was operated at Mount Sinai Hospital in New York in 1987, but that transplant failed within a year. Baba had another transplant operation performed on him in 1988 and his doctors at Mount Sinai advised him to visit New York every year for an annual check up. That kidney lasted until November 1992, when Baba finally relinquished his mortal frame at the Mount Sinai Hospital in New York.

In pursuit of his social aims, Baba would speak to all those who came to him. All were welcome to him, and with all he discussed even the most mundane of their concerns. Baba's teachings were, therefore, imparted more through everyday conversations rather than through sermons. Later in his life, when the Sarveshwari Samooh turned into a huge organization and people wanted him to give formal talks, Baba began to do so, and some of those words have been published in various books, as well as the newsletter published by the organization, 'Sarveshwari Times'. It was during his time spent at the Mount Sinai Hospital that Baba asked me to compile his words into a book that will have the essence of all his messages, first in Hindi, and then in English. The Hindi book was published in 1991 as 'Aghor Vachan Shastra' a year before Baba left his mortal frame at Mount Sinai Hospital in Manhattan. This is the English version of the same book.

Aghora: A Brief History

It is not always easy to sort out the various traditions that constitute the Hindu pantheon; nonetheless, a look at the cosmological structure of divinities in Hindu theology helps to place a particular tradition in its larger philosophical and historical context. In the Hindu understanding there exits the formless Brahm or Brahman, a single entity from which the creation emanated, and into which it all dissolves ultimately. The desire of Brahman to create the world brought forth its creative energy, conceptualized as a feminine energy, which led to the emergence of the Hindu trinity — Brahma, the creator; Vishnu, the preserver; and Shiva, the one who destroys so that the world can be created afresh. These three are the primary gods of whom only two are worshipped by most Hindus, but it is also understood that their powers are animated by the feminine creative principle, the goddess, who is worshipped either on her own or as a consort of each one of these gods in her various forms and with various attributes.

The two gods of the trinity most worshipped by Hindus are Vishnu and Shiva. The worshippers of Vishnu are *Vaishnavas*, and the worshippers of Shiva are *Shaiva*. The worshippers of the Goddess are *Shakta*, although elements of Shaktism can be found in both *Vaishnava* as well as *Shaiva* traditions; the degree of its prevalence depends upon the proclivities of the particular sub-tradition of these two primary streams. Brahma's worship is not so widely prevalent; in fact, there exists only one major active temple to Brahma in all of India, at Pushkar in the state of Rajasthan. Historically, the worship of Vishnu is a result of the primacy attained by the Brahmanical Vedic religion after the Aryan advent into India, while Shaiva-Shakta traditions are generally regarded as being pre-Aryan, indigenous to the land, representing traditions which have greatly influenced other streams of worship within Hinduism, and which have themselves become modified with the passage of the centuries. Yet, one of the primary gods described in the Vedas is Rudra, considered by many to be a pre-Aryan deity, also regarded as an earlier conception of the God Shiva of the Hindu Trinity.

The Shaiva-Shakta Tradition

Aghora represents a tradition which, in the present day, can be placed within the Shaiva-Shakta school of thought. Without going into the debates about the finer nature of its myriad streams, we will take a broad look at the Shaiva-Shakta tradition as enunciated by scholars based on the written sources derived from various scriptural texts consisting of the Vedas, the Upanishads and the Puranas, that describe the nature of Shiva and his relation to Shakti. For example, the *Rig Veda* (approximately 1200 BCE)[5] describes a fiery and terrifying God named Rudra, a god who is fierce but who provides blessings and rules benevolently over herbs. The *Rudradhyaya* chapter of the *Yajur Veda* describes Rudra's auspicious form, which is innately united with his feminine power, and is called Shivâ (Shivaa). Within this description, Shivâ is embellished with the adjective Aghorâ. According to followers of the tradition, this illustration implies that Rudra is Shivâ, and Shivâ is Aghora, a Sanskrit word which is known as 'Aughar' in the present times. Another name for Rudra-Shiva in the *Rig Veda* is Pashupati, a God who protects the sheep, cows and horses. Agama and Tantra scriptures consider Shiva and Shakti to be inseparable. The illustration mentioned above from the *Yajur Veda* leads one to the conclusion that Rudra is Shiva only because he is inseparably joined with the feminine Shakti, Aghorâ. A huge cornucopia of Tantra literature has been composed to expand upon Rudra's Shivâ/Aghorâ

---

[5] The four Vedas, the earliest-known Sanskrit literature from the Brahmanic period, are hymns compiled from an earlier oral tradition. The *Rig Veda*, the earliest book, probably dates from between 1700 to 1200 BC; the fourth, the *Avtharva Veda*, dates from 900 BC and consists chiefly of formulas and spells; the *Brahmanas*, associated with the *Vedas*, are ritual instructions from 700 to 300 BC. Hindu epics are popularly dated as: the *Mahabharata* (500 BC), and the *Ramayana*, between 200 BC and 200 AD.

form. It can be said that worshippers of Rudra's Shivâ or Aghorâ form are, interestingly, Shakti worshippers. Aughars, observers of the Shaiva-Shakta tradition, therefore, are regarded as a personified embodiment of Rudra's auspicious form, which is in constant union with his feminine power Shivâ. Other scriptures mention several other names for Rudra, namely Sadashiva, Ishana, Tatpurusha, Aghora, Vamdeva, Sadyojata, Harparvatirupa, Mrityunjaya, Mahesh, Dakshinamurti, Neelkanth, Ardhanarishwar, Panchanan, Pashupati, Neelagreeva, and Chadeshwar. Quite commonly Shiva is attributed with five faces, namely — Sadyojata, Vamadeva, Aghora, Tatpurush and Ishana. Each one of these faces, according to the *Vihsnudharmottara Purana*, is associated with one of the five constituent elements of the cosmos. Sadyojata is associated with the earth element, Vamadeva with water, Aghora with fire, Tatpurush with air and Ishana with space. When these five faces of Shiva are thought of in conjunction with these five constituent elements of the cosmos, then emerge the five names of Shiva which are widely known today, namely Mahadeva which represents the earth, Bhairava which represents fire, Nandi representing air, Uma for water and Sadashiva, space.

Based on the specific doctrinal inclinations of practitioners, in the context of the various forms of Shiva, ancient scriptures delineate four major Shaiva sects named Shaiva, Pashupat, Kaladaman and Kapalika, or Pashupata, Shaiva, Kalamukh and Kapalika.[6] The major literature of these four Shaiva sects is known collectively as Shaivagam. This literature, though, is sometimes further locally subdivided in the regions where they became popular, such as Pashupata thought, propounded by Nakulish or Lakulish, popular in Gujarat and the Rajputana in the 3rd or 2nd century B.C., Shaiva-Siddhanta, revered in the Tamil region of South India, Vir-Shaiva thought, known in the Karnataka region of South India, and the Pratyabhigya thought, which was centred in Kashmir and which is said to have been propounded primarily

[6] Chaturvedi, Yagyanarayan: *Aughar Bhagwan Ram*, Shri Sarveshwari Samooh, Parao, Varanasi, 1973, p. 58; Lorenzen, David: *The Kapalikas and the Kalamukhas*, University of California Press, 1972, p. 107.

by the son of Rishi Durwasa, a sage by the name of Tryambak. All these names of Shiva and the various sects associated with them mentioned in the Vedic, Tantric and Puranic literature point to the fact that the populace worshipped Rudra or Shiva in various forms through a large part of India over the centuries, leading to many different traditions of Shiva-Shakti worship. One amongst these was that of Aghora.

The Aghora Tradition

Followers of the Aghora tradition in the city of Banaras believe that this tradition was started by the god Shiva himself, and was propounded further by Jagadguru Dattatreya (a historical figure who may have lived about 4000 years ago by some estimates,[7] also mentioned in the epic *Ramayana* as the son of Rishi Atri and his wife Anusuya), Baba Kaluram (during King Harishchandra's time in ancient India), and by Baba Kinaram since the 17th century. Chaturvedi, in fact, mentions several well-known personalities from Hindu scriptures as having been a part of the Aghora tradition. These include, until the 10th century C.E., Vishwamitra (said to be the *mantra* seer in the Kaushika Sutra of the *Atharva Veda*), Vamadeva (a propounder of the left-handed path of Tantra and an important personality in the epic *Ramayana*), Vashishtha (the guru of the Raghu lineage in the *Ramayana*, and regarded to be a worshipper of Goddess Tara), Queen Churala (wife of king Shividhwaj mentioned in the *Yogavashishtha*), Emperor Vikramaditya (a popular king whose stories are still widely read in the Sanskrit text *Vetala Panchavinshati*), Aghoracharya (mentioned as having lived 1300 years ago, a personality popular with the Buddhist Lamas in Tibet), Bhairavacharya (said to be the guru of King Pushpabhuti, mentioned in Banabhatta's *Harshacharita*), and Abhinavagupta (the chief propounder of the Kashmir group of Agamas, said to have lived around the 10th century C.E.).[8] Chaturvedi also mentions Sarvanand Thakur (born about 600 years ago in Mehar village of Tripura), Avadhut Nagalingappa (born in the

[7] http://www.clas.ufl.edu/users/gthursby/tantra/datta.htm.

[8] Chaturvedi, *op. cit.*, pp. 13-16.

Nizam kingdom in 1860), and Aghoracharya of Tarapeeth, Bamakhepa.[9]

The Four Shaiva Sects

Let us consider the aforementioned four Shaivite traditions to trace, very briefly, how scholars have shown their development. Mishra writes that Shrikanth propounded the Shaiva school of thought where the living being is regarded as a *pashu*, a bound animal, who can realize its Shiva nature by transcending the limits set by illusion. Here Shiva is Brahm, the ultimate cosmic reality that can be found by meditation and other ascetic practices.[10]

Regarding the Pashupata school, U.P. Shah[11] notes that some sources such as the epic *Mahabharata*, the *Shiva Purana* and the *Tantraloka* ascribe this school to Shrikantha (seen as an incarnation of Shiva), while others consider it to have been established by Lakulisha or Nakulisha. He writes that Lakulisha was the twenty-eighth and last incarnation of Shiva, born into a Brahman family at Kayavarohana (modern Karvan) in the Baroda district of Gujarat. Images of Lakulisha holding a staff in his left hand, a vase in the right hand and a bull looking up at him have been found from Ujjain dating back to the third or second century BCE. He also states that the Lakulisha sect spread as far as to Kashmir, Nepal, Assam and Orissa. The reason for its popularity could have been that both celibates and householders could join it; there were no caste restrictions on who could be a member, and some of their meditative practices included laughter, dance and music. Shah writes:

> The Lakulisa-Pasupatas maintained their individuality by dress, by philosophy, and by mode of worship. Like other Saiva ascetics, they smeared their bodies with ashes, wore

---

[9] Ibid., pp.16-20.

[10] Mishra, Dr. Saroj Kumar: *Aghor Mat: Siddhant aur Sadhana*, Aghor Sodh Sansthan aur Granthalaya, Aghor Parisad Trust, Avadhoot Bhagwan Ram Kusth Sewa Asram, Parao, Varanasi, p. 74.

[11] Shah, U.P.: "Lakulisa: Saivite Saint" in *Discourses on Siva*, ed. Michael W. Meister, University of Pennsylvania Press, Philadelphia, 1984.

> a loincloth, kept matted hair, and wore the sacred thread. They used *yogapatta*, rosary beads, neck ornaments, armlets and bracelets or *rudraksa*. Unlike other monks, the ascetics of the Lakulisa sect used black dress...[12]

David Lorenzen mentions that the Pashupatas were the predecessors of the Kalamukhas, and hold Lakulisha in high esteem. They also smear ashes on their body and carry a staff.[13] The Kalamukhas seem to have been a part of the Shaiva scenario from the 11th to the 13th centuries in the Karnataka region of South India. He cites sources that mention Pashupatas and Kalamukhas to have originated in Kashmir and then to have migrated to the Karnataka region.[14] They had a very strong presence in this region and were divided into two main sub-groups, the *Shakti-Parishad* and the *Simha-Parishad*.[15]

Regarding the Kapalikas, Lorenzen writes that they seem to have originated in the Deccan or South India somewhere around the 5th or 6th century, but became extinct by the 14th century. Most probably, they were assimilated into other Shaiva-tantric traditions such as the Kanphatas and the Aghoris. The Kapalikas are understood to have followed a socially transgressive, left-hand path based on tantra,[16] which included the use of Panchamakaras.[17] As compared to the staff carried by the Kalamukhas, the Kapalikas, he states, carried a trident. The Kapalika worship also included eating from a skull bowl and offering of wine to the gods. They too eschewed caste principles and regarded mere initiation as sufficient to start one off right on the spiritual path. Lorenzen notes the description of Bhairavacharya, a Kapalika ascetic, from the *Harsha-Charita* of Banabhatta:

---

[12] Ibid., p. 95.

[13] Lorenzen, David N.: *The Kapalikas and Kalamukhas*, University of California Press, 1972, p. 5.

[14] Ibid., p. 108.

[15] Ibid., p. 97.

[16] Ibid., p. 3. "The five Ma-sounds which designate the principal ingredients of the central tantric ritual (*pancha-makar-sadhana*): *madya* (liquor), *mamsa* (meat), *matsya* (fish), *mudra* (parched grain or posture), and *maithuna* (coition)."

[17] Ibid., p. 53.

> Bhairavacharya, the saint who befriended Harsa's ancestor Puspabhuti, was also from South India (*daksinatya*) and also performed a tantric ritual appropriate for a Kapalika. One of his three disciples, Karnatala, was a *Dravida,* and another, Titibha, carried a skull begging bowl (*bhiksa-kapalika*) in a box made of *kharjura* wood. Bhairavacharya's name indicates that he worshipped Siva as Bhairava, the form of the god held in especial esteem by tantric groups such as the Kapalikas. Bana introduces him as the 'great Saiva saint named Bhairavacharya, almost a second over thrower of Daksa's sacrifice, who belonged to the Deccan, but whose powers, made famous by his excellence in multifarious sciences, were, like his many thousands of disciples, spread abroad over the whole sphere of humanity.[18]

Lorenzen further explains that in the legend of the Daksha's sacrifice, that ceremony had been disrupted by Shiva himself, and that Shiva-Kapalin or Kapaleshwara is the divine archetype of the Kapalika ascetic. It is doubtful if Kapalikas were ever so organized as to have lived in large, organized groups; rather, they are thought to have been individual ascetics roaming the countryside practicing their unorthodox religion. Dr. Dharmendra Brahmachari Shastri points to the *Rudrayamala Tantra* story of how the sage Vashishtha tried hard to attain enlightenment following the path propounded in the Vedas, but did not succeed. He was then directed by the goddess to follow the path propounded in the *Atharva Veda*, and the one followed by the Buddhists, to realize the knowledge of *Kula* (the Kundalini energy). Followers of the Aghora tradition consider this to be a very important story because, as Shastri writes, the main sources of this tradition can be traced back to the *Atharva Veda* and the Brahmanas, Sutras and Upanishads associated with it, but that their practices are influenced and modified by Shakta-Tantra and Buddhist Sahajayan schools of thought. These have found a place in the Aghora tradition in a highly transmuted form.[19]

[18] Ibid., p. 20.

[19] Shastri, Dr. Dharmendra Brahmachari: *Santmat ka Sarbhang Sampradaya*, Bihar Rashtrabhasha Parishad, Patna, 1959, p. 29.

Historically, the most important centres of Aghora teaching have been Mount Abu in Rajasthan and Girnar in Gujarat in western India, Bodhgaya in Bihar and in many parts of Assam in eastern India, Kashi in north India, Madras in south India which has a large temple to Kapaleshwar, and at Hingalaj in Sindh.

Today there are two main streams of Aughar saints, namely Himali and Girnali. Since Himalayas are regarded as an abode of God Shiva, the *himali* stream believes the Aghor tradition to have originated in the Himalayas, and is said to have been propounded by Gorakhnath. The second stream, *girnali*, regards Dattatreya, the son of Rishi Atri and his wife Anusuya, as the propounder of the tradition. At Girnar is the most holy pilgrimage place for aghoris, called Datta Paduka and Kamandalu Tirth. Baba Kinaram, the founder of the Kinaram Sthal in Banaras, is said to have been initiated into the Aghor tradition by Dattatreya at Girnar.[20]

While it is certainly difficult to pinpoint any single source for the preponderance and continuation of an ancient stream of philosophy and practice such as that of Aghora, especially since followers of this tradition consider that God Shiva was the founder of this tradition, it is worthwhile to look briefly at the two traditions which do seem to have carried it forward. As mentioned, one can be said to be the Jagadguru Dattatreya tradition, the other, that of Guru Gorakhnath.

Dattatreya

There are many stories about the birth of Dattatreya. One tale found in the *Markandeya Purana* tells that there was a Brahmin named Kaushika who had fallen from his sacred path. His pious wife, Shandili, still loved and venerated him. Kaushika used to frequent a prostitute, and one day, when Kaushika did not have any more money, she kicked him out of her house. The heartbroken Kaushika came home and his wife tried to make him happy. He asked her to take her to the prostitute's house. As Shandili was doing so, through a set of accidental circumstances, her hus-

[20] Chaturvedi, *op. cit.*, pp. 76-77.

band was cursed by Rishi Mandavya to die at sunrise. Shandili, who had great spiritual power due to her piety, stopped the sun in its tracks. That led to the whole business of the world come to a screeching halt. The gods went to Vishnu for advice in this matter and were directed to seek help from Anusuya, the wife of Rishi Atri. Anusuya persuaded Shandili to let the sun progress on its course, thus returning life back to the world, while at the same time saving Shandili's husband from death. The gods — Brahma, Vishnu and Shiva — were so pleased with Anusuya that they asked her to request a boon. She asked that the three gods be born from her womb as her children. The gods agreed and in time she had three sons — Soma, an incarnation of Brahma, Datta, an incarnation of Vishnu, and Durwasa, an incarnation of Shiva. Datta renounced all attachment and took refuge inside a lake, but his followers waited for him outside for a 100 celestial years. To dissuade them Datta came out of the lake with a beautiful lady. His followers were not dissuaded. Datta then proceeded to drink wine with the woman. Even that did not help. Finally, Datta was pleased with their devotion and gave them the knowledge of the absolute.[21]

The *Bhavisyat Purana* narrates the story differently. The wives of the three gods are envious of Anusuya's piety and ask their husbands to test her. The gods go to her ashram and demand that she serve them food while nude. Anusuya sprinkles holy water on them and turns them into babies, and proceeds to serve them in her lap. When the three gods do not return, their wives then go to her and beseech her to give their husbands back. In return, Anusuya asks them to be born as children from her womb. Later on, the tradition of Dattatreya developed to include worshippers from both the Vaishnava and the Shaiva traditions. As Joshi writes:

> In the *Bhagavata Purana,* Dattatreya is considered to be Yoganatha. His school is not a stereotype, is still developing. The idea of trinity has developed fully into the form

[21] Joshi, Hariprasad Shivprasad: *Origin and Development of Dattatreya Worship in India*, The Maharaja Sayajirao University of Baroda, 1965, pp. 57-58.

> of Dattatreya. Dattatreya, in the present form, is worshipped as an incarnation of all the three principal gods of the Hindu pantheon, viz. Brahma, Vishnu and Rudra. His triple nature is shown either by three heads or six hands. This school has always stressed the idea of equilibrium — the idea of synthesizing the two opposites very effectively and positively... The need of the times becomes, as it were, the main problem before the school and their promulgators though the spiritual side is never forgotten. (p. V)

As is evident from the passage above, it is in Dattatreya that all of the trinity can be perceived. He is a figure worshipped equally by the Vaishnavas, the Shaivas and the Shaktas, for he is also said to have developed all the schools of tantra that exist.

Gorakhnath

Regarding the influence of Gorakhnath's tradition on the Aughars, George Weston Briggs writes:

> Aughars are followers of Gorakhnath who have not undergone the final ceremony of having their ears split. A legend is current, which serves to justify them in not completing initiation. Once two Siddhas (perfect Yogis) tried to split the ear of a candidate who had been at Hing Laj;[22] but they found that the slits closed as fast as they were made. So they gave up the attempt. Since then Aughars have dispensed with the custom.[23]

Briggs lists several legends of the origin of Gorakhnath. One story says that God, the formless creator, produced Gorakhnath

[22] A holy place in Baluchistan province of Pakistan, which is sacred to the followers of the Aghora tradition. According to legend, when Shiva was roaming the earth in grief, carrying the burnt and disintegrating body of his wife Sati who had immolated herself in the sacrificial fire of her father, Daksha, after he had neglected to invite her husband Shiva to it, her limbs fell at various points in India. Each one of these places has become a *shakti-peetha*, a place charged with her creative power. It was at Hingalaj that her forehead is said to have fallen.

[23] Briggs, George Weston: *Gorakhnath and the Kanphata Yogis*, Motilal Banarsidas, Delhi, 1982, p. 10.

from the sweat of his own breast. Another legend from Nepal states that Shiva recited the Yoga doctrine to Parvati once while they were at the seashore. Matsyendranath, the future guru of Gorakhnath, was a fish in the sea at that time and heard the teachings. At that time he gave a woman something to eat with the promise that she will bear a son. The woman did not eat the substance but cast it upon a dung-hill instead. Twelve years later Matsyendra passed by the same spot and asked to see the child. When he heard what the woman had done they searched in the dung heap and discovered a boy of twelve years. That boy was named Gorakhnath and Matsyendranath became his spiritual master.[24] Briggs cites another version of this story from the *Tahqiqat-i-Chishthi*, where a devotee of Shiva desirous of offspring received ashes from Shiva's sacred fire. The devotee's wife was to swallow the ashes but she, instead, threw it upon a dung-hill. Eventually a child was found there who was named Gorakhnath by Shiva.[25]

Gorakhnath is supposed to be a true Siddha, a perfect yogi with powers over his own body and mind, over nature, over people as well as over gods. In fact, there is even a legend where Dattatreya and Gorakhnath are portrayed as playing at power. Briggs cites from Dabistan:

> ...the record of a contest of power between Gorakhnath and a sannyasi, Datateri, in which Gorakhnath disappeared in the water in the shape of a frog. But the sannyasi was able to find him and bring him forth. Then Datateri concealed himself in the water and Gorakhnath in spite of all his searching could not discover him, for he had become water, "and water cannot be distinguished from water".[26]

Many attempts have been made by scholars to find the exact dates when Gorakhnath existed. Some relate him to Kabir, some with Madhusudan Saraswati, and some with Jnana Deva:

> The age of Goraksa or of his Guru Matsyendra is not known with certainty. The tradition connecting him with Kabir

[24] Ibid., p. 182. [25] Ibid., p. 183. [26] Ibid., p. 191.

> (1500 A.D.) and with Madhusudana Sarasvati (1700 A.D.) is not probably of any historical value. But Jnana Natha, alias Jnana Deva, who is usually assigned to the thirteenth century, mentions his own spiritual pedigree, in his commentary on the Bhagavad Gita in which Goraksa Natha appears as his third predecessor — thus: Adinatha, Matsyendra Natha, Goraksa Natha, Gahini Natha, Nivrtti Natha and Jnana Natha. This would place Goraksa in the beginning of the 12th Century A.D. This date agrees with the tradition which makes Goraksa and Dharmanatha contemporaries and pupils of the same Guru. Dharmanatha is generally assigned to the 12th Century A.D. But there are other views according to which Goraksa lived in 500 A.D. or 700 A.D. or 1000 A.D.[27]

However, Briggs even cites a source that dates him back to 78 C.E.[28] It is significant to note here that legends of Gorakhnath place him as hailing from Punjab, Bengal, and even Nepal. His guru Matsyendranath is believed to be the Buddhist yogi Avalokiteshwara or Padmasambhava, and their stories form a substantial part of the Buddhist tantric lore. Shastri[29] is of the opinion that Aghora and Sarbhang[30] traditions have sprung from the pre-Vedic streams of thought, are supported by Vedic tenets, and are mediated by the tantra scriptures and Buddhist tantric principles. The philosophical tenets of the Buddhist Siddhas, such as the concepts of *shunya* (void), *shunyalok* (the world of nothingness), *sahaj* (natural, easy), *khasam* (husband), moon, sun, *samras* ('constant flavour'), and so on, are found in ample evidence in the Aghora and Sarbhang literature as well. The tendency to contradict fossilized social traditions of Hindus as well as of Muslims, seen among Aghora and Sarbhang ascetics, is also found amongst the Buddhist Siddhas. The tendency towards infinite faith in guru, and non-reliance on scriptures, is found equally in tantra literature, Buddhist Siddha

[27] http://www.clas.ufl.edu/users/gthursby/tantra/aspects.htm

[28] Briggs, *op. cit.*, p. 240.

[29] Shastri, *op. cit.*, p. 37-41.

[30] See section on many streams of Aghora tradition.

tradition, and the Aghora-Sarbhang traditions. The use of *pancha-makaras* is found amongst Buddhist Siddhas as well as Aghora-Sarbhang ascetics. In the Buddhist tradition, *pragya* is a form of Shakti, and Shakti is the primary goal of worship in tantra. Within the Buddhist traditions there exits a unique sub-stream of tantric Buddhists whose philosophy and literature are very similar to the Shaiva-Shakta tantric literature. Thus, it appears that the Agamas and tantras influenced Buddhism, and the tradition of Buddhist Siddhas influenced the Aghora and Sarbhang traditions.

Like Shastri, scholars like Mishra find ample evidence of the fundamental building blocks of Aghor philosophy and practice not only in the Vedas, Upanishads and the Puranas, but also in the tantras of the Shaiva-Shakta tradition, as well as in the Buddhist tradition. He considers Aghora to be a 'unique' tradition, which cannot be subscribed exclusively to either the Dattatreya, or the Gorakhnath traditions. In his opinion it is an ancient and valuable link not only between the Dattatreya and the Gorakhnath traditions, but also an important link between the tantra practices and philosophies of the Hindu and the Buddhist streams.

Since Aughar seekers have elements of tantra in their practice, and as their dress, appearance and behavior resembles that of the ascetic Shiva, they are also called *avadhut*, ascetics who wear necklaces of bones, live naked, apply either ashes from the cremation ground or the paste of red sandalwood on their body, carry a staff, or deerskin or Shiva's hourglass drum in their hands. In fact, the words Aughar, Avadhut and Aghora are often used interchangeably for the same kind of Shakti worshipper. Some even think that it is impossible to be an Avadhut without being an Aughar. Seekers of the Kinarami tradition use clay utensils and live a self-imposed life of poverty. They wear white, saffron or khaki clothes. They also wear a red loincloth, a *jhool* (a one piece long shirt made from rags) and a *lungi*, while some also go about without clothes. Shastri explains that Baba Kinaram and his followers regard a true saint to be an Avadhut. Etymologically this word implies 'one who is discarded'. But followers of this tradition do not use it as this adjective, but as an adverb, which implies 'one who controls his senses and desires, and discards this illusory world'. In a sense, an *avadhuta* acts as discarded by the world, which is to say that his life and behaviour are unique: they are of his own making. The world can call him names, criticize him, but all that matters not to him. He lives in the world, but he is not of it.[31]

Baba Kinaram

The hagiography of Baba Kinaram, founder of the Kinaram Sthal in Banaras, gives important clues to the lifestyle, practices, and powers of Aughar saints. Baba Kinaram was born in the Ramgarh village near Banaras in the year 1620 according to the Vikrami calendar (approximately 1563 CE). He is regarded as a spiritually enlightened person who had taken a physical form to complete what he did not finish in his last life. According to the custom of that time, despite his resistance he was married when he was just twelve years old. However, three years later, a day before he had to go and bring his wife to her married home, he insisted on eating a dish of boiled rice and milk, a dish considered particularly inauspicious on such occasions because this dish is used only in death rituals. The next day his family got the news that his wife had died the night before. This made the people wonder about how he came to know of his wife's death in advance. He neither enjoyed the chores of the home nor was his heart into getting educated. One day, disenchanted with home life, he set out to wander and reached Karo village in Gazipur district, where saint Shivaram of the Ramanuja sect lived. Kinaram devoted himself to his guru's service and was later initiated by him.

Shivaram Ji was a householder saint and when his wife died he decided to marry again. Kinaram did not like this and told him, "Maharaj, if you bring another wife, I will find another guru". Shivaram asked him to leave and Kinaram walked away. He reached the village of Naidih where he saw an old woman sitting alone, crying. On asking the reason for her sorrow she told him her son had been taken away by the *zamindar*'s henchmen because he

---

[31] Ibid., p. 97.

couldn't pay the taxes due. Baba Kinaram went to the *zamindar*'s place and asked him to release the boy. The *zamindar* said, fine, if you can pay me the amount that is due, you can free the boy. Baba Kinaram asked the landlord to dig the ground where the boy had been standing, and when they did so, they found a whole treasure trove of money. The *zamindar* not only freed the old woman's son but also paid his respects to Baba. The old woman was so impressed by this deed of Kinaram that she insisted he keep her son with him. Kinaram had no option, and he started his journey towards Girnar with his companion, the boy named Bijaram.

At Girnar, Kinaram went alone to the top of the mountain to meditate, and it is said he not only met with Guru Dattatreya there and received divine knowledge from him, he was also initiated into the Aghor tradition by him. He wrote the essence of that knowledge in a book called the *Viveksar*. Baba Kinaram came down from the mountain and went to Junagadh with Bijaram. It was the year 1724 by the Vikram calendar (approximately 1668 CE) and something very interesting happened when Bijaram went out seeking alms according to his ascetic practice. He was caught and imprisoned by the Muslim ruler of Juagadh. Bijaram saw that the jail was full of ascetics and seekers who were all made to grind grain on hand-mills. There were 981 hand-mills in the jail and Bijaram also got one. When Bijaram did not return, Baba Kinaram, in his meditative state, discovered the reason for it and thus himself went begging for alms in the city; he too was caught and put in jail. He looked at the hand-mill given to him in the jail and asked it to move. Nothing happened. Then he struck the hand-mill with his staff and all the 981 mills began to move by themselves. When the ruler got to know of it, Baba Kinaram was brought before him with his disciple Bijaram. The ruler showed his respect to Kinaram and presented him with some gems as a gift. Baba Kinaram popped two or three of them in his mouth and then spat them out saying, "These are neither sweet nor sour", implying, of what use were these to him. The ruler asked Baba Kinaram to give him another chance to serve him. Baba Kinaram said okay, if that is what you want then give two pounds of flour in my name to every ascetic and seeker who comes into your town. The ruler agreed and by Baba Kinaram's blessing he begot children to continue his lineage.

From Junagadh Baba Kinaram went into the Himalayas where, after a long time spent in ascetic practices, he came to the city of Kashi and reached the cremation ground at Harishchandra Ghat. An Aughar saint by the name of Baba Kaluram used to live there. His particular trait was to converse with, and to feed chick peas to, the skulls of the corpses waiting to be cremated. Baba Kinaram was amazed to seeing this, but using his own yogic power he prevented the skulls from answering Baba Kaluram. Baba Kaluram found out what had happened through his divine vision and Baba Kinaram asked him to stop playing and go to his designated place. Baba Kaluram said he was very hungry; could Kinaram feed him some fish? Baba Kinaram looked at the river Ganges and said, "Ganga, give me a fish". He said this, and a big fish jumped out of the water onto the riverbank. Baba Kinaram roasted it and the three of them had a meal. As they moved forward Baba Kaluram pointed to a corpse floating in the river and said, "Look, that corpse is coming our way". Baba Kinaram said, "Sir, that is not a corpse, it is alive". Baba Kaluram challenged him saying, "If it is alive, call it here". Baba Kinaram yelled out to the corpse from the riverbank. The corpse floated to the bank and then stood up. Kinaram asked him to go home. When the mother of the corpse who had been brought alive heard of this miracle she came to Kinaram and said, "Maharaj, you gave him a new life, from today he belongs to you". Baba Kinaram took that man with him and named him Ramjiyawanram. This incident is supposed to have happened around 1754 Vikram Samvat (approximately 1698 CE). After seeing all that Baba Kinaram had done, Baba Kaluram revealed his divine form to him and took him to Krin-Kund at Shivala in Kashi, and told him this was Girnar, and that all places of pilgrimage were present here. One belief is that Baba Kaluram initiated him at Krin-Kund with the Aghor mantra, the other belief being that he was already initiated into the Aghor tradition by Guru Dattatreya at Girnar. From that time onwards, Baba Kinaram began to live at

Krin-Kund. He established four Vaishnava ashrams in the name of his first guru, and four more Aghor ashrams in the name of his second guru. He is said to have relinquished his mortal frame in 1771 (1714 CE) at the age of 151 years.

Gupta mentions several other stories related to the life of Baba Kinaram.[32] One story relates an episode from the life of a barren Brahman woman who used to serve an old saint. She asked the saint for children but the saint told her that children were not destined in her fate. One day she met Baba Kinaram and when she asked him to be blessed with children, he hit her with his stick four times. In due course she gave birth to four children.[33] Another story Gupta mentions narrates an episode that took place in Darbhanga with the Maithila Brahmans. Kinaram, with a cat on his shoulder, riding a donkey reached Darbhanga and asked the Maithila Brahmans to give up their food restrictions. The Brahmans, naturally, were curious and asked him to show his authority by bringing their dead elephant back to life. Baba Kinaram threw his cat on the elephant and made his donkey kick the dead elephant. The elephant stood up and the Maithila Brahmans began to eat meat and fish from that day on.[34] Yet another story takes Kinaram to Surat in Gujarat:

> Kina Ram was also a defender of women. One day in Surat, Kina Ram found out that the people of the village were planning to throw a young widow and her illegitimate child into the sea. Kina Ram forbade them to do it but they insisted, saying that she was a corrupt woman. Kina Ram said, "okay, but only if you throw the father of the child along with her. Just give me the word and I will name him for he is here and is one of you." All of the men walked away with heads bent in shame. Kina Ram ordered the woman to live near the tomb of Nar Singh. Later on, a tornado destroyed Surat City, and to this day it is said that the people there fear the name of Kina Ram.

[32] Gupta, Roxanne Poormon: *The Politics of Heterodoxy and the Kina Rami Ascetics of Banaras*, Unpublished PhD. Dissertation, 1993.

[33] Ibid., p. 132.

[34] Ibid., p. 133.

Baba Kina Ram

The theme of Kina Ram as the protector of fallen women persists in Banaras as well, where he has been looked upon as the patron saint of prostitutes. Even as recently as the 1950's, the prostitutes and *nautch* girls used to make offerings at the Sthala once a year.[35]

Another story tells of Baba Kinaram's arrival at a religious feast organized by Baba Lotadas of Banaras, to which all saints of the city but Kinaram had been invited. Kinaram went to the venue anyway and the vegetarian dishes on the plates of the guests turned into fish, while water in their cups turned into wine. Lotadas came out to investigate and found Kinaram sitting outside. He invited Kinaram to come inside and with the use of a mantra, Kinaram turned the food back to its original state. Lotadas began to serve Baba Kinaram but all the food that he poured from his sacred magical pot into Baba Kinaram's skull-bowl disappeared instantaneously. Lotadas apologized to Baba Kinaram and everyone feasted well.[36] Gupta narrates another interesting story dealing with Raja Chet Singh of Banaras and Baba Kinaram:

> One day Raja Chet Singh was sitting in his palace when Kina Ram passed by wearing one wooden sandal with a dancing bell attached to it. The Raja, who loved music and dance, taunted Kina Ram by saying "What does a *sadhu* have to do with dancing bells?" Kina Ram replied, "What do you have to do with rulership?" He then cursed Chet Singh that his lineage would be barren and that before long he would have to abandon his beautiful palace; nothing would be left except shitting pigeons. A few years later Warren Hastings drove Chet Singh across the river and until 30 years ago, no heir was born to the family. Today it is said that the present Maharaja of Banaras had to ask the forgiveness of Avadhut Bhagwan Ram in order to break the curse and obtain his son.[37]

---

[35] Ibid., p. 134.

[36] Ibid., p. 135.

[37] Ibid., p. 136.

The Many Streams of the Aghora Tradition

The Aghora tradition is also related indistinguishably with the Sarbhang sect, mostly found in Bihar. Shastri enumerates six streams of this tradition started by six different preceptors, namely, Kinaram of Kashi (Varanasi); Bhinakram, Bhikhamram, Tekmanram, Sadanand Baba and Balkhandi Baba of Champaran district in Bihar, and Lakshmisakhi of Saran district in Bihar. By enumerating these names separately it does not imply that they these traditions are totally different or exclusive from each other. At most, Baba Kinaram's tradition can be regarded as different from rest of the five traditions because it is widely prevalent and influential.[38] Within the Sarbhang sect, the tradition started by Baba Bhikhamram is old and popular. Baba Bhikhamram was born in Champaran district of Bihar and one of his disciples, Tekmanram, is very well known.[39] These Sarbhang ascetics are said to perform their penance in the cremation grounds whereby they begin to control various kinds of ghosts and spirits, and become endowed with many kinds of miraculous powers. Those Aughar or Sarbhang ascetics who have obtained these powers are called Siddha (the realized ones) and the populace expects them to help in curing many kinds of physical and non-physical ailments. In the *Atharva Veda*, Rudra has been portrayed as a great 'doctor' who is sought after to cure troubles caused by ghosts and spirits. Dogs are regarded as his companions. This representation of Rudra translates into the persona of the present day Sarbhang or Aughar saint.[40]

Aughars can be further divided into two categories, Nirnavi (*nirvani*) and Gharbari. While the Nirvani stress renunciation and lone practices in places like the cremation ground, the Gharbari can be married, householder ascetics who continue their practices in the tantric way at home. Baba Kinaram and Baba Bhinakram belonged to the Nirnavi category, while the tradition started by Bhinakram had householders in it.[41]

---

[38] Shastri, *op. cit.*, p. 116.

[39] Mishra, *op. cit.*, p. 81.

[40] Ibid., p. 9. [41] Ibid., p. 67.

Aghora Philosophy

Of the five faces of Shiva, Aghora, the fiery one, has generally thought of as being a terrifying form of Shiva, especially for those who look at it from outside the tradition. For those who follow the tradition, however, Aghora is the simplest, most direct route to unity with the divine. Often, it is said that the Sanskrit word 'ghora' means 'that which is terrible or very difficult'. As opposed to that, adding the negative prefix 'a' turns this word into 'Aghora' which means 'that which is simple and easy'. True to its nature, Aghora reveals a direct path to the divine, one which becomes very easy as soon as one relinquishes the fetters of the mind, but one which becomes difficult if one tries to follow it while still clinging to the desires and aspirations fuelled by the senses, shaped by the mind, and sanctioned by enculturation. It is a tradition of the *avadhuta*s that transcends all physical limitations to reach the state of union with the divine. An aughar is called an Avadhut because such a seeker transcends all category distinctions, all prescriptions and proscriptions of the 'normal' social structure. He remains constantly imbued with the 'Mother' vision; therefore, whatever he sees in the outside world appears to him as beautiful as the Mother.

In the Vedas, the Aghora form of Shiva is mentioned on the one hand as beneficent, and on the other it is juxtaposed with his terrifying form called 'Ghora' in the mantra — '*Aghorebhyoth-gorebhyo, ghoraghoratrarebhyaha*'. Such a vision of Aghora is understood to be a non-dual, formless form, a *nirgun* form. In its formless form, as Baba Kinaram mentions in *Viveksar*, the living being (*jivatma*), the God (*paramatma*) and the created world all are one and the same; there is no distinction between them. This ultimate reality, *nirgun* Brahm, is free of the three fundamental qualities, or traits that form this world — *sattva*, *rajas* and *tamas*. This formless god pervades all things and beings just as the sky or space pervade the cosmos. However, when *nirgun* Brahm is looked at from the point of view of *bhakti*, the tradition of devotion, the same *nirgun* Brahm becomes divided into separate categories of devotee and devoted, worshipper and worshipped.

At this point the *jivatma* is called *hansa* (the swan), while Paramatma, God, is called Paramhans (the Great Swan). When a *jivatma*, a swan, attains complete liberation, it transcends to the category of the Great Swan. The distinction between *jiva* and Paramatma or Brahm arises because of the intervention of *avidya*. *Avidya* is the act of imposing an imagined characteristic on the innate or natural character of something. One of the most popular examples is the difference between a rope and a snake. The nature and character of a rope is very different from the nature and character of a snake, but when, in the dim light of dusk, a rope is perceived by the mind to be a snake, this imposition of an imagined characteristic on the true nature of the rope is *avidya*. Another name for *avidya* is *maya*, or illusion. Baba Kinaram mentions that the five *pranas* ('life-force') and their 25 characteristics (five characters for each *pran*), as well as the sense of *jiva* and *Ishwar* (God), are all so perceived because of *maya*, illusion. To be in a state of illusion is regarded as a shackled state called *upadhi*. To become free of this state and to perceive one's true nature as god is *samadhi*. Thus Avidya, Maya and *upadhi* are regarded as synonyms. The contrary state of *samadhi* is reached by dissociating the mind from the illusions of *maya* and allowing the *jiva* to realize its true nature, the Brahm nature.

The world generated by illusion is extremely nascent; it is ephemeral. Even human body is ephemeral. The body has five knowledge instruments or organs — the eyes, ears, nose, tongue and skin; and five actions instruments or organs — the hands, feet, anus, genitals and mouth; and finally there is the last constituent, the *antahkaran*, variously translated as the soul, the heart, the consciousness or the inner self. This inner self is further divided into four sub-categories of mind, intellect, conscience/desire, and ego. According to Baba Kinaram, in the mind exists the desire, which motivates the senses. The mind is supported by *pran*, life-force; the *pran* is supported by breath, breath is supported by Shabd-brahm (or Brahm conceptualized as the primal vibration), and *shabd-brahm* is supported by its own natural state. While *brahm* is ever-existent and indestructible, the body is ephemeral and mortal. All our relations, emotions, desires end with the body; therefore, keeping the ephemeral nature of the body in mind, one should not be proud of one's form and beauty, nor get into egotistical involvements because of it. Controlling one's mind, then, to wean it away from ego-identification with the body, and to inspire it towards one's *Brahm* form, is the goal of ascetic practice.

This illusory distinction between *jiva* and *brahm* is a product of the process of creation itself. Baba Kinaram describes the process of creation thus: In the beginning was the formless, nameless primal being, Satpurush. With its own desire, a word exploded from that Satpurush (Nad-Brahm or *pranav*) which gave birth to the trinity of the three male gods Brahma, Vishnu and Mahesh (Shiva) and a female power. With these emerged the five fundamental elements that constitute the cosmos — the sky, the water, the fire, the air and the space or ether. The process of creation of the cosmos came into being. The female power Adi-Shakti took the form of creative action and arranged for the creation, nurturing and destruction of the created world, with the help of the five fundamental elements and the three traits, (the *gunas*, that is, *sattva* being light and knowledge, *rajas* as action and motivation, and *tamas* as illusion and attachment), and with the support of the trinity of Brahma, Vishnu and Mahesh. Since everything is created by these primal elements, what exits outside in the world also exists within every being. The *jiva* and its soul, the *atma*, is perceived to be limited and fettered only so long as the senses motivate it to remain engrossed in the perceived world which is ever-changing and ever dissolving. With the practice of *sadhana*, yogis dissociate their senses from the outside world and focus it to look inside, where they find the constant world of the everlasting *brahm*. It is this ability, then, which makes the yogis omniscient and omnipotent.

Such a realization comes from true love for one's divine entity. Love here implies faith, devotion, practice and discipline. The knowledge of enlightenment, *vidya* (as opposed to *Avidya*), then, is a practical matter; it is a matter of experience. Such knowledge is not incumbent upon reading the scriptures but, in fact, is dependant upon experiencing the divine within one's own self. To inculcate the practice and love for a union with oneself, one should continuously remember the name, the mantra, given by the guru. This process deepens the love of the seeker for his divine, and focuses him inwards. Baba Kinaram has mentioned that 'So-Ham' is a mantra that is very easy to remember and focus continuously upon since it vibrates naturally with each inhalation and exhalation performed. This name remembrance can be of two kinds, spoken and unspoken. The unspoken method is called *ajapa jap*, which happens silently within the seeker.

Aghora Practice

Typically, followers of the Aghora path try to cultivate a state of mind and social practice which is totally non-discriminatory, just as fire does not discriminate whether something put into it is pure or impure. It is the nature of fire to either burn or purify, and Aghora does the task of absolute purification for the seeker, making his mind and spirit so clean that he is able to see a glimpse of the divine within him, and then extends it to the divinity resident in all beings of this creation. Once the seeker begins to see the same divine element in all beings, even the thought of such mentally and socially generated constructs as high and low, purity and pollution, pure and impure, or male and female, do not taint his mind or modify his behaviour.

Since Lord Shiva is thought of as an itinerant ascetic inhabiting cremation grounds, indulging in intoxicants, ruling over spirits, ghosts, and every other class of terrifying spirit, Aghora seekers also try to mould themselves on the imagined behaviour of their deity. They live in cremation grounds, they are ascribed power over all kinds of ghosts and spirits, and they are supposed to use (and, indeed, to be immune to the effects of) intoxicants. Chaturvedi cites some common practices recommended for Aughar seekers, such as touching the earth as soon as one wakes up in the morning, because the earth is treated as mother, and this action allows her energy to infuse the seeker; to mumble mantras on sitting up in bed; to meditate on nothing, but to repeat one's mantra as much as possible; and to strive for nothing, yet to not remain inactive.[42] To attain an absolute focus onto their own spirit, Aughars can perform a special mode of meditation called 'the meditation of the cremation ground'. Five kinds of cremation grounds are enumerated: a *peepal* tree (*ficus religiosa*) outside the village, a cot made of *moonj* string, a prostitute's bed, one's own wife's bed, and the cremation ground. On special occasions, Aughars also use *panchamakar* in their meditations. Normally, the seekers wear a red loincloth because it signifies the feminine creative energy. During their penance period they wear blue or black clothes because it protects them from many troublesome forces. On transcending the period of penance, the Aughar seeker is advised to wear white clothes because it represents a pure and clean consciousness.

As will be evident from our discussion, Aghora is known to be an ancient tradition for seeking enlightenment, one that has been influenced by many other streams of spiritual thought from within Hinduism as well as from Buddhism. What is socially important is that Aghora tradition believes in interacting in a non-discriminatory manner with all beings and things; in more recent times, the demand of social service from realized Aughar saints has been given a new and comprehensive form through Baba Aghoreshwar Bhagwan Ram. This new turn to the Aghora tradition makes it much more accessible and useful for the common people to interact with (and to identify with) Aughar seekers, and derive physical as well as spiritual benefits from their actions. Before Baba Bhagwan Ram relinquished his body, he established Baba Siddhartha Gautam Ram as the abbot of Kinaram Sthal, the temple where he himself had received initiation in 1951. Readers will recall that it was to this place that Baba Kinaram was led by his guru Baba Kaluram, the place where a sacred fire lit from the wood brought from cremation grounds has been burning constantly for more than 400 years. The society for social service named Shri Sarveshwari Samooh, founded by Baba Bhagwan Ram, still carries on social work under Baba Gurupad Sambhav Ram. Baba's

[42] Chaturvedi, *op. cit.*, p. 50-52.

other disciples have opened ashrams in other parts of India to continue social work, such as Baba Priyadarshi Ram's ashram at Banora (Chhatisgarh), and Baba Shavak Ram's ashram at Mussoorie, Uttaranchal. Some of Baba Bhagwan Ram's disciples have started ashrams internationally as well, such as Baba Harihar Ram's ashram in Sonoma, California, and Gurubaba's ashram in Mezzago, in Milano (Italy).

Baba Bhagwan Ram is credited to have changed the place that Aughar ascetics occupy in society. While earlier they were regarded as being, literally, on the social fringe, inhabiting cremation grounds, today they have become a part of the mainstream of religious life in Banaras and elsewhere, using the powers of their spiritual practices for social benefit.

The Mother

In the Indian context one of the most important symbols of love, life and nurturing is the mother. But that is not all. The mother figure is only a part, albeit an extremely important one, of the totality of the feminine figure. True, people react differently to the feminine figure depending upon their conceptual, social and experiential backgrounds, but this figure, nonetheless, is regarded as one that has the power, the energy, to energize all those who come in contact with it. This is an important spiritual tenet also. This chapter describes the Mother — the particular female entity whose mere wink of an eye overwhelms with attraction every being of this earth. She also knows all the weaknesses of human beings, and she is also the one to provide restful sleep in the form of the night (Nisha). The society which Baba founded, Sri Sarveshwari Samooh, espouses the glory of females and the feminine. One more statement of clarification: Shaiva Avadhoot, Shakta Avadhoot or Vaishnava Avadhoot all have the Divine Mother, the creative energy, the Shakti, as the object of their worship and devotion. A special time for all of them to contemplate upon and worship the mother is during the Navaratri festival, which is observed twice a year for nine days each.

1. If you ask me who can be pleased most easily, I will say it is the Mother. The father figure and the family represent austere strictness and discipline.

2. If you want peace, go to the refuge of the Mother.

3. O living human being, life is ephemeral! Worship the Mother who nurtures and provides fulfilment. In this way you benefit yourself and inspire others.

4. Salute the Divine Mother in all four directions, for it is She who exists in the form of All Directions.

5. Whenever we have to perform a prayer of adoration we address the Mother first: "You are the Mother and You are the Father" (*Twameva mata, cha pita twameva...*).

6. The Mother is present everywhere, and in all living beings.

7. The true form of the Divine Mother is Creative Energy, *Shakti*. It expresses itself as many different kinds of energy, and therefore, it is understood in different ways in different countries and times. But, in reality, there is no difference, it is one Creative Power.

8. Thus, at Brahma's place, assuming the attributes of Brahma, the Divine Mother is known as Brahma; at Vishnu's place, She is known as Vishnu; at Shiva's place, Shiva; so in the places where saints and great beings dwell, She manifests Herself as the behaviour of these beings. As daily activities, thoughts, and the ideals of a particular time, place and condition mould one's character and behaviour, so the character and behaviour of a great being becomes, itself, the Divine Mother.

9. But the Divine Mother is not of the caste of Vishnu, Brahma or Shiva. Neither is She of a particular nation, race, religion, class, or time.

10. A matured intellect should try to know the Divine Mother as Shakti, a single Creative Energy. However, if one cannot yet do that, one should try to see Her, to understand Her in Her various forms. At a minimum, one should strive to know Her in at least one of Her forms. This striving, itself, constitutes one's worship, one's prayers, one's meditation, one's unbreakable faith.

11. Those who are dear to us, close to us, who wish us well, are addressed in very few words, often in two or three letters. For example: "*Ma*" (Mother).

12. So, also, divine Shakti of the mantra (a sacred word to meditate upon) is addressed in not more than a letter or a syllable. That is known as the one-lettered (*ekakshar*) or seed *mantra*. In reality, however, it is not one-lettered; it has half an 'R', or half an 'I', and half an 'M' sound in it [such as in *mantras* like *Hrim*, *Shrim*, *Dhrim*, which represent the Divine Mother].

13. The mantra of the Divine Mother is already supercharged. You do not have to bring it to life. What is important is that you make a promise to yourself and keep that promise. Do not be crooked in your ways toward others. Especially, do not deceive yourself.

14. Ma (the Mother) is the presiding deity of all our senses. She is very close to us. She is very affectionate towards us.

15. The Mother, who we worship, who we meditate upon, that very kind Mother is found in many forms, with many names. Saints have said: She is Durga, She is Kali, She is Parvati, She is Uma, She is Tripurabhairavi, She is Chandika. And so, people worship her in many ways. In reality, She is One Shakti (Energy). It is the same Shakti which is in Brahma, in Vishnu, in Shiva, as well as in you and me. It is because of the flow of this Shakti that we move and walk, that we maintain personal energy within ourselves. When we worship The Mother, we are engaged in the worship of Shakti. We contain Shakti within us and we want to enrich ourselves with more Shakti.

16. There are three primary forms of the Divine Mother (as Daughter, Wife and Mother) in the form of Mahakali, Mahalakshmi, and Mahasaraswati. In the present age called Kaliyuga, Kali is the primary deity.

17. When we are afflicted by pain, agony, or mental distress, when there is darkness all around us, nobody is to be seen but the

Divine Mother. She is the only one visible, whether it be as the Earth Mother or as the earth itself, whether it be the Mother in the form of the sky, or in the form of the directions, or even whether She comes in the form of an agonized sigh! That sigh, then, will take us across life.

18. However wrong we may be, however wrong we may become, by Her all is forgiven. She forgives everything. But if we become so wrong that we can no longer justify being known as Her offspring — if we don't belong to Her, what can Mother do?

19. The Divine Mother is all-pervasive. If we try to express this, or understand it, we learn that She does not have any beginning or end. How can you measure something that does not have a beginning or an end? It cannot be gauged. How can you measure something that is immeasurable? It cannot be measured.

20. The Divine Mother is a part of the play, excitement and joy of Mahabhairava.

21. Mother Mahakali, Mother Mahalakshmi and Mother Mahasaraswati — all whom we worship — are a single threefold Creative Power.

22. The original form of this Creative Power is Sarveshwari, which means 'Mother of All', whose grace provides everything.

23. Sarveshwari is the one *shakti* which permeates every particle.

24. Our adored, respected, dear Divine Power Sarveshwari has no expectations from anyone. She is neither a form nor a sound. If She is to be found as form or sound, it is in the aggregation known as *samooh* (collectivity). Into this *sangha* (aggregate), She subtly infuses Her life force.

25. Nothing can be said about the grace of Sarveshwari, the Divine Mother. We cannot say what She will show to whom or in what way.

26. This Supreme Mother, this life force, is not merely a subject of contemplation. She is not merely a subject of speech — how can you speak of Her? She is invisible — how can you see Her? Particle by particle, in every particle She *is*. That is how She is. This is the Truth.

27. Where is Ultimate Good? It is in the company of the Mother, Mahamaya (Supreme Illusion).

28. The Mother, in the form of their Livelihood, is busy taking care of all beings.

29. The Divine Mother is, Herself, an aggregate — a *sangathana* — an aggregation of many divine forms. She is the Collective *shakti* of all the Divine Entities contained within Her. For example, Ganga (the sacred river) absorbs the drainage, pollution and waste of the cities and purifyes them; she is also the Divine Mother. Through innumerable drains, the pollution of humankind flows into Her, through Her, and becomes purified. Thus, She becomes the redeemer of humankind. At Her source (in Gangotri in the Himalayas), Ganga would be redeemer of but one individual, not the redeemer of all humanity. The Ganga of Gangotri cannot flow for the welfare of all until She embraces all waters eager to join Her, all 'drains of the city' eager to merge with Her. If She did not absorb this great multiplicity, if She did not incorporate all of them within Herself and continue to flow with them in Her, She would run dry at Her source. She would be the redeemer of but a single person, not the Redeemer of Humanity. By the collective redemption of all, She is known as Ma Ganga. Her act of absorption is known as *aghor-shakti*. She can be the sacred divinity called Ganga only by absorbing and purifying

all men and women: warrior women, prostitutes, devout women, valiant men, lechers, ascetic men — the Holistic Entity formed by the incorporation of all these is known as Aghor-Ganga.

30. When even the earth, the cosmic bowl, the directions, *everything* disappears, when creation ends and nothing remains — neither you nor I — Mahabhairavi keeps performing her *tandava* (dance of the dissolution of the creation), the dance from which the sounds of "*Dhrim*, *Dhrim*, *Dhrim*, *Hrim*, *Hrim*, *Hrim*" resonate.

31. Mother Mahabhairavi removes fear from Her devotees. She protects them in every way. Even Yoginis regard Her as their presiding deity.

32. *Shakti* is known as Yogini, a yogic state of absolute unity. When enriched with *shakti*, even a man ascends to the Yogini state.

33. A woman who, in her quest of the Supreme Truth, has reached the pinnacle of spiritual practices becomes a member of Mother Kamechha's group of friends, and is referred to as a Yogini. She can fulfil all wants and every desire.

34. There is nothing beyond *shakti* in this world of action. Every action in the world is accomplished through *shakti*.

35. "*Baba*, are all women referred to as *devi*s, the Feminine Divinity?" "No wise one! Only the representatives of Shakti are called Devi."

36. *Devi* (the Feminine Divinity) is the one who grants you a desired wish or gets it for you from someone else. She can also take away what she has given to you. Devi is known as Shakti, as Heroic Energy, as Iron Strength: iron's strength protects gold. Know Her to be so as well.

37. As iron is referred to as a measure of strength, think of Devi in the same way — as a measure of strength.

38. We attempt to face Shakti headlong, or we stand opposing this Divine Power. The result is that we either remain unsuccessful or it destroys us.

39. It is essential for every being to store *shakti* within themselves.

40. The original being, Shiva, is enfolded by Shakti. Without it, even Shiva is like a corpse.

41. Every being in the cosmos embodies Shakti.

42. *Shakti* is nothing external to us. She is with us; She is between you and me, but we may be unable to recognize Her true form. Or perhaps we are unable to understand how to worship Her. Don't limit Her worship to fruits and flowers, candles and incense, foods and other gifts. These are mere physical objects, not Divine Entities by which to get to know Her. Until we are able to cultivate pure thoughts, pure *bhava* (faith and feelings), as well as pure behaviour, until then, that Sacred Entity and the virtues of that Supreme Sacredness will not come to us. But, keep in mind, this Sacred Entity keeps looking to find us so that we may find It.

43. Know the forms of the Creative Energy that you worship. Energy can be destructive. One who gets *shakti* can be destroyed by ignorance or misunderstanding of that Power. For example, fire's energy can burn you, but if you treat it with respect, you can cook food on a fire and derive heat from it when you are cold. So, also, the train is a power. If you leap in front of it, it can kill you, but if you approach it from the side, you can ride on it safely to distant places. It is necessary for the seeker to know the various forms and the characteristic behaviour of the Creative Power worshipped.

44. We say that we want to see the Mother. We see Her every day. All that we see around us is Her form. But in our mind is a different conception of Her; we think of a thousand different forms.

45. We have never tried to see the Mother in the trees and vines, in the plants and bushes, in the shine of the grass — in the rays that emanate from the shine of the grass. In all the pictures we have tried to make of Her, She appears as the cartoon of a person. She will never be visible in this way.

46. The night, Nisha, is another form of the Mother. From Nisha's darkness we see the light. She is the night. When She comes all the lamps are lit. Taking all creatures in Her lap, She puts them to sleep and imbues them with new inspiration. After night has provided new energy to all the beings of this world, then dawn, Usha, makes them industrious and diligent.

47. Between earth and sky lies 'emptiness'. In this 'emptiness' exists the world. Not only the world, but also the solar system. Beyond this sky is more sky, and beyond that sky, more sky, and beyond that sky, more sky. When you get to know this, you will know the Divine Mother who is easily known and understood by *bhava* — the deep emotions of faith and love.

48. Our life-play exists because of this 'emptiness'. Within it one can see houses and castles, cities and towns, plants and trees, rivers and mountain tops — everything is breathing in and breathing out in this 'emptiness'. From this 'emptiness' is derived the warmth and energy which makes everything appear and disappear.

49. 'Emptiness' contains that Creative Energy within which we move about, within which we move our limbs, breathe in and breathe out. If this 'emptiness', somehow disappeared, our life-energy would end; our life-play would end, too.

50. This 'emptiness' is bounded on all sides, but hollow in the middle. Since it is hollow, we can sit within it, perform our actions, do our work. This is how one can know the Mother.

51. We have no idea how many souls are born and disappear in the 'emptiness' that lies between the earth and the sky, in the vast empty sky. This is the womb of the Mother; it is the place of growth through which all beings progress, including you and I.

52. The 'emptiness' between you and me, the 'emptiness' between the earth and sky, this 'emptiness' is the place of Ma's origin. In the Scriptures, 'Emptiness' is described as the Mother Herself.

53. The Mother is the empty space between the earth and the sky from which we derive our life-energy. To find Her we will have to give up everything and nothing.

54. The glory of the Mother in the form of the life-force (*pran*) is not limited solely to words of poetry. Energy, latent deep within us, is the primary evidence of Her power.

55. Many people do not know how to perform rituals, how to pray, how to meditate. But they still try by saying: O Mother Ashtabhuja, I know neither worship nor prayer, but nevertheless look kindly at whatever I am able to do. I know I have not served my Guru, nor thought deeply in his company, nor tried to learn from him, nor tried to learn the scriptures, nor tried to keep good company. I know these, my failings. Even so, I have faith in You. If I have faith, that faith is You.

56. Mother Ashtabhuja, I do not know how to pray and meditate. I know only how to remember You. I know only that You are The Mother. I just repeat Your name, saying "Ma, Ma, Ma...." I don't know anything more than this.

57. Ma, if I am worthy of You, please accept me as I am. If I am unworthy of You, then my life is wretched. Only You can show me how to remove this unworthiness, this wretchedness from my life. It is not something dependent on my intelligence or my own efforts. It is not subject to my mind.

58. The Mother can be worshipped, known, seen only by our feelings of faith and love (*bhava*). Where these feeling are lacking, She will not be present.

59. There is a great difference between hearing something from somebody and experiencing it one's self. If you have an other-person-dependent view of life, how can you find the Divine Mother?

60. The Mother is hungry for our emotions of faith and love. With these feelings, whatever you offer Her — water, fruit, flowers — their essence reaches Her, through the medium of air, through the medium of fire.

61. Our biological mother has an unfathomable heart for her progeny. She bears all kinds of troubles for her children. She controls her senses, checks her desires, goes through intense pain for the baby in her womb. After birth she controls her diet so her milk will be good for the baby. Her love for her children is so great that it cannot be adequately described.

62. Nor can we describe our other-worldly Mother. She keeps us happy in this world and in the other world, too. She protects us in this world and in the other world, too.

63. We would collapse if She removed Her supportive hand, Her supportive grace from us. We may have no place to go in sorrow but to the lap of Mother Earth. It is to Her refuge that we go. Even when we cannot forgive our own sins, the Mother forgives us, supports us. She supports us in the form of Mother Earth. She supports us as Infinite Compassion.

64. Great veneration is to be performed in this life: veneration of the mother who gave you birth. You owe to your worldly mother more than you owe to your other-worldly Mother.

65. We should have respect and affection for our other-worldly Mother. We should serve Her all our lives. How do we serve Her? In the same way that a hen incubates her eggs.

66. If the Divine Mother wants to meet you, She will manoeuvre you so that, somehow, wandering through life, through living in various environments, by meeting saints and great souls, She will get you to stand in front of Her door and She will say to you: "Look! This is Me and this is My Knowledge. This is My Vision. All these are My Powers. These you can have."

67. When the Mother comes before us, we hide from Her. We remember our weaknesses, our minds become polluted with negative thoughts, our hearts begin to hate us. We say: "Alas! I am unable to lean toward this Divine Power. I do not realize I am totally unattached — totally without internal conflict, internal dilemma, internal divisiveness, totally faultless, totally egoless — thus I remain deprived of Her." We never say, "I promise myself, starting today, I will not behave in any way to make myself unhappy".

68. We should say to ourselves, "O my 'Self', I promise you I will behave nicely with you and never deceive you. I promise never to let you fall." A person who makes such a promise to himself actually makes a promise to the Mother. He makes a promise to God. His promise, then, is very valuable. On hearing of his promise, God immediately comes to meet him.

69. As needed, the Mother distributes Her energies for creation, preservation, and dissolution into Brahma, Vishnu and Mahesh respectively. The first duty of life is to absorb oneself

in the worship of the Mother in the form of this *sangathana*, this Aggregate of the Gods that is The Mother.

70. Mother Saraswati, O Beautiful One, please make our speech beautiful. Make it so beautiful, so sweet, so fine and melodious that even a wild beast may relinquish its savagery on hearing our voice. May the wild beasts become tame and make friends with us so that we may share each other's affection.

71. First, recognize the fundamental Self. Knowledge comes later. The supreme element is *shakti*, the creative energy. Only the one who recognizes the Creative Power of one's Self-element can recognize the Creative Power of the Supreme Element. Before starting prayers and the ritual of purification (*achmani*) we say '*tatsat*'. *Tat* means 'element' and *sat* means 'the Truth' i.e. 'that element which is the Truth'. Saying *tatsat* is known as 'the cleansing of the past'.

72. The Divine Mother is with us: She is eager to meet us, friends. But, until we know the practice of prayer and meditation, we have not met the basic conditions to know Her.

73. The ocean that is on the earth is saline. The ocean of Mother's love is like *kshirsagar*, the ocean of milk. Narayan, the Supreme Being, resides in this cosmic ocean, not in the saline ocean. The women of earth are an embodiment of *kshirsagar*. The rapture of *kshirsagar* is much deeper than that of a saline ocean.

74. Divine Mother! I do not wish to worship You as my wife. I want to see You in the form of my mother or daughter. It is this kind of affection I want from You. I am not afraid of seeking this love from You.

75. Sarveshwari asks you to respect the ways of your ancestors, *rishis*, and divine beings. In the absence of such respect, it is possible that we will lose our culture, our civilization.

76. Sarveshwari does not ask you to perform ritual *pind-dan* — to appease the ancestors with gifts of food — but to perform *punya-dan*, acts of virtue and charity.

77. The various physical forms that exist are that of the Mother, aren't they? It is only through this physical form of the body that we can achieve the company of the Mother, the Shakti. That great *shakti* is achieved through action, and action reflects the source from which it originates, the life-force (*pran*).

78. Any activity is the worship of Mother Kriti, the Divine Mother in the form of Action.

79. Mother Kriti, please give me divine knowledge, divine hearing and divine speech.

80. I request the Soul of the Supreme Soul to infuse new virtues, new thoughts, new sentiments in each soul so that, in this period, in this time, in this moment, each soul may receive new inspiration.

81. Divine Mother! Make us full and complete so that we do not feel the lack of anything. If we do not feel a lack, we will not beg You for anything.

82. Why should we not ask something from Her which, upon getting, we will not need to ask for anything else?

83. Pray to the Divine Mother that our faith not only support and cooperate with our heart and mind, but that it keep them stable and in check. If heart and mind become unstable and fickle, it can cause turbulence in nature and in the solar system.

84. The life of human beings is like a wet cloth. When you spread a wet garment in the sun you anchor it with a stone or a clip so that it does not blow away in the wind. Similarly, in human

life, an anchoring brick or clip of *shakti* is needed or our life will blow away like a wet garment.

85. It is not that whatever we want is good for us, for what we want can, in fact, be poisonous for us. For this, O Mother, do whatever is favourable for us!

86. To try to know one who is unknowable is the worship of Mother Lalita. We search for that which is not ours. We find that which is ours.

87. The Shakti whom we call Durga is not an external being. Durga denotes those queens who, like the Divine Mother, fought and destroyed those of beastly behaviour who attacked them. These queens achieved success where males were not able to succeed.

88. She is an eternal maiden and she is not limited by any race, religion or country. She belongs to all countries, at all times. She always remains a maiden, like the five virgins [who are worshipped in India]. She always, always, remains a maiden.

89. It takes great effort to understand what it means to come close to the Mother, Her deeds and Her embrace. Many people have sacrificed themselves many times and yet have not recognized Her.

90. We do not have the stability of the mind through which the Mother is found, so that we can know Her, hear Her, and understand Her.

91. She does not accept even an atom of whatever is brought before Her. She does not take it. She does not taste it. It is our desire that accepts it, our thoughts that taste it, our motivations that take it and use it.

92. Mothers! Just think of it, you are not inert like the rocks. You are the living and walking source of the Divine Mother.

93. In many lifetimes we have been unsuccessful because we do not accept the Mother in the right way, the Mother who gives us all success.

94. The Mother will meet you, find you if your thinking remains steadfast, if your ways remain right and if you keep the promise made to yourself. The time you were lost, the time you were in darkness doing many things you should not have done, She will forgive all that.

95. How beautiful is Mother's love! How big is Her heart that bears pain and trouble. She has only the welfare of Her children at heart.

96. What joy we receive, what affection we receive, what love we receive! What don't we derive from the Mother's power? It is the Mother's power which, in various forms — sister, wife, daughter, daughter-in-law, mother, Aunt — helps us, encourages, and inspires us. In various forms and by various names She directs our *shakti* in the best possible way.

97. One who is favoured by Ma's creative power, one who is respected by Her, becomes full of *shakti*; this one becomes powerful. One from whom She takes Her grace, who falls from favour, becomes an object of criticism and, despite being innocent, is beset by a thousand troubles.

98. We are unable in our human lives to mould this Creative Power favourably, all the time and in all places. This is why we must think about Her, ponder over Her, study Her again and again. We have to speak to Her and hear from Her. This song [of experience] is not sung. It is different from poems that are sung. It is not *Gita*. This is a song which, not sung, can only

be experienced. Where? Don't look for it when alone, but when sitting in a group. Look for it in the *sangha*, in the resonance of unity. What? This song, this *sangita*, this is the *sangha*. This unity, too, is music, the music and song of *sangha*. What is the meaning of music? The resonance of good thoughts in good company for the welfare, peace and happiness of all beings, this too is music.

99. Friends, we have hope. With hope we also have faith, a divine faith, a faith in the loving Divine Mother who shows us our path and helps us to complete those actions She wants us to complete.

100. When Lakshmi, presiding deity of wealth and daughter of the Ocean, was sent from Her home at the time of Her marriage, Her father gave Her the sands as a wedding gift, for all the other gems had been given away to the guests. Thus, She brought sand to the house of Her husband. Wherever She goes, Lakshmi dusts sand from Her clothes. This dust provides material needs and great wealth. It also gets in one's eyes. Then one cannot see clearly. Especially one cannot see the poor, those who have less than oneself.

101. If we are able to receive food, water and clothes regularly and on time, it is due to the grace of the Mother. It is Her kindness, for many beings are deprived of these.

102. Mother! Our heart is not so noble, our mind is not so noble, our senses are not so noble, our soul is not so noble. Who does not want to live like a compassionate human being? But our brothers, relatives, friends, neighbours distress us; mental agony agitates us. So Mother! Give us strength to understand and to bear with these things.

103. We worship Mahakali, we think about Her, meditate on Her, ask Her to expunge all the dark thoughts, the tainted thoughts

that arise in our minds, the dark emotions that arise in our hearts, so that they may not afflict us again.

104. Mahalakshmi comes in the fourth stage [of *Navaratri* ceremonies]. She fulfils all our desires and wants.

105. Mahasaraswati, she is the beautiful one. She imparts power and vigor to our speech. She makes our speech beautiful. She makes our speech very sweet. The worship of Saraswati begins on the seventh day [of *Navaratri*].

106. Whatever time we take to think about and meditate on the Divine Mother, The Mother of the Cosmos, whatever time we spend in Her service, this will accumulate; one day, it shall become an immeasurable wealth. It will become a great treasure, imparting to us a great heart. When such a heart rises in us, all our friends, well-wishers, and everybody else will derive joy, happiness and peace from us.

107. The quest for Her is a joy in itself, which ends on coming face to face with the Divine Mother. The pain of separation from the Divine Mother is better than an actual meeting. Because, after meeting Her, everything ends for a human being. But living in hope of Her, with faith in Her, waiting for Her, we have a happy, joyful life, a life akin to the joyous sounds of babies at play.

108. We should strive to know her in some form or other. This striving itself constitutes our worship, our prayer, our meditation, and our unbreakable faith. In the absence of this faith, we lose so much.

The Practices

All spiritual paths have certain practices designed to aid the seekers on the path. Aghor tradition favours the practice of self-discipline and thought discipline to quiet the mind. A mind that has been stilled has the potential of seeing the reflection of its own soul in the ocean of its own consciousness. But Baba also spoke of a practical path of spirituality. Instead of asking seekers to give up their mundane life and duty, he asked them to live in the world, yet apart from it, so that they may perform all their social duties, and still be able to pursue their spiritual goals.

1. Aghor is the path of simplicity.

2. The cultivation of right speech and expression is known as the worship of Vagishwari, the Mother of Wisdom.

3. The cultivation of right speech begets a sweet temperament.

4. O tonsured ascetic! The pursuit of good character and good behaviour turns a human into God.

5. Dear Sudharma (one who performs meritorious deeds), we should have the ability to cope with things. We are on the path of the ascetic [a life of discipline with a spiritual goal]. We should accept whatever we get, if it is appropriate. If it is not appropriate for us, we should reject it.

6. With determination and practice we get to know the unknown.

7. The married males of our *samooh* (society), Sri Sarweshwari Samooh, are worshippers of Creative Energy (*shakti*). This, by extension, makes all males worshippers of Creative Energy. A man becomes whole only by contact with Feminine Creative

Energy. It is only by contact with this Creative Energy that men derive the talents of intellect, strength, patience, competence, charity and compassion. The sorrow that often seems evident in this contact between male and female is a weakness due to the male's attachment to illusion.

8. We do not need external ostentation to please God. The method of worshipping or pleasing the Isht, the divinity dearest to one's heart, is kept confidential. Your *Isht* is hungry for the *atma-bhava* — the thinking of yourself in the image of the Supreme Soul — and desires only the flowering of your beautiful heart.

9. If good thoughts are not put into practice, they fall into disuse and cause pain.

10. Human beings have a separate plane of existence — that of thought. Here exists the unique Creative Energy called intellect. With the help of the intellect human beings can face the problems of the world.

11. Worship not the past but the future, so that you may attain the divine light of the present.

12. We do not just speak about equality. We practice a holistic yoga that generates balance and equality.

13. Assure your soul and your life-energy that you will search for the Supreme Soul (*Paramatma* or God), that you will dispense divine virtues among the people of this world.

14. Philosophy is merely a text until it assumes a pragmatic shape which is practiced in behaviour.

15. You will find divine knowledge only when you will lose your egotistic attachments.

16. By thinking about your 'Self', vices will not come to you. Your body and mind will become pure.

17. Don't allow your vision to become tainted. Then, as long as your eyes are open you will be able to see your friends and relatives, as well as saints and monks. Keep your sight so clean that you are able to see reality, and understand it.

18. There is power in the mantra. There is immense effect in the word.

19. Awaken the divinity within you. Then only will you derive true joy.

20. Human beings are one. Whether they be men or women, Hindus, Muslims or Christians, the omnipresent soul is present in all of them.

21. To be unstable is not in the character of a yogi. It is not his innate nature. A yogi's character is to be stable. That is why yogis speak about keeping their unstable eyes closed. Only when they are closed can you see the spark of the fire burning within you, the fire that burns away our sins and makes us fearless, the fire that bestows upon us a pure, radiant, blue light. To become pure is a great state to achieve. To become so is the goal of spiritual practices. This is what is known as the Eightfold Yoga.

22. O seeker! Stop feeding the fire of material desires to escape from attachments and jealousies. On doing so, this fire goes out. To attain the state of liberation (*nirvana*), these actions are necessary.

23. All practices can be practiced, but all practices are not practicable for everyone. The choice of your practice will be made by your Guru for you.

24. Give up amassing material things for your own benefit, not through fear of worldly ridicule.

25. O seeker! Destroy all attachments. Become transcendent to them all.

26. Whatever comes to you without desire, of its own accord, is right and appropriate for you.

27. Working for social welfare and fulfilment of appropriate social goals is a great service to the Cosmic Energy. There is no spiritual practice, *japa* (chanting the *mantra* or the divine name on a *mala* — sacred beads), yoga, knowledge or salvation greater than this.

28. Do not voice the deep knowledge residing within you. It will express itself in your behaviour. Transform 'meaninglessness' in life into 'meaningfulness' for the purpose of everyone's happiness and everyone's welfare.

29. Never express anything without a specific purpose.

30. O Seeker sitting in meditation! That one, The Supreme Soul, the ever-active Cosmic Energy, will not think of you in this way. Your meditation on an inactive form will just make you an embodiment of inactivity yourself. It is better to walk than to sit down. Make a resolve to walk and you will start to walk. You will leave all kinds of paths behind. Yes! You can even leave death behind and move forward!

31. Darshi (one who sees with discerning vision), tell Sambhav (the potential seeker) to practice 'vibrationlessness'. This is a state beyond either wakefulness or sleep.

32. When we think about the sayings of saints and *munis* (forest-dwelling ascetics) in a different way from what we have thought

about them until today, only then will we understand the power and appropriateness of their sayings.

33. Only that is acceptable, O Sudharma (one who practices acts of virtue), which does not make tremble your heart, or that of someone else.

34. O Sudharma, focus and concentrate. Do not be careless or negligent. Do not repent later. This is our discipline.

35. Always remember, there should be an absolute lack of the firewood of worldly attachments. The fire of many desires is extinguished when the firewood is missing.

36. This path found with great effort should not be taken lightly. By those full of desires and jealousies it is not understood easily. Deeply, with reverse flow, the subtlest it will show. For those attached to darkness it is not possible to be known.

37. Clear insight or knowledge cannot be achieved by indolence.

38. Live within society; live without ego. Do not lose the greater part of your valuable life hankering after prestige or recognition. All this is also known as meditation.

39. Accept and cultivate the virtues of saints and soldiers.

40. With great attention focus on yourself. Fulfil the inspirations arising from within. Do not worry about the many obstacles on this path. If you have confidence in yourself, you will journey along the path of your life without difficulty, without dilemma, without internal strife, without ego.

41. Do not just speak of the idea of controlling desires, but practice it. Only when your behaviour speaks of 'desire-control' will you have accepted the ideas of the great saints.

42. Never do anything only because others are doing it. "One who does yoga as a copycat weakens his body and ruins his health." Encourage your mind to mature. Avoid that which should not be done.

43. With personal vigilance there is no scepticism. Wherever the Guru wants me to go, you can go.

44. Display of spiritual powers is in bad taste. You have received powers neither to deter people from their own action nor to produce easily for them whatever they desire. Such displays weaken your spiritual pursuit.

45. If something comes to you by itself, without your having desire for it, such as grains and cereals, then you are not made guilty by accepting it, nor will anyone think so. But if you desire something and act on that desire by pulling something to yourself with effort, that effort is not correct.

46. Amass the wealth of peace, equanimity, non-attachment and equal sight.

47. Real happiness lies in giving up even giving up.

48. Whatever is gone, is gone. Keep whatever you still have.

49. Struggle is necessary for success.

50. Act according to the inspiration from within. Do not be artificial. Don't harbour conceit.

51. Wishing does not beget anything. Act for it.

52. Live a natural life. You will achieve the clear vision of knowledge.

53. Do not amass too much by your livelihood. Share what you have with those who are without resources. This is the spirituality of equal vision; this is known as encompassing empathy.

54. O virtuous one, O Sudharma! Teaching without initiation widens a gap between Guru and disciple.

55. Vamdewanagar, the home of Aghor knowledge, is beautiful. It has been the Aghoreshwar's place of spiritual practice. It is ever-resonant with mantra. It has been the residence of Aghoreshwars, Aughars, saints, great souls, and good people. Spiritual practice here during appropriate times leads to great knowledge and merit. Here, one can even glimpse the Aghoreshwar; one can even glimpse the Kapaleshwar.

56. Understand the indications sent by all-liberating Tara. O seeker! Let spiritual unity generate within oneself during sleep. This will create absolute knowledge. What can be better than this?

57. One who has given up the quest for prestige, status and praise needs neither to wear ashes on his body, nor to do austere practices, nor to look for recognition. Such a person keeps himself free even from the chains of caste, of lineage, and of regional, national or linguistic identification.

58. I do not ask you to understand only this and no more. Such is not a state of complete understanding. There is more beyond this, which you have to know and make your own. For complete understanding, you have to end all notions of ownership.

59. Sudharma! Roam freely in a state of limitlessness. Accept the state of non-acceptance.

60. You can find a lot within yourself which you cannot find in history or literature, or in inscriptions or through rituals and devotion. What you can find by an exploration of yourself is

better and higher than things achieved through other mediums. I exhort you to be active toward this reachable goal.

61. Free yourself from illusions induced by hearing, misunderstandings produced by seeing, doubts created by smelling, tasting, touching and speaking.

62. It is better to remain unburdened by metal [i.e. gold and silver] or stones [gems and jewels] or papers full of ink [scriptures, the Vedas, the Puranas] than to lug them about. The mind should have to bear the burden of too many books.

63. By doing *pranayama* (breathing exercises) and *pranav* (vibrations of the seed mantras), electrical currents are generated which will end the lethargy of your senses.

64. When you meditate with a strong resolve you achieve all the things, substances, resources that you desire. How do you achieve them? Through the medium of vibrations. This is true. This is a characteristic of the truth. It is to achieve this knowledge that scholars, ascetics, and yogis do austere practices.

65. What is wealth? At the beginning of prayers we say the mantra '*tatsat*' ('that which is true'). Your fulfilment of duty, your sweet words, your good character, your inner absorption in spiritual strength — this is your wealth. With this wealth you acquire all the riches of divine existence.

66. Let your prayers, practices, mantra-recitation and meditation remain a mystery within yourself. By this effort only, by silent acceptance, one can achieve many special things which one cannot obtain by opening one's mouth.

67. Pray and meditate upon the inner soul of the Supreme Cosmic Force, the Divine Mother. Keep performing your worldly

duties so that your friends and relatives, children, grandchildren and all those who come in contact with you do not suffer in any way.

68. By performing prayers to that Supreme Creative Power, by taking time from your daily activities to meditate, you awaken your inner nature, your inner comprehension.

69. Fully devoted to the great unknown, I never became restless; I had an unshakable faith that my vision would be enlightened, that my speech would be enlightened, that my voice would be invigorated to inspire the intellect that seeks reality.

70. The *Brahm* (God) that you look for so eagerly is within you. By forgetting the distinction between 'I' and 'You', you will achieve *Brahm* and will, yourself, become *Brahm*-imbued. The feeling of "I am *Brahm*" (I Am That) is very far from the distinction between 'I' and 'You'.

71. Sitting in meditation, the seeker becomes a triangular instrument. As a triangular instrument, whatever thoughts come to his mind, appropriate to the time and place, he offers to the Divine Mother. He prays to Her. He meditates on Her.

72. If he has a physical image to meditate on, it is good. If he does not have a physical image then he, himself, becomes a physical image of the divine and a special vibration begins to happen in his heart. That vibration remains with him. And, as soon as he sits in meditation posture, whether he meditates or not, whether he prays or not, that special vibration remains with him.

73. The prayers and meditations we perform never go to waste. In one form or another they bear fruit and we will achieve the supreme gift of limitless peace and contentment.

74. Things become available to people in different places in different ways, depending upon the way in which you make your resolve, and the strength you apply. Often, things happen the way you want them to, and then they are good for you. One can never say exactly how, where or in what form the Divine Mother will bestow her grace on us, or how she will reveal different things to us.

75. If we remember the Divine Energy for even a moment while performing our daily activities — by stabilizing our mind, by controlling our senses, by staying within ourselves — for that moment it will truly qualify as 'remembering the Divine'. It will bestow tremendous creative energy and insight on us. It is this creative energy, then, that takes us to different places and causes us to meet good people.

76. Understand Her as the same Creative Energy that is everywhere, in every form. If one cannot do that, then try to understand Her in Her different forms. But, definitely try to know Her; try to be knowledgeable about her in one form or another. This very effort is devotion, prayer, meditation, and unshakable faith. If this effort is absent we lose so much that could be ours.

77. Who do we pray to? We pray to the great unknown, the Supreme Cosmic Force, or we pray to ourselves. We say, "O my Self, if you are in a good state, if you are full of love, then I am not worried about anything". Then I do not have any reason to give place within me to thoughts and acts that are ephemeral.

78. In a state of deep meditation, the seeker remains absolutely quiet. He lets the vibrations of his heart communicate everything. Within this vibration, the mantra given to him by the Guru resonates. Then, he manages everything in life easily.

79. Our inner being should remain constantly with our Divinity while we perform our duties with our eyes, nose, mouth and hands.

80. O Sudharma! Devoted to the unknowable Divinity, you will have to explore and experiment in *particular* ways, because if philosophy does not become practical, it is incomplete. Philosophy alone keeps us, and our understanding, separate away from the truth. Truth and the grace of that unknown Divinity are matters of ultimate practicality.

81. Aghoreshwar seekers do not have body-oriented intellect or understanding. Their intellect and understanding are spiritually oriented. Because of this, and due to their strong resolve, Aghoreshwar seekers can reach the deepest places, the deep understanding of everything. On reaching such a place such seekers become humble, and their voices then express only the best for everyone. They no longer have a place for distorted words in their vocabulary; such words do not arise in them.

82. Aghoreshwar seekers do not wear specific attire, nor are they confined by caste, class or category. Nor do they have any great concern to fill their bellies. Because lay people do not understand this, they think the *aughar* seekers eat anything. This is not so. Aghoreshwar seekers take many forms for survival.

83. It is said, "For twelve years a seeker lives with the monks to learn to think and speak". Speech, here, signifies the speech of welfare for everyone. The thoughts of such a person, their aura, their electrical charge, their vibrations are self-activated without performing breathing exercises or rituals. They achieve the Divine in the flow of thought itself.

84. Know the straight path. The straight path is the path of the dear *Isht* (the divinity dear to one's heart). Dattatreya,

Abhinavagupta, king Harshavardhan's father's Guru Aghor-bhairavacharya, Kaluram and Kinaram: all these self-realized beings achieved success by walking the straight path. If you walk on a crooked path, you may hurt yourself; you might break your limbs; you will become a victim of distortions. You may be trampled by the unwary on the path. All these things are possible.

85. The faith and devotion that you show the Divine Mother in her many forms is of utmost importance: She is none other than that faith itself. By worshipping Her, you worship your own faith and devotion outwardly. Faith and devotion arises within you and prompts you to worship.

86. I want to be blessed with everyone's blessings. Whether they be young or old, rich or destitute, I have respect for everyone. This is the greatest worship. It is this devotion that manifests during the period of *Navaratri*. We performed these rituals in times gone by, we perform them today, and we will perform them in times to come.

87. If you are married, observe the principle of 'one spouse and a disciplined life'. Then you will not have untoward desires and you will begin to understand the Mother Principle. Your heart will become simple and attuned to the Mother Principle. Whatever you undertake then, you will succeed at.

88. To achieve the great grace of the Supreme Soul, Cosmic Energy, all that we need practice is self-control. Performing violent austerities does not qualify one as a true seeker. Maintaining good character and self-discipline are the mark of a seeker's authentic quest. Such a quest has great meaning. In Hinduism people who maintain good behaviour throughout life gain the respect of even Brahma, Vishnu, and Shiva, as well as other Divine Beings. They bow their heads to such a seeker. If one strays from good behaviour, one may beseech the Divinities,

but they will not come. If one loses self-discipline, one cannot follow one's quest. If one cannot follow one's quest, one will not achieve the company of The Divine.

89. True seekers resolve to accept the way of life of great souls. They do not relinquish this resolve under any circumstances. Such seekers worship Mother Lalita. She is the mother of intelligence, knowledge, and expression. The voices of seekers of Lalita become so sweet, so beautiful that those who hear them melt at the sound. Such seekers do not say "we will do this" or "we will do that". They remain quiet within themselves. This silence is their biggest seed, their primary teaching.

90. In our prayers, in our enunciation of words, in the things expressed by our speech there is great energy. This energy travels throughout the cosmos very quickly. In the same way that modern scientific tools produce electrical currents that travel very quickly, our acts also produce vibrations. They vibrate through the whole cosmos instantly.

91. Everything is favourable. Behind this 'being favourable' is the hand of the Great Unknown. If one maintains the balance of one's mind, heart and intellect, then one can achieve this Great Unknown. But if we lose our balance, become unbalanced, and do all kinds of unwarranted deeds, then how will we achieve this Great Unknown?

92. Lalita, the divinity with the beautiful sweet voice, blossoms in our hearts with Her grace and our voice becomes like Hers. You know when it has blossomed as soon as you begin to speak. You have no doubt about your ability. You become fearless. Your love and affection begin to grow continuously. You are happy, you achieve peace. You are known as the person with the beautiful voice. Your voice has strength. It is refreshing to the ears. It produces happiness in those who listen. Full of pure thoughts and sentiments, you lead a wholesome life.

93. We have wandered in the jungles of the mind so long! We do not even know for how many lives we have been wandering. We are still wandering. O God, how long will we keep wandering in ignorance? God, we have been through much. We are tired of wandering lost. Give us a path. Show us on the path. We are so tired of wandering lost.

94. Our ignorance, our poverty of knowledge shows that we have associated with people who are not alive; they are like the walking dead. The dead stink. That stink bothers us. Our hearts and minds, then, do not feel free. The practices we do will not bear fruit.

95. We perform our meditation, our mantra-recitation, and our pure thought processes, and we refine these continuously by keeping our senses quiet and our mind focused; we do this to gain this state which has no profit and no loss. It is a state beyond considerations of profit and loss and it can be achieved within ourselves.

96. We achieve Creative Energy only by listening — and after listening, by pondering over it, and then finding expression for it.

97. We save our strength by taking the vow of remaining with one mate. This is a great austere practice in itself. What practice can be more austere? It is a greater vow than worshipping divinities, than going to the doors of saints or *fakirs*. This vow also pays respect to your Guru. If you want to cultivate Creative Energy, you must rely on the creative strength within yourself. You must save the strength within, refine the strength within, incubate it like an egg.

98. If we worship Divinity out of inhibition or greed or some other mundane reason, then our fear and greed remain intact. Many kinds of desires will continue to rise within us. When

these remain in us, we will not be able to destroy the suffering of happiness and sorrow. These desires can be destroyed only by the grace of the Great Unknown and by intense discipline.

99. By performing mantra-recitation, by meditating, by reflecting — by doing these things, strength is added to our speech. This strength accumulates and gives us the ability to succeed in everything. Mantra is the friend who takes us to our soul, which, though we have always lived with it, we have suppressed. Unable to discern this, we keep looking for our soul outside ourselves and among various divinities.

100. I meditate on the Divine Mother. I meditate on solitude. I do not think of this and that within myself. I do not listen to the internal noise; I do not argue with it, I do not hold sentiments at all. I draw on the ambrosia within, I count on the *mala*, and I drink the ambrosia of that exhilarating energy. I close my eyes and I am absorbed in it. I have nothing to do with illusions.

101. During meditation, devotion and reflection, that Entity being contemplated comes very close, then goes away after visiting you. That moment will not come again. Therefore, give the utmost attention to that moment.

102. I do not like living in villages or cities. At times, in the summer at sunset, I would sit with well-wishers absorbed in thought. Or we would discuss good acts and the welfare of the people. When currents rose in my mind for seeing pure sights, I would call up visions and think about them. At times I would try other mantras. I would reflect on the knowledge imparted by the different mantras. I used to think of myself in the form of the mantra as well.

103. O Sudharma! Like the sage Durwasa, remain free of attachments; remain the same through profit and prestige, respect

and disrespect. Perform everything without expectation; walk on the path of liberation. This is better than walking the path of desire-full action, getting tired, and sitting down on the path.

104. O Sudharma! I do not ask you to become merely a performer of ritual acts. In that lies an enmity towards real devotion. There are no stopping places on the path of desire-free liberation. There are many stopping places for the tired on the path of desire-full action.

105. After contemplation and prayer, after practices, we perform the act of dissolution (*visarjan*). After dissolution we acquire the goal of our practices, which is very close to us. Friends! Dissolution does not mean that we forget that Divinity, or what we have been contemplating.

106. We express devotion to Creative Energy in three ways. When one worships Her in the form of a child, a daughter, it is a devotion full of joy and happiness — She is dearest to one's heart. One neither expects nor accepts any gifts from the Creative Energy. Rather, one gives something to Her. One always gives to one's children. There are no obstacles in contemplating Her in the form of daughter. When one worships Her in the form of mother, one knows She will not listen to or do everything one asks of Her. That is because a mother knows what is good for her child and what is not. However, when you worship Her in the form of a spouse, there are many acts, practices and rituals one can perform. There love and only love exists. Nonetheless, being devoted to the Divine Mother in the form of one's spouse creates many obstacles, because love does not follow rules and regulations. Therefore, one may have to bear deep sorrows and troubles. That is why seekers have been asked to think of women as mother, sister and daughter to attain absolute absorption in them. If a seeker projects any form of spousal love on others, he commits a kind of aggression.

107. Therefore, seekers should attain absolute absorption in Her in the form of daughter, mother, and sister. Even respect has its own rules and regulations. But you love only the one who is your own. There are no obstacles in contemplating her in the form of your daughter. How heavy our heart becomes on the day when our daughter leaves the home!

108. The place where practices are followed, resolves are made, devotion is expressed and prayers are performed, this is a sacred place. Live in such a place humbly. All paths lead to the same goal. Paths are not very different. They all rise out of the same source and end in the same place. We should be humble, gentle, and virtuous in contemplating Cosmic Energy, our Supreme Consciousness, our object of devotion. Whatever is happening within us is all that is going to happen. It is a gift from the Mother. It is her blessing. It is her grace. Without her grace, human beings have no strength at all.

The Truth

For anybody pursuing the path of devotion and spirituality, 'Truth' matters the most. It could be the truth of the social world we live in, or the eternal truth of life that seekers try so hard to find. Baba also spoke about the truth. His simplest advice was to seek the truth within one's own self. For there it lies, waiting to be discovered.

1. Look at yourself with utmost attention. In yourself you can find everything in its wholeness, without lacking anything at all.

2. To see what exists within you, will be as the real truth for you.

3. The reality within you, absolutely yours, is worthy of devotion.

4. Peace and happiness are achieved by exploring the soul. Listen to the voice of the soul. Listening to the mind, full of desires, can bring sorrow.

5. Truth is not known by mind, intellect or body. Knowing he knows but acting as if he does not know, this one knows the truth.

6. What is known as the truth is but a mere part of reality. [Social] truth is not the same in every country or period.

7. Human effort implies divine Power. It infers the supremacy of good thoughts.

8. One who speaks the truth, acts. Unaffected by the weaknesses of society, the truth-speaker achieves success.

9. People who keep an eye on their feet are aware of what is beneath them. They do not stumble on their paths. They regulate their whole body and system with ease.

10. Consider the deep mystery: while you live only for yourself, your life is useless. The day you come to know that you live for others, your life becomes meaningful.

11. When something is right in your hand and you are still unable to see it, this is known as a state of darkness.

12. Without deciding on what should and should not be done in life, one remains unfulfilled and ignorant.

13. The inspiration or sacrifice of a few people can lead to the fulfilment of a goal.

14. Shyness, fear and doubt taint a human being. Shyness, fear and doubt are among the five repugnant traits.

15. All of our despicable deeds — robbing, killing, all violence and crime — are seen by the Divine Power in the sky, in the wind.

16. A livelihood involving malice, cunning, deception, thievery, robbery, bribery, smuggling or unjust appropriation generates fear, discontent, rancour and sorrow.

17. A king cobra with a jewel on his hood denotes unfathomable wealth. He also bears poison. Such wealth can take away the life of living beings.

18. Rancour is a cause of sorrow. This spite flares up due to momentary greed, egotism and useless pride. This rancour has grown so much that it has given rise to castes and classes among us. It is this rancour that makes us powerless in our towns and homes, amongst relatives and friends.

19. If one's life and body are continually assaulted by terrible shocks [to the senses] and one keeps quiet, this specious calm is useless. It is only an attempt to deceive others.

20. One who is afflicted by laziness, torpor, and too much sleep becomes a victim of sorrow and mental agony.

21. Troubles tell you to regain your balance. Difficulties and problems take you to the right path and show you the way.

22. Neither be kind nor expect kindness from anyone. Kindness does away with human effort, and effort is the real expression of truth.

23. Charity given from the earnings of hard work bears good fruits. Charity given from plunder does not bear good fruit.

24. A crooked one lives like a malevolent spirit in his own house, among his relatives, mother, father, children, wife, and especially with himself. Because of this ghost-like existence he remains deprived of wholesome food and pure water. He runs here and there, spurred by relentless desires.

25. One who does not really live with himself will not find a place to live anywhere else. Such people are bereft of the electrical impulses that can be found in the human body, with the help of which one can ignite the eternal light.

26. Whatever becomes [something else] gets destroyed. Do not become anything. Then you will have no fear of being destroyed.

27. Becoming anything produces attachment. Attachment produces infatuation with things or position. Eradication of attachment and infatuation is a truth.

28. Anything associated with illusions, desires, praise, and prestige will exhibit ups and downs, cause and effect, trends of waxing and waning.

29. Attachment is neither ignorance nor sin. It is an intoxication; it wears off.

30. For anyone who is born, for all who live, it is necessary to die one day and leave this world.

31. Be it God or a representative of God, whether it be a divinity or a representative of a divinity, whether it be a pair of divinities — whomsoever — *nobody* is spared the causal effects of their actions. And nobody *ever* will be spared the causal effects of their actions.

32. In the Kaliyuga era, we don't recognize 'mental sins' (crimes of thought). But we certainly do recognize 'mental virtue' (thoughts of piety).

33. Very greedy are the small divinities that have made our ten senses their home. They give us sorrow and force us to live a hellish life full of guilt. They thrive on indulgence. They try to convince us that they give us happiness, peace, comfort, joy. But all these pleasures are momentary — so momentary that often we cannot even speak about it.

34. All physical pleasures are ephemeral.

35. Delicious food does not provide as much taste as hunger.

36. Indulgence prompts the senses towards more indulgence.

37. Do not expect divine consciousness from inert matter.

38. Greed is the progenitor of sin.

39. A person who is fed up with material desires is a trustworthy person.

40. To forget one's limits is to forget one's self.

41. There is no such world as heaven. Good action, itself, is a form of heaven.

42. Inactivity achieves nothing but mental agony.

43. Regard all actions as useless that do not benefit the spirit.

44. The essence of the 'whole' is truth. Even its residue is true.

45. Untruth is not healthy. Give it up.

46. Human effort ornaments this body of dust.

47. The Great Unknown has no name.

48. If we help ourselves a little bit, the Divine Power will help us a lot.

49. Before God, flattery does not work.

50. How can you achieve peace if you have not experienced the Self?

51. One beset by illusions is amassing what is already amassed.

52. One-upmanship, rising in us, generates illusions and destroys us.

53. Our own little hut, our own doorstep is better than the palace of another.

54. Just as the wheel of a chariot rotates, we will inevitably arrive here again. We will definitely meet again in successive lifetimes.

55. God has nothing to do with particular diets and dress.

56. One who does not display the basic traits of a human being, is inhuman.

57. One who has fallen cannot lift others.

58. It is an absolute truth that everyone born will die.

59. Action prompted by injustice leads to fear.

60. Those who are frightened produce fear.

61. A life full of suspicion is a life of torment.

62. Bad habits are the devil himself.

63. The only cure for bad habits is death.

64. The thoughts expressed in the revered *Bhagavad Gita* arose on the land of the Kaurawas, amidst a battlefield. How can peace, harmony and tranquillity be derived from thoughts born in conflict, born in war? At that battlefield, even after listening to the *Gita*, war and fighting were the most dominant thoughts.

65. Religion is like a huge banyan tree. It provides shade to everyone, no matter what class or religion they belong to. Religion respects people; religion attracts respect to people. Without such guiding principles, distortions arise, ignominy takes birth and grows. Without guiding principles, the behaviour of human beings resembles that of animals with horns.

66. One who deceives himself deceives everybody. His knowledge is like unrestrained babbling. It is merely a voice [without any worthwhile content]. O Seeker! He does not know the ideals of religion or their practice.

67. True religion fosters friendship between people. It overflows with affection, for people who are truly religious do not have doubts about themselves or their religion. True religion is charged with empathy.

68. Regardless of the specific religion or faith shown by whichever guru or saint, all paths ultimately converge at a common confluence.

69. For each moment, time and place are significant.

70. Every nation, moment, period, is merging into itself and passing with every passing moment.

71. The Eternal One has given the same rights to all, has given the same rights to all to express those rights to all natural wealth, whether it be material or spiritual.

72. There is nothing sinful or virtuous in the world. There is no happiness or suffering. The world is pure, like fire and water. The feelings and experiences of sin and virtue, happiness and sorrow are generated by the senses. Human beings burn in the fire they create.

73. The children of the One 'Eternal' Power of the cosmos have individually declared their Gods to be unique. Their individual Gods give them conflicting social systems in different languages. Each declares as God-given the system they desire.

74. No book or scripture is dictated directly by God. A book given by God must be in a Godly language, but people of every religion regard their own language as the language of God.

75. Human beings, in each passing moment of their lives, are attracted to new things, new substances, and new thoughts, whether they are right or wrong.

76. Letters [of the alphabet] do not say anything. But they speak volumes.

77. The word is truth. The word is described as Brahm. The sequence of its emanation is letter, word, action, Truth, Brahm. A letter exists. From the letter sound rises. That sound is Brahm. The word is everything. With particular words, sounds we call each other. All economic interaction, all business is carried out with words. By words, we buy things and chase away unwanted things. Through words, global quarrels and wars can be settled peacefully. Everything happens because of words.

78. *Vaikhari*, the emanation of vibration and its expression in one's speech, is an instrument through which every truth is reflected. The vibrations from one's *vaikhari* are the only instrument that resonates everywhere, brought to light everywhere in one simultaneous moment.

79. The word '*pandita*' does not denote a Brahmin, nor does it denote a scholar. A Pandit is an expert or a specialist in any field.

80. There is nothing everlasting on earth. Everything is swallowed by time. But the words spoken by saints never die. However, over time, the forms of their words and expressions do indeed change.

81. This earth has never been empty. Nor has it ever been full. On it have dwelt many living beings who vigorously began to search for the secrets of life, but got tired and turned back.

82. O Seeker! We understand the certainty of our birth. So, also, is our death absolutely certain. If one leaves the world after giving birth to great ideals and practices, they will remain on earth as one's everlasting life. This is what is known as immortality.

83. We are alighting into a pure, clean lake [of divine feelings]. The joys of this lake will wash the darkness away.

84. Liberation from *samsara* (the cycle of birth and rebirth), to be not born again, is the fruit of devotion.

85. The germ of a species begets seed, flowers, or fruit, according to its nature. So do human beings and animals. They are formed by action. A species reflects the character and form of the action from which it came into being.

86. To picture baby Krishna as sucking his toe (thus forming a circular flow of energy) cannot be mere imagination. All this [vibration and flow of energy] happens within us like the energy of a whirling top. It is this very same wave, this very same vibration, this very same impulse which is a million times faster than the speed of light. It goes around the whole solar system in a circle within the span of a minuscule moment.

87. Many beings receive the gift of life. Of the many forms, the highest form is to be a human being. Human beings receive special insights about their obligations in life. Vibrations rise in them; vibrations of an affectionate, motherly aspect clarify perceptions and feelings to their minds and hearts. Affection, love, joy, satisfaction, coolness, fulfilment: every thought and feeling is available to human beings who perceive their duties clearly.

88. Animals and birds have progeny. Beyond mere progeny, human beings recognize sons and daughters, grandsons and granddaughters, aunts, uncles, cousins. The children of human beings have a gentle nature. They have conscience and a soul. If, after acquiring wings, they fly away like the progeny of birds, they, too, can be regarded as mere progeny as they abandon their parents who bore all troubles, all difficulties for them, who nourished them with great care.

89. Even if we give all the wealth of this rich earth to our mother and father, we have done nothing to favour them, nor have we paid them back.

90. There are devotees of Divinities. There are devotees of humans, too. There are devotees of serenity. There are devotees of agitation, too. There are devotees of the Mother. Practice good actions, good deeds, and understand 'goodness' consciously. This will make you live like an un-limited, un-measurable person.

91. One who has an all-encompassing vision, one who sees God and Guru in himself, one who remembers my words and does not ignore them, is like a personification of ambrosia. By keeping company with such a person, many worldly diseases of human beings — hunger, thirst, desire and ambition — are dissipated.

92. In the same way that one enjoys the pleasures of night at night, and the pleasures of day during the day, the pleasures of light are in the light, the pleasures of the earth are in the earth, the pleasures of the sky are in the sky. They are all different. One cannot experience them all at once.

93. Like a grand imperial path, Ramayana presents an easy path of devotion and duty that leads to *Ishwar* (Supreme Consciousness).

94. Silence is the strength of the soul. Self-absorbed silence is equal to achieving the unblemished, unattached, absolute state. It is the single essence, *Brahm,* of non-dual reality.

95. Pure faith leads you to the divine essence of the Guru.

96. Before inauspicious, impure, inactive, unjust, unsavoury creation came into being, only 'I' was there.

97. Only after 'I' have tasted the world first do all other beings taste it.

98. Like a shadow, I and my heart are always with you.

99. A sovereign cannot be eternal. Only the timeless ideals and practices of a saint can be eternal.

100. A saint inhabits a higher place beyond the joys of luxury, or God.

101. Action is one, but it has different effects. Saintliness has no particular characteristics.

102. A person practicing Self-welfare and welfare of the other is a true human being.

103. Great souls, saints, do not belong to just one nation. They belong to every nation; they have everybody's welfare at heart.

104. A pen that records the experiences of great people has a very long life.

105. You must have noticed while walking on your path that your shadow never falls to the south.

106. In traditional India it is a sin to accept either interest or gold.

107. An understanding of category distinctions is also needed in life. The Feminine Essence is One, but some women are regarded with those considerations due a wife, and some with the considerations due a mother, or a sister, aunt, grandmother, etc. [This distinction tells you the proper way to relate to them.]

108. Women are not bound by distinctions. That is why they are a form of the [transcendent] divine energy.

Conduct

For a seeker on the path of spiritual enlightenment, be they an austere ascetic or a householder, their mode of behaviour while pursuing their spiritual goal is of utmost importance. Baba always stressed good conduct as a prime spiritual trait — conduct that does not hurt anyone in anyway, but in fact helps them derive love and happiness. To achieve spiritual enlightenment, Baba said, it is very important that one incorporate basic traits of wholesome behaviour, for those humans who do so become divine.

1. In whichever corner of the earth you live, be it in a jungle or a city, or a village, make friends with all living beings around for a thousand miles to the east, a thousand miles to the west, a thousand miles to the north, and a thousand miles to the south. Always keep this thought constantly alive deep within you that you have to become a well-wisher of all, you have to become a friend of all.

2. Within our worldly lives, in our social life, we should constantly examine our behaviour, and we should do constant self-analysis.

3. After the autumn season, a tree acquires new leaves. Give up old ideas and live freely in the city with new ideas. Be sure that illusions and attachments do not grab you.

4. Even if you are cheated, do not cheat others.

5. Duty and its *modi operandi* should be explained keeping in mind the needs of the time, the country, and the person concerned.

6. If you have to criticize someone, do it with a well-wishing heart.

7. Good people do not harbour feelings of revenge within them. O Darshi! You will also have to live such a life. Even amidst the most trying conditions we will have to take the shelter only of a healthy mind, a healthy conscience, a healthy body, healthy senses and good conduct. You will always have to keep in mind that you do not humiliate anyone through your words, or insult anyone in any other way, even if they consider something good as bad. This is saintliness, this is true humility, this is all-encompassing vision.

8. If your pure heart does not permit you to do certain things, do not force it to do them; do not incite it to do them, or it will become very heavy, very difficult to carry around, very difficult to bear. If you put undue pressure on your mind to do unjust things it will have a very bad effect on your mind and intellect, and your speech will lose its forcefulness.

9. Make your life useful and active.

10. Always pay attention to two things — if you can do something good for someone with this body, definitely do so; and if someone does something bad to you, ignore it. Suffer patiently, eat less, and do not let your Self-respect die.

11. To be liberated from this world and the sorrows of this world, members of the Sarveshwari Samooh —followers of the Aghoreshwar — should live their own life, and should satisfy the hunger of their family and dependents with discipline and modesty.

12. One who has a short life should try to establish new ideals through his behaviour, through his mind-action-speech and his disposition, in his society, in his place of dwelling, and in the place where his well-wishers reside. He should keep in mind that he does not inflict any injury on anyone through his behaviour and through his speech.

13. Not everyone who lives in or is dependent upon the ashram is a saint. It will be naïve to regard them as true Aughar-Aghoreshwars in character and action merely because of their similar dress, posture and attire.

14. A marriage performed in the mode of buying and selling, with gifts and dowry, indicates that the bride is only wanted for sex. Children born of such a marriage favour only money. It never fosters an inclination towards righteousness or the spirit.

15. People receiving the grace of shelter in the ashram should, through their behaviour, not encourage consumption of alcohol, overindulgence, or rancour amongst people.

16. Service of the nation and society is greater than worshipping sculpted idols. Such service is also akin to worshipping yourself.

17. "Welfare of all, happiness to all" is a noble and normal behaviour. To fully accept this is the best human duty.

18. There is a great devotion to be practiced in life — devotion to the mother who gave birth to you. Regard the debts to your earthly mother as greater than the debts to that other-worldly Mother. In ancient times, very old, greatly respected people were in fact referred to as the 'mother'.

19. You have to save yourself from the ills of bad company.

20. Listening to criticism of others reduces the spark in your own life. It does not provide any positive encouragement to you.

21. The company of those who are fallen will not take you across the ocean of life.

22. A person who — despite living in the ashram — keeps jealousies towards others, does not use his thoughts and speech

carefully, and whose temperament it is to disrespect others, lives like a very poor person.

23. It is not improper to live with a beautiful woman in this world. But it is very dangerous to lose oneself in it. Like an ant, one should remain apart from it despite partaking of the sweet syrup, not like the fly which just goes and falls in it. The ant is better than that monkey who has two feet, for she makes her nest for proper living, so that she may be able to cope with the cold in the winter, with the heat in the summer, and with water in the rainy season. And that monkey who has two hands and two feet roams homeless from one treetop to another.

24. The person who is criticized for doing good deeds is a very fortunate person. The person who expects thanks or praise for his good deeds is a very unfortunate person. That is because he sells away his very valuable deeds for a very little price.

25. Speak sweetly; it costs you nothing.
The wealth of kindness, knowledge, devotion, virtue, contentment, wisdom, and detachment that one has, this cannot be stolen by anyone, this cannot be burnt by fire, nor does the ruler of the country have any rights over it (for taxes!). Humility — the person with this wealth is a very rich person indeed.

26. In this world no one is either your friend or your enemy. Here, it is your behaviour that creates friends or enemies for you. The affection of a good person is like that iron chain which bonds two people together. It never breaks.

27. O human being! Do good for others. It lifts your own heart very high.

28. Facing up with difficult situations provides great power to the spirit.

29. Only that person really lives who is devoted to his duty.

30. The path of ill-action is the worst kind of leprosy.

31. Do not close your doors for your mistakes. It is your mistakes that will eventually take you to the right path.

32. It is a great sin to look down upon an unmarried, pregnant woman. Whichever religion you follow, if you can, try to reassure her. If you do something to protect her baby, you achieve the merits of worshipping God. If you want to eradicate this weakness of society, then work to make such an unfortunate woman a fortunate one with your assistance. It will be an act of great merit. But if we insult such mothers, then there is no place for us anywhere.

33. Say something with conviction only when you yourself are fully convinced about it.

34. To move forward means to work with constant evaluation of time.

35. We should resolve to happily cross some difficulties on the way [of life]. Only then can we reach our goals.

36. To deter from justice is a crime against God.

37. I am a critic of *sadhus* (monks, mendicants). Is it proper to escape from life if you cannot manage your domestic duties? What can we expect from such people?

38. To neither know, nor see, nor hear about to the weaknesses of others is a meritorious act.

39. When you cannot find soft, sweet and beautiful fruits on old trees, new trees should be planted in their place, O Sudharma.

40. Old people say that one should go to the woman after midnight, when food in the belly has been digested. If your semen is mature, you will have a healthy child.

41. Anywhere in the world one is a saint by one's actions, and one is a thief by one's actions. One is a priest and a scholar by action, one is a warrior and ruler by action, and one is a person who does service to others by action.

42. O Sudharma, never, even by mistake, partake of water, fruits, food and other offerings made to a religious idol established by a smuggler or profiteer. It takes your own inner strength away.

43. Listen! Do good to everyone. If someone does any disservice to you, pray for that person. If someone walks a mile for you, then you should walk two miles to benefit that person.

44. May the consciousness of the people become mature; may their vision become clear. May they be able to walk on the path shown by Rama and the Buddha.

45. The biggest goal of human life is humanity. Only when the human being adopts the religion of humanity does his dear Divinity become pleased with him.

46. We should all be practical in our behaviour. Practical behaviour is the biggest achievement of social success.

47. A patient is given medicine not according to his likes or dislikes, but according to his condition.

48. A living being who has limited needs is always happy and prosperous.

49. You should never keep yourself inactive. The person or

organization or party that does not have a clear goal or project, ultimately perishes.

50. Moral action and faith: these are the two greatest treasures of life.

51. There is no doubt that, once each individual overcomes his weaknesses, the ills of the world will dissipate by themselves.

52. In whichever corner of the world be a human being, it is his duty to stop the one who exploits others, to boycott the exploiter, and to save the exploited. This is the biggest worship of God.

53. Keep rancour, jealousy and petty contentions far away from your family.

54. To have simplicity in life is very important.

55. An individual does wrong and society is blamed for it. How, then, can we pretend to be improving the society? If we would improve society, then each individual will have to improve themself. Let every one of us individuals throw away our weaknesses. This is real social service, real social improvement.

56. If you want to live, live with love and goodwill.

57. Divinities, saints and prostitutes: these should only be seen, not touched.

58. Fully use your free time. If you do not have anything to do, then go sweep and clean the neighbourhood. If you have some time after all this, then remember God as well. One who has spare time after both these activities will think of futile things and will create troubles for others.

59. Hurt nobody, neither by your speech, nor your acts, nor your behaviour.

60. Human beings should not lose their faith. Make yourself believe in yourself. This will raise morality. This is the only medicine to eradicate the darkness in your heart.

61. Regarding every person as a child of the only mother of all human beings, Mother Sarveshwari, forgetting caste and class and high and low, let us progress towards the truth so that we may adopt secularity in our behaviour, and be proud of being humans in this world.

62. To criticize others is ignorance. Look at things with a good vision. Be mindful of what words you use for whom, and what effect it has on the person. Understand all this, and then evaluate yourself. Act only after carefully considering your actions.

63. You will need to give up a few more things — weaknesses. Selfless renunciation is the foundation of our life. You do not need to give up your home and family.

64. Dig out the roots of ill-feelings and cultural aberrations with strenuous effort.

65. Crime makes your heart fall very low. Take the vow with your mind, word and action that you will not commit any kind of crime.

66. Most of our ills are generated by [succumbing to belief in] the categories of caste and class. Because of this burden, many people of the Hindu society are not able to achieve their full physical and mental potential.

67. To serve the suffering is to serve God. Real service is done by good actions and wholesome inspirations of the mind.

68. You should adopt good conduct with your mind, speech and action.

69. If you are experiencing injustice, be it from any element of society, or from the leaders or administrative officials, you must oppose it. To do this, it is necessary that you live a disciplined life and have good conduct in life.

70. Rama practiced the ideal of "One woman, ever celibate".

71. We have to learn the temperament to give. We should learn to give something. On doing this we will have friends, well-wishers, dear ones, pals, everyone. By giving I do not mean giving money. Give pure behaviour. Give pure actions. Give pure conduct. And teach all this to your little children too.

72. Neither should you get into fights unnecessarily, nor should you unnecessarily ejaculate. It weakens your strength immediately.

73. Bad thoughts and bad actions are like a demon that always keeps you perturbed and frightened. If you want to be fearless, make your life pure.

74. If you are following pure conduct, even if you are punished for it, understand that you will thereby find your goal very soon.

75. Commensality generates love. When we live together, we are equal and same.

76. To criticize anything with your speech, whether that thing be good or bad, is not good. It denotes our own weakness.

77. How can we evaluate someone else's life and conduct? You cannot measure even a blade of grass against a mountain. A blade of grass has its own importance in its place.

78. Save yourself from ostentation. To accept gifts and dowry on the occasion of marriage is a grave misdeed.

79. If you begin to oppose marriage gifts and dowry everywhere, in every home, then no one will dare to even talk about it before you, nor would they be able to boast that they have accepted such gifts.

80. Those who live on unjust interest find that their heart falls very low. If we help someone with money in their time of sorrow, then to take interest on that money, or to expect anything else in return, shall cause our own downfall.

81. Keep beautifying this organization, in the same way you beautify your hair.

82. To look back upon some of your past actions in life will give you sorrow. Perform pure actions in the present or it will lead to retrogression.

83. To want more, is greed.

84. May God give us the strength to bear with things.

85. To use your experience in your own way will be beneficial.

86. The word *shudra* (low caste) does not mean impure. Actually it means 'pious and respectful'. The day you begin to look at Shudras with the sentiment of them being 'pious and respectful', you will achieve indescribable heights, your personality will have a great aura, you will generate wholesomeness. O Sambhav seeker! This is what is to be known, that you too have to know.

87. Tell a sick person about his diet and way of life also, not just about the medicine, to help him recuperate fully... With the

medicine of knowledge, we must also have good conduct as a way of life.

88. Because you eat grains and derive nourishment from your country, if need be, relinquishing all love for your life, sacrifice yourself on the sacrificial altar of your country and your nation.

89. I hope you will keep yourself free from all tensions and stress in every way, and will pay attention to your health, to your cleanliness, and to your good behaviour.

90. To hoard those things that are necessary for saving lives, in any nation or society, is an indication of the weakness of the administrative structure.

91. You will have to keep yourself carefully separate from the retrogressive tendencies that are prevalent in society today, amongst those people competing to paint the truth as a lie and a lie as the truth.

92. [In the Hindu context,] vermilion is the symbol of a woman's blessed state of life when her spouse is alive; it is indicative of her husband's valour. Ignoring this, many Kshatriya women are enacting the husband-destroying form of Mahadevi these days.

93. In the same way that it is a heinous crime for a very greedy person to gamble with his friend and thereby claim all his money, so also it is a heinous crime to accept someone's daughter after wrenching money out of him.

94. How can a man, after neglecting his duty to nurture his family, be called a true 'head of the family'? Such a person is definitely not worthy of being addressed as a father, or as a head of his family, or as the ruling authority of a country.

95. It is not good to keep oneself in darkness. One should strive to achieve glory. One should have unfailing trust in God, and one should have this sentiment — long as I want to be friendly to myself, the extent to which I am friendly to myself, I will be friends with others too.

96. The ashram in which you live, the little hut in which you live, everything in there is worthy of respect, not neglect. When you live with this feeling, then you will achieve that vision of the Guru, the experience for which saints and great souls keep searching, that entity who is addressed as God. All these you will find right here.

97. May my speech become eloquent. May my speech become highly efficacious. May my speech have that supreme ability of patience. May my speech neither hurt anyone nor generate any feelings of regret in anyone. Let this be our constant endeavour throughout life: that our speech should remain ever-sweet and pleasant for others.

98. Be polite towards all your friends and relatives, and accept humility in your life. Then you will learn to live with politeness and love and affection with everyone — the love and affection which have in them no trace of cunning or deception. This should be the ultimate goal of our life, and this should be our religious duty in today's day and age.

99. The kind of behaviour one metes out to others, it is certain, shall be received in return. Our actions keep trailing behind us. They spare no one. They do not spare even the gods or goddesses, or their representatives.

100. If, like the dung-beetle, we carry our ego with us wherever we go, then we will remain deprived of that supreme happiness and peace; instead of enjoying this, we will only keep criticizing each other.

101. Let us not turn away from this duty of ours (to experience supreme joy). Let us not wash our hands of our duty. Let us not overlook this duty of ours. We have to search for it. Then it arises in us. Then we feel its vibrations in us. Then we hear its sound within us.

102. We say that we are going to become a devotee of the Divine Mother, we say that we shall propitiate her, that we are going to her to establish our rights with her. What is our right? Our children, our friends and relatives, our well-wishers, they have a right to get some love from us. Are we able to give that love to them? People of such cruel temperament, people involved in such cruelty, will not find shelter anywhere on earth.

103. Divinity is nothing separate from us. Human beings themselves are divinities. Human beings themselves are demons, as well. If their behaviour becomes so, they become demons. If their behaviour becomes good, they become gods.

104. We will have to now with certainty that these idols [i.e. these living beings] in whom God himself has infused life are the idols we shall respect. We will give them love, we will receive love from them, we will receive affection from them, and we will feel great pride and satisfaction in receiving all this from them.

105. Salute to the divine; the way is the truth. Neglecting the way of our ancestors and our *rishis*, and by presenting the reality to others in a greatly distorted way according to their own convenient viewpoint, the priestly class has fomented retrogression within our society. Now, they have nothing to teach about the way anymore, nor do they have any knowledge of the scriptures or Puranas with them. These have grown unfamiliar to them, and are becoming increasingly unfamiliar every day. May God save them.

106. We, the people of India, had such ideal behaviour and character once, that we had no need for any rules and regulations.

107. One who desires someone else's wealth for his own convenience remains dependent on that person. In the same way, we are indebted to our mother and father, to our guru, to our nation and to our society. And there is only one way to pay this debt back — to never turn away from our duty of "welfare of all, happiness to all".

108. One who leaves his own home and keeps to roaming around other people's doors, he loses his own self-respect and becomes an object of ridicule everywhere. Then, no one will even come to sit with him.

The State of Being

The state in which a person is at any given point of time is of utmost importance for their success and balance in life. If one has a stable state of mind, calm and patient, it will not be difficult for them to either understand or solve the problems that come before them. On the other hand, if they are in an agitated and confused state, then the simplest problems will become insurmountable for them. Therefore, one needs to cultivate a state of being that is in keeping with one's spiritual goals, because it is in that state that divine knowledge permeates into the person.

1. O devoted seeker! [The realized person] remains absorbed in himself, remains untouched by tastes and enjoyments, remains in ecstatic enjoyment within himself. In ecstatic enjoyment within himself, he sees everything, hears everything, does everything, his behaviour becomes different from common behaviour . His acts may be unintelligible to the laity.

2. Neither the sky nor the earth is heaven. Neither is heaven [in] the directions. There is neither any cause nor purpose for any heaven.

3. Non-duality begins when one is [established] within one's self in supreme solitude, in mind, speech and action, despite being in a crowd. This is a supreme achievement.

4. The person who ends his sense of duality and distinction becomes God. As long as remain any distinctions or differences of 'pure' or 'impure', he does not achieve divine energy.

5. The solitude gained in a crowd is more intense and deep than the solitude attained in a desolate place. In a desolate place, many illusions and unwanted activities arise. Contrasting with

this, the solitude gained in the midst of a crowd is great; it is pure. It is beyond dilemmas and uncertainties. In this solitude one does not feel as if one is doing anything at all special.

6. As far as realization is concerned, human beings can reach any place. However, if they do not remain [one-pointedly fixed] there, then know that their actions are ill-advised; their thoughts are impure.

7. The non-attached seeker considers wealth, jewels, property — everything — as insignificant as straw.

8. The word 'ours' has a big meaning: this is to be done, that is not to be done. All this is decided in your consciousness by itself.

9. 'Non-attachment' is not a path one follows. It is a stage, a position achieved by Aughars and Aghoreshwars.

10. Recalling acts of kindness and acts of joy in the form of words, in the form of the mantra, I remained absorbed in myself into the last hours of the night.

11. Treating everyone equally, the nation, country or society without excesses creates people with stable minds and hearts, desires, knowledge and science.

12. Your (the Guru's) words have carved and moulded this raw form — me — and have given me the ability to reach myself, and to help others to reach a high place.

13. Be *with* time; do not be swept by its flow. I am with the flow: I am not stagnant.

14. Those who are simple, with beautiful speech and beautiful minds, those who can endure things, these are the people who

achieve non-duality. Those who cannot endure anything are the people who usually produce misery.

15. If you give up what is flowing and changing — the unreal — it will be good. Best is the stage where, once you close your ears, nothing arises nor sets in you. Achieving this stage, one's vision becomes fixed; one begins to live a life free of turbulence and full of practicality. This vision is a complete vision. It is known as "I Am That", as "I Am *Brahm*", as "*So'ham*" ("As is that, so am I").

16. I do not talk about the world generated by the mind. A person who achieves the *turiya* stage becomes the owner of the innumerable solar systems found in each atom within him.

17. At that place there exists no *yantra*, no mantra, no spiritual practices, no worship, no divinity, no one to revere; nothing exists except the guru. Then the distance between the guru and the disciple also disappears.

18. The 'non-conscious state' is a name for the ecstatic mind (*samadhi-chitta*). One who attains this state no longer suffers pain.

19. Neither coherent nor confusing vibrations arise in a 'non-conscious' mind.

20. "O Gurudev! When you accept my humble requests, I am delighted. My numerous vibrations wane. My mind progresses towards balance and ecstasy."

21. You will know not only the eight-fold yoga, you will know yoga itself. You will become knowledgeable and capable. Sitting in the lap of that Super-nature, you will experience not only the joys of love, but you will see the truth face to face.

22. That time and period is described as a separation from that which is dear, a separation from attachment. There will be liberation (*nirvana*) from that which 'Is', and liberation, also, from that which 'Is not', and the dissipation of all tendencies. When consciousness of the body is gone, this state will be described only in these words.

23. When one becomes stable within, understand that this time, this moment is a momentous time, a great period, because it is at this moment that the Unknown Friend appears to us, reveals itself to us.

24. If, from within, one becomes aware of this threefold state (stable, aware and detached) and establishes one's Self within one's self, then one realizes that within is the guru, within is the creative energy. Within, one's soul itself prompts one toward virtues and good actions.

25. Whatever prayers and practices, meditations and reflections that we do in a disciplined and regular way do not go to waste. They will blossom within us and we will know grace, which bestows contentment and peace.

26. We do not have to seek the happiness, joy, and enthusiasm that we look for in nature, in these bushes, in the open air, within these walls, in these clothes — in the vibrations that all these have. Rather, it will appear to us by itself if we look in the right way, with the proper eyes and a clear vision.

27. Those who speak sweet words develop self-control. Then, only good words come from their mouths.

28. Only when we achieve a realized state will we understand our reality. Only then will we understand the words and thoughts, the counsel of saints and great souls.

29. It is difficult to understand how a being gains redemption by the dissipation or non-dissipation of sins, or through the possession or absence of certain virtues. This is not a full redemption. A complete redemption is a state in which you actually reach the Great Unknown, see the Great Unknown, meet the Great Unknown, converse with the Great Unknown — and, likewise, the Great Unknown with you. You sit with the Great Unknown and the Great Unknown sits with you. This is called adoration. This is the same state of existence as that [i.e. of the Great Unknown].

30. Then, It reassures us that It has now made us Its own, and that we, too, should consider It ours. That I, which is in you, you understand. It is my soul, the very same. It is the one who has forced me to this special stage. When this happens, we become absolutely drenched in Its love, Its affection, Its joy, Its happiness. This is the state of an Awadhut, of a saint, of a *mahatma*, of a *mahapurush* (great person). This state is a million times higher than that of an incarnation.

31. An incarnation — as you must be aware since you are aware of scripture — is forced to adhere to the social organizations and the religion of its time; it can not go beyond these limits. If it does cross, break or remove those limits, society criticizes it by calling it an idiot, stupid, foolish. Then, society describes this situation (of social transgression) as hell.

32. Great souls, great people, they have crossed all limits. When you see saints and seekers, they do not have a little ponytail, they do not have a sacred thread, they do not have any attachment for rituals. If rituals can be performed, good; if not, then there are no regrets. Such a person is not concerned about pure or impure, edible or inedible, where to sit, when to rise, if he has prayed on time, whether two hours before or two hours after. He does everything. He respects everyone. Yet it is as if he does nothing. He keeps himself detached. He is not bound by limits.

33. What is the human condition today? Again and again human beings try to find the Supreme Truth. They begin to see things, to think, ah! it is in this scripture, in this worship, in this ritual. It seems as if they can see it, but they do not find it. They are not able to find the Supreme Truth.

34. O silly human being! What you look for does exist, but it is not what you think it is. And the way to find it is absolutely not the way you are going about it. It is difficult but not impossible to find. It can be found. You will find it, too. But you will not find it in doing the things that you are doing now. By doing what you are doing now, you find only what is found by all living beings — who are born in excrement, who play in it, roll in it even before birth. They are sad. "Why, why, why", cries the baby, "why have I entered this place of excrement". Your present condition is like that of a newborn baby; it is not different.

35. If a person is overwhelmed by impurities, how can his spiritual energy (*kundalini*) awaken? He lies in a state of torpor. He is not fully conscious.

36. You are known as householders (*grihastha*). You bear the weight of a family. If you are among the good householders, and if there *is* an entity such as God, and if He is influenced by your efforts, then all good householders will attain a high place. But if there is no such entity, or these efforts do not matter to it, nevertheless these efforts are sufficient in themselves. In a little corner of his heart, a householder has a big space. He can accommodate hundreds of people in that space and still find space for himself. What could be greater than this?

37. We need to be measured in our ways. When we are measured in our ways our awareness grows, our intellect grows. Then a carefree spirit will come into us.

38. A superficial person does not stay in one place. There really is no place for a superficial person. Superficial, loquacious, untrustworthy, ignominious people never achieve knowledge, they never achieve capability. They do not make a history of their own. They are born like insects, and like insects they die in darkness.

39. Young people suffer at the hands of the demigod Kama (Desire). They suffer today; they will always suffer. It is inevitable.

40. Contact with excrement does not make one impure. If one ingests excrement or alcohol, these do not make one impure. Impurity arises when the initiatory rites of purification have not been performed for that person.

41. There are only eight initiatory rites. These rites do not exist only among the Hindus. They exist among everyone: the Muslims, the Christians, the Buddhists. In the absence of these sacraments, a person is not a Muslim, a Hindu, or a Christian.

42. Although we are ready to be Brahmin, Kshatriya, Vaishya, Shudra, we are never ready to be human beings until these rites are performed for us. If the rites have not been performed, we cannot attain the highest state.

43. Midway between praying and relinquishing, I rest. Rama himself prays *to me*; I relax.

44. We are afflicted by many thoughts of sin and virtue, heaven and hell, actor and non-actor, receiver, non-receiver. As long as these dualities find a place in our minds, our minds will be contaminated. Remaining contaminated, faults will rise in our minds.

45. Nobody can catch the sky. But everybody can see the sky, everyone can experience the sky. Nobody can catch the wind. But everyone can experience the wind. A fragrance, an aroma, this has neither colour nor form. But it can be perceived.

46. When we touch another's skin we perceive a strange experience within us. It is really not there. That perception is not reality at all. It just seems to be so.

47. When a fire begins to burn among a group of learned people, in a group of scholars, in a city, in a village, and someone there begins to burn, he shouts "I am burning, I am burning!" and he runs away from the fire. When he is out of the fire, he experiences some coolness, respite, peace, solitude. Then he begins to say "Mine is burning, mine is burning". What of yours is burning? "My trunks, my boxes," he says, "my sons and grandsons, my cow, my home, my city, everything is burning". To save his things, he runs towards the fire. Reaching it, he feels the heat again and cries: "I am burning, I am burning!" Again he runs from the fire. Again he feels peace, coolness, respite, solitude, stability. Then again he remembers "Mine is burning, mine is burning". Thus at times he thinks "I am burning," and at times he thinks "Mine is burning". He is like the one whose mind is contaminated. When he experiences the feeling "I am burning", he makes an effort and comes out of it. He becomes stable. But when he says: "Mine is burning," he again becomes embroiled in the same illusion. So he burns and burns until he turns to ash. In this way we have progressed toward failure through many lives.

48. Since the time you were born, in all the time you have been on earth, you have never made a promise to yourself. Even if you gave your word, you broke it. So, having broken the promise you gave yourself, how can anyone else trust your word? How can your mantra, your meditation, your prayers, be believed?

49. How do we achieve the power to make things happen? You may break your promise to someone else. You can say: since the other did not keep his side of the promise, I broke mine too. But what happens when you make a promise to yourself?

50. "O my Self, I promise to behave nicely with you, I will never deceive you, I will never take you into the holes of hell, I promise you."

51. We do not need to make a promise to the Unknown Friend; we need to make a promise to ourselves. I don't ask you to make a promise to God or to the Divine Mother or any such entity. I ask you to make a promise, and that you never break this promise to your Self.

52. We think about this and that all day, we speak about this and that all day. We speak so much more than we need to. We have a disease of speaking jibber-jabber, jibber-jabber all the time. Can this gibberish do anything for the upliftment of the soul? Never! Never, at all.

53. The more you keep yourself disciplined, the more you keep your mind stable, the more you internalize sorrows, the less you eat, the more you will be permeated by [spiritual] strength. People who have such strength have a very stable mind.

54. We face our divinity with our back. We never face the divinity we worship. When we do try to face it, it is with a stance of opposition as if the divinity were an oncoming train that will surge at us, crush us, cut us and leave us behind. We never understand that if we stand to one side, we can climb into its coaches.

55. All this subtle and ever more subtle knowledge is derived from keeping good company and listening to good words — by keeping the company of your guru. When you find such

company, you must listen. To understand what you hear, you must have a stable mind. To reflect on what you hear and understand, you need time. This is an arduous and unique effort.

56. Time does not punish anyone with a stick. It takes away one's lustre, it takes away one's strength, it takes away one's intellect, it takes away one's reason.

57. First we need sight. After sight, we need hearing. After hearing, we need a nose to smell — so that we may smell the presence of our Unknown Friend, the way an animal smells out a mate.

58. How engrossed I become at times. Engrossment is a manifestation of That. When That manifests, we become engrossed, we achieve peace. Work which seemed on the brink of doom appears possible, appears headed towards success.

59. When what you have undertaken is about to come to fruition, you see indications of it beforehand. If we observe closely, we can understand that the desired entity is about to arrive. We should become very careful; we should become very alert. If not, if we lie lost, then we will remain lost.

60. We are crooked ourselves. We stand crooked, we sit crooked, we walk crooked, and we think crooked, so why shouldn't our life be crooked? It remains crooked. Then life becomes very difficult.

61. Regarding the arrival of the divinity: first we get indications of it within. Our heart feels the manifestation. Yes, it will happen this way. Our heart can feel it before it actually happens.

62. When your heart does not feel it, you should think: "I have a fault somewhere within me. Because of that fault, I can see far in the distance, I can see darkness far in the distance. How should I rectify this fault?" Ask this of a great soul.

63. When one is to be afflicted by ignominy, it will come one way or another. The reason for this coming is something that can be known only through God. Other than that, however far one runs, and despite that one keeps running and running, wherever one goes, their fate will follow.

64. I have been cheated by many people. I have never cheated anyone. I have been cheated by divinities, I have been cheated by demons, and I have been cheated by my own intellect. Every kind of circumstance has cheated me. We have not been helped by circumstances. Nor have we been helped by our intellect. Our knowledge has not been helpful either. And we will certainly not be helped by our religion. It does not help anyone.

65. Look, there are people right here. There are houses, homes. But despite being here, how far away these people are from us! It seems as if they are sitting far away in Pakistan. We are sitting together in this room, we are talking together, but a person's mind can be flying to some other place. A person can be thousands of miles away while sitting right here. And not being here, he does not understand what is being said. And when he does not understand it, he says, "Oh, that person was just speaking nonsense. He was just saying nothing."

66. We may live in a temple, yet be thousands of miles from that temple.

67. Friends, if between us I say something harsh about you, by criticizing you I am not hurting you in anyway. By criticizing I am going to become co-sharer of that sin of yours. I am going to share that unwanted deed with you (to lessen its effect on you.)

68. You say to somebody — "Oh Sir, I made this mistake". At that moment, you become absolutely clean and pure. By that

admission you have unloaded the burden within you. Now it becomes the burden on the head of the person you told it to. If he is not clever, he will keep lugging it around and distributing it to others. He will leave some of it in one house, some of it in another house, some of it in someone else's house...

69. There is a big difference between hearing something about somebody and seeing something about somebody. If you keep jumping to conclusions, how will you be able to find the Divine Mother? How will you find God? You will remain entangled within yourself!

70. Extricate yourself from these sins. If you hear something unwanted, forget it right there and then. Say to yourself — "this is not true", because if you believe it to be true, you will keep distributing it amongst others.

71. Achieving spiritual power (*siddhi*) means that you become very straight, very simple, and very good-natured. You become gentle. But you can be tough and hard, too. If you need to chastise somebody, you will be able to do that, too.

72. What comes to us in our imagination will come to us in reality, too.

73. We are so steeped in ignorance that we deceive ourselves. There are many beings who, without a doubt, torture themselves.

74. We have been asked to achieve a state of spiritual ecstasy (*samadhi*). We have been asked by the *munis* to develop a good intellect, to become strong, to become wise, to be courageous. This will happen only when we keep ourselves under control, when we keep ourselves disciplined, when we remain ever-alert.

75. Then you will become a good human being and all you perceive will fit like an *amla* fruit (*amblic myrobalan*) in your palm. In the same way that the *amla* fruit fits in your palm, the nectar that flows through this fruit in the months of *Kartik* (November-December) and *Agahan* (September-October) can be yours. This nectar can make your life very long.

76. We seek answers because of our unfamiliarity with ourselves. Being so close to one's self, the seeker who keeps wandering away becomes stable not when he just comes back within himself, but when he actually sees himself.

7. The reason for this [wandering] is neither balance nor imbalance. Curiosity arises only in a balanced person. A vision from within is the only reason for this.

78. Even God is an ancient being. Gurus are ancient beings. Tradition is very old. The new that we see is also very old. This serial motion that you perceive is a representation of Chethariya Vir Baba.[1] Consider Chethariya Vir Baba the beginning of the series, not the end. The end will be found somewhere at the end of the earth. We lie somewhere between the two.

79. [About Chethariya Vir Baba]: I found him happy, ego-free, content in the joy within.

80. In the end, what is heaven? Heaven is nothing but a decrepit, decaying, artificial make-believe.

81. If beings know even one moment of their transience, they know all.

---

[1] Baba has talked about a very old, even ancient, divine being, a personality, who is in rags, yet brave enough to conquer all limits of the world. Literal translation of Chethariya Vir Baba is 'An old, brave ascetic, in rags'.

82. If you start looking at the surface, will you find anything? That which 'Is not' actually 'Is'. It is what you are looking for. This understanding is knowledge.

83. The end of faults is a great treasure. The treasure of virtues can be derived only in company. Company represents *satsang* (good company).

84. Peace is achieved by solitude in the quiet cave of the heart. It is not achieved by contemplation of the senses.

85. Peace is achieved by contentment in the soul.

86. Even in great pain and sorrow, one can experience joy and happiness. I am living. Whatever is happening within, whenever I feel the vibration, the joy, the affection of that 'Unknown'; it is more than the pain of sorrow.

87. One unconcerned with transient things in the world, including the physical body, achieves ecstasy, knowledge of the Self, knowledge of the Unknown, and the rise of a knowledgeable consciousness. In knowledgeable consciousness, thoughts about anyone else do not arise. Consciousness thinks of consciousness only. This is not merely a representation, but a complement of the whole. Once this state is achieved, music rises with an unspoken voice within the physical body vibrations rise, senses get controlled, and the dried fibres of the mind become active again. As a result, the seeker attains indestructibility, peace, tranquillity, stability and happiness. The seeker also achieves unique sight. When their gaze falls with a smile on anybody, then that person experiences coolness, be they even burning in a raging fire.

88. To get away from, to be liberated from worldly ties is what is known as saintliness. What else is saintliness? If there is anything else in saintliness it is the saintly way of life: simplicity,

humility, patience, discipline and forbearance. Such a person should listen to everything from everyone, but should not express anything of his own.

89. All human beings perform janitorial work for themselves every morning. They clean their own dirt with their own hands. That same work, when done by a janitor, is looked down on by people. They address the janitor as if he was of a lower category. When the same work is done by a saint, he is known as a *paramahansa*, an *awadhut*, a carefree and joyous person.

90. He who delves into the depths of consciousness, who sees good signs in the sky [of the depths of that consciousness], good pointers, he who hears, sees and understands and makes others see and hear, and who himself walks on those paths — such a stable, self-controlled person we call a saint. Such people are found in simple huts.

91. Divinity is nothing separate from you. Divinity is *bhava* (feeling in totality), and divinity hungers for *bhava*. Your parents and your guru do not expect anything from you except that *bhava*. They have only this desire, that you will be full of good *bhava* and that you will be able to do something for others with those good feelings.

92. The word '*puja*' (worship) means fullness, wholeness. One who is never full, remaining empty and spurned by desire, keeps running after things. He has never worshipped, for he has never been full. In the background of not being full or fulfilled are the absence of forbearance and the keeping of undesired company.

93. If we are devoted to ourselves, we can have devotion for everybody else. That is because devotion is a sentiment. Devotion does not denote your subservience. It also denotes the state where the master becomes the slave because, day and night,

in sleep and while awake, every moment of his life he is concerned about the one devoted to him.

94. You will achieve your goal only when you are disciplined. Then, you will not be deadwood and you will not wander lost after every desire.

95. Saints can appear in a deceptive form — in disguise. Saints do not have any special form or colour. Our parents and relatives can be saints. Our neighbour, too, can be a saint, and those who until today we considered our enemy can be saints as well.

96. In rituals, the purpose of a sacred pitcher is for the divinity that we desire to come into it and do favourable things for us. But what is favourable for us and what is unfavourable is not for us to decide. If we do, we can make a wrong decision.

97. Divinity is achieved through use of a mantra, actions and herbs. In all regions and at all times one can perform prayers and become imbued with energy.

98. Our prayers and worship depend upon our mood. If in this ashram, if in this *aghorachal* you persist in your old ways of talking about this and that, thinking about this and that, you retain your old habits. Unless you come alone, by yourself [leaving your desires behind] you will not achieve anything.

99. If your heart is within your heart, and you are not heartless, then you will not be afraid of swimming across the ocean of death.

100.
Let the world look for me
Let there be no sign of me
Let me have a grave
battered to illegibility.

101. All the streams, rivers and drains coming together take the form of Ganga.

102. A Philosopher's stone does not discriminate. Whether a piece of iron is from a temple or a butcher's house, when touched to the Philosopher's stone they both turn to gold.

103. Better than achieving power on the earth, better than going to heaven and having suzerainty over all three worlds, better is the joy of the saint who remains active in the flow of the stream of life.

104. You cannot satisfy every desire, even if it rains gold coins. Every happiness ends in pain. An *aughar* who has wealth (of this knowledge) is to be appreciated; he is to be respected.

105. There is no fire stronger than desire. There is nothing worse than hatred. There is no pain greater than internecine acrimony. And there is no joy greater than pure *nirvana* (liberation). Health is the greatest wealth. Contentment is the greatest treasure. Self-confidence is the best friend, and pure *nirvana* is the pure joy.

106. One who gets to know the solitude of silence, one who gets to experience the joy of silence, this one remains free from acrimony, fear and sin, and is ever joyous.

107. If you ever find a saint who is stable, who is devoted, who is aware of the light of his inner consciousness, who is contented, who does not lug around a book in his mind, who is simple, who has a nice temperament, then, O Aughar, follow such a person like a calf follows its mother.

108. One who is free from happiness is free from fear and pain. It is happiness that generates sorrow. One who is free from the desires of the senses is also free from fear and pain.

Aghoreshwar

An aughar ascetic who transcends all limitations of life — physical, mental, emotional and spiritual — becomes an Aghoreshwar. An Aghoreshwar is a spiritually enlightened person, one who has transcended all dualities in life. For such a person there is no hate or disgust towards anything in the world. All that he has are feelings of love, acceptance and welfare for all.

1. A true disciple is one who is devoted to the Aghoreshwar, disciplined, as a child is akin to his parents in form and character.

2. Aughar-Aghoreshwars have unlimited compassion and sympathy. They are hate-free. Avoiding discrimination and hate, Aughar-Aghoreshwars are concerned and active for the welfare of all, for a better organization of society and the nation. They live and dine with people regarded as socially inferior. They believe in the Self, and they have a spirit-oriented (Self-oriented) intellect.

3. The random words of Aghoreshwars [spoken as mantras] do not constitute a language [that is linguistically understandable].

4. Aughars are not overactive. Nor are they inactive. In a middle state between being a doer and a non-doer, they provide oblations to the *vaishwanar* (the creative energy present in all) in the form of their *pran.*

5. You may have heard that Aughars indulge in magic and exorcism. But what they do is not magic; they embody good thoughts for all. They play the role of attracting good deeds and good people.

6. Every morning, Aughars embrace their life-force.

7. Yogi-beings who relinquish all illusions and roam in the unfettered state of the *pran* are known as *abhayadhar*. They are known as Abhayadhars ('holders of fearlessness'), not as Aughars.... Only a person beyond the entanglements of ambition is known as an 'Abhayadhar', and an Aughar is a person who has established harmony between the strings of his heart and mind, one who is a knower of the mantras. "Is a 'knower of the mantra' an Abhayadhar?" "Yes. Abhayadhar. It is a complement of the word Aughar, and Aughar is a complement of the mantras [i.e. mismatched, random words]."

8. In a particular time and situation, the good ideas put forth for the benefit of human beings as well as for the villages, cities, and society constitute the vision of the Aughar-Aghoreshwars. Desiring everyone's welfare and happiness even before desiring God, Aughars stay away from shallow philosophical knowledge. They live a normal life among people, keeping a watchful eye on their happiness and sorrow. Benevolent saints, Aghoreshwar-Aughars consider service to others their greatest action.

9. Aughars stress celibacy and asceticism, and so, are ignored by the so-called high lineages.

10. Even if turbulence exists, even if an army and ruler pass by, real service means one's attention does not waver, and one remains absorbed in one's service. One's mind and heart remain stable. This is known as *aghorachal* [*aghor* + *-achal*: unmoving, stable]. One who is unmoved is Aghor; they are stable.

11. Aughar-Aghoreshwar do not distinguish between a dog, an undertaker, or a cow. They have the same vision for all. They teach us to recognize our own real Self. Aughars go everywhere in society. They provide free advice about how to make good use of time and how to gain liberation from the slavery of the senses.

12. Whatever is made and exists is devoured by time. Time does not spare anything or any being. Even the sky and the Earth disintegrate over time. That is why a saint, a Mahatma, an Aughar-Aghoreshwar feels no attachment, sorrow or unhappiness when hearing or seeing others.

13. O seeker! Aughar-Aghoreshwars, saints, Mahatmas should be like this. Ask me, "Like what?" Like the Earth (which neither insults nor respects anyone).

14. Shiva is referred to as Aughar-Aghoreshwar. The word '*Shivom*' is associated with welfare and beneficence. Within the stories of Aughar Mahatmas lie concealed the goal of life: living with peace and happiness, without ego, the necessary goal of this life.

15. One who possesses the grace of an Aghoreshwar can, with a kick, bring the dead back to life. An Aghoreshwar is a supremely alive person. It is said that Aughars are the boatmen who ferry you across this world, and the other world too. They were once addressed as boatmen. Because they kept fires burning on the *ghats* people began to call them Aughars. Earlier, the word 'boatman' was added to their name.

16. An Aughar's character is practical. It is praiseworthy, it is beautiful, it is publicly acceptable. Aughars do not dwell on little thoughts and practices propelled by selfishness. They do not prompt crowds to violence. They do not divide people by caste or religion, nor by other narrow means which dissolve the nation into small territories. They do not prompt people toward bombings and arson. Those who follow Aughar thought do not live as deadweight on society. Unlike today's doctors and lawyers, they perform actions for the welfare of society, such as giving medicine, *vibhuti*, words of advice and words of inspiration without charging fees. In their thought and in their way of life, they show the right path. Their

livelihood depends upon alms. Faith, belief, affection, love are the only fees they charge.

17. Aughar-Aghoreshwars have a spirit-oriented intellect, not a body-oriented intellect.

18. The behaviour of Aughar-Aghoreshwars is not merely one option among many. It begins at the point where people practicing other options, tired, have turned back.

19. Those who are unfathomable, who cannot be measured, are Aughar, Aghor, Aghoreshwar. They are like those beings who materialize into existence by their own divine will (*ayoni-janma*).

20. Aughar-Aghoreshwar do not neglect their duties even for a moment. Nor do they stop for anyone else's actions. They move continuously, like the Sun. They are always performing actions. They keep the same vision for everyone.

21. The senses of the brave and courageous are under control like an Aghoreshwar's. Every Aghoreshwar has conquered his senses.

22. The soul of an Aughar-Aghoreshwar, from the atmosphere, enters the body of the child born of a truthful and meritorious woman.

23. "When Aughar-Bhabbar grows angry, it is like an earthquake. Human beings are frightened off. Many people became targets of his anger."

24. Saints, Aughars, Aghoreshwars are always inwardly oriented. They remain unattached, every day, at every moment. However, at times, to inspire their devotees and disciples, they may become outwardly oriented.

25. Aughar-Aghoreshwar are not a weight on society. They are not the garbage of society either. They are a force of consciousness in society. They assume responsibility within the society. They are a crucial link in a fragmenting society. Aughar Mahatmas are like grass that is not destroyed despite being trampled a thousand times. They have no attachment for either praise or criticism. If they suffered from attachment you would not see them performing their actions as they do today. They are fond of wasted things and discarded clothes; they live in cremation grounds; they spend their lives with anyone who comes along. They do not like to live beneath people high like the toddy tree.

26. Non-attachment is not a path. It is a stage, a position achieved by Aghoreshwars and Aughars.

27. Aughar-Aghoreshwars practice equality toward all. They do not differentiate between people. One who practices such equality is a model of love.

28. Aughar-Aghoreshwars have beautiful hearts. They are like those flowers with so much delicious pollen in them that deer — those beings with beautiful eyes — are attracted to them due to their delicate sense of smell. There the deer derive so much joy and happiness that, in a state of ecstasy (*samadhi-chitta*), in a state of intoxication, they become quiet and peaceful.

29. The childlike vision which does not differentiate between a rope and a snake is the kind of vision that Aughar-Aghoreshwars acquire. They no longer make a distinction as to whether a thing is an edible sweet or excrement or sacred Ganga-water, or whether a person is male or female.

30. Aughar-Aghoreshwars do not have a concept of heaven or hell, sin or virtue.

31. An Aughar belongs to the 'other house', a different state of existence. He is the only one who, despite being surrounded by wealthy people and prestigious people proud of their bodies, appears as detached as a dwelling in the cremation ground.

32. A provider of beneficence, happiness, peace and dedicated to living within the discipline of the Aghoreshwar, an Aughar is more virtuous and talented than normal people.

33. Laziness leads to no good. One who gives up laziness is known as an Aghoreshwar.

34. Our life-breath itself is the Aghoreshwar, the Aughar, the Sarveshwari, the one with equal speech, the one who does not hate, the one who is without difficulty.

35. If a person drowning in the ocean of the world remembers the Aghoreshwar, soon his hand comes up, his head comes up, the Aghoreshwar takes hold of him with the rope of his words and rescues him from the ocean of the world.

36. There have been great Aghoreshwars before this time. Aughar saints who have not known the thoughts and words of those old Aghoreshwars do not know what it is to be an Aghoreshwar.

37. The person who is content with food and lodging that comes without difficulty is content in me, the Aghoreshwar.

38. Full of worldly compassionate virtues are Aghoreshwars, Aughars. Aughars pay respect to women and strive for their welfare.

39. The Aughar who hears good words and remembers them is dear to the Aghoreshwar. An Aughar saint does not try to deceive people through magic or sorcery.

40. Aughars and Aghoreshwars are few in numbers. The Aughar who lives with the joy of alertness and self-control, who fears base thoughts, is kissed by victory. Liberation welcomes him.

41. One with an undeluded, unbounded mind and heart is close to the limitless sky; his heart and mind are like the sky. One with mind and heart bound, one who is beset by duality, his heart and mind are horrible. He experiences fear, he experiences the sky as apocalyptic. But Aughar-Aghoreshwars fly like birds in the sky of the consciousness.

42. Aughar-Aghoreshwars rise like bamboo here and there on the earth — in small numbers, one or two at a time.

43. The Aughar seeker who keeps the company of good people, who sits with saints, who follows the Aghoreshwar, who measures himself by the standard of the Aghoreshwar, and who does not believe in magic and sorcery, he is a real Aughar. It is the thought stream of Aughars that flows through the thought-stream of the Buddha.

44. Power inherent within the mantra is not achieved by crooked people. Those who are not strong, who have no faith and devotion, who do not work hard, they achieve the powers of the mantra, the divinity of the mantra only after a long time. If they accept the words of the Aghoreshwar, that is me, and practice it for one year, they will achieve in fifteen days what they would have achieved in fifteen years.

45. Aghoreshwars and Aughars who belong to a good lineage, even if they do not get food, stay respectfully in their caves in a state of ecstatic joy.

46. Nobody remains the same all the time. Neither cause-and-effect nor change happens in an Aghoreshwar.

47. An Aghoreshwar considers neither the transient to be eternal, nor the perishable to be imperishable, nor effect as non-effect. Becoming unattached from all effects and outcomes, from sorrows, from attachments, *mahapurush*, saints, *mahatma*s and Aghoreshwars live freely, and consider only the everlasting as everlasting.

48. Neither change happens, nor effect, neither increase nor decrease in the activities, conduct, behaviour, or disposition of the Aghoreshwar. He remains the same, unmoved. Aghoreshwar has the same vision for all. He has compassion, friendship and kindness for all.

49. In Aghoreshwar nothing is lacking, no change happens, there is no increase or decrease. There is no such other person in the world.

50. In the way that the great ocean has just one taste, the taste of salt, so also the ideal words of the Aghoreshwar have just one taste — the taste of freedom.

51. O Aughars! Accept this. Accept with faith and dedication the path, the way of life shown by the Aghoreshwar.

52. Aughars belong to a different house. What is that different house? In it self-control exists, alertness exists; therein is forbearance, equanimity for all, the same behaviour for all, a spirit- [Self-] oriented intellect. One who revels in the life-breath of his soul is the one who belongs to a different house. One belonging to a different house is disciplined, vigilant. He has comprehensive consciousness, comprehensive knowledge. His actions are comprehensive. He has comprehensive knowledge of the mantra. This is the different house of a real Aughar. The different house is eternal; is ever-new. It provides strength; changeless, it is free from desire and from Self-conceit. It is spiritual — it is a place where the spirit resides. Consider the different house to be so.

53. We saints, we Aughars should not give any place to undesirable words or invective. Let what belongs to others remain with them.

54. One who stays away from the guilt of bad actions is known as an Aghoreshwar. A sin-free, guilt-free person is known as Aghoreshwar.

55. One who refrains from the enjoyment of the senses, from the enjoyment of the world, from the guilt of the world, is known as Aghoreshwar.

56. An Aughar is a master of many spiritual powers. As one he becomes many, as many he become one again. He appears; he disappears. He passes through walls, across boundaries and goes away having touched all. He walks in water and on water. While sitting cross-legged he moves on the earth and in the sky like a bird. He touches the Sun and the Moon with his hands. He reaches the domain of the divine with his physical body.

57. There is a saint by the name of Aghoreshwar who remains changeless. Such a person is a person who cannot be measured.

58. Aghoreshwars have a spirit-oriented intellect. They do not have a body-oriented intellect. That is why, even after the body dies, they continue living in the cosmic bowl, in the skull-bowl. They keep meeting and protecting the seekers who have control over their senses, control over their mind, control over their desires.

59. Those who revel in the mantra '*Aghorannam Paro Mantrah*' ('greatest is the name Aghor') are Aghoreshwars.

60. The ability to pay attention to all the pain of humanity is a tradition of Aughars and *awadhuts*. Dedicate yourself to change this poverty into the richness of wholesome sentiment.

61. When difficult situations arise — like a covered hut, like a rock — we should stop our speech; we should not let our speech out. This is the gospel of Aughar seekers.

62. The Aughar who has lost his position can commit any kind of bad action; he can turn away from his social responsibilities.

63. Disciples must prevent the loss and disappearance of the tradition of easily obtainable knowledge, the stages of Aughar-Aghoreshwars, the mantras. They should practice them as disciples. Only then can the tradition be prevented from disappearing.

64. This is the truth I know
This is the truth I know
You are away from wealth and prestige
You are away from wealth and prestige
Aghoreshwar-Aghoreshwar.

This is the truth I know
This is the truth I know
You are so very humble
You are so very simple
Aghoreshwar-Aghoreshwar.

This is the truth I know
This is the truth I know
One who desires wealth
One who desires praise
insults himself on this earth.
This is the truth I know
This is the truth I know.

65. Aghoreshwar seekers do not have body-oriented thinking. They have spirit-oriented thinking by which they reach meaningful places. On reaching those places they become so humble that they speak only pleasant words. They have no

place for distorted words in their vocabulary. Such words do not arise in them.

66. It is not strange that one can cross the ocean of life with the name [of God, as in a mantra]. But, merely the name will not take you across. Such a boat also requires oars, and knowledge of the depth, length and breadth of the ocean. You can cross the ocean on the boat of a knowledgeable person, the Aghoreshwar's boat.

67. At the midday of life, at the Sun's midpoint in an Aughar's day, nothing can provide shade for his head.

68. Whenever my body is touched by Aghoreshwar, I experience a state of super-consciousness (*samadhi*). Then, by being stable within I see and know the desired [divinity].

69. I will request Bhagwan Ram's soul to protect you with its light rays, with its aura.

70. Friends, I am away from you only physically. But we are never far from our inner determination, our inner voice. Your voice is never far from mine, nor from the soul of the One I worship.

71. Aughars do not have only equality in their regard for all, they manifest equal behaviour towards everyone. In their greatness they accept food and drink in anyone's place. Like the Sun, the Moon, fire, Earth and wind, they lack physically-oriented thinking. They are non-dual. They do not perceive duality. They see non-duality everywhere.

72. Aughar-Aghoreshwars have befriended the Truth. According to the times, they say good words and welcome realities. They like to breathe in the air of happiness, peace and equality. That is the reason why they talk about living in the body made of the five elements. Otherwise they let the bird of their

life-force fly out of this cage, and let it rest in the Cosmic shell — at the place of the Kapaleshwar [when the time for leaving the body-cage arrives].

73. If you are involved in prayers, in contemplation of That [Divine Friend], then there are things deep within which pass before you a thousand times, which you do not understand and which you let go. If you understood, you would achieve happiness, peace and respite, and I would achieve happiness, peace and respite, too. What is the reason for my suffering through these troubles? It is because I keep sharing your troubles and sorrows with you. If I try to put out the fire that burns you, then my face will burn too. Look at the result. I am deprived of you for many days, for many years. I do not know when your fire will die down, when you will achieve coolness, so that, in that coolness of yours, in the cool shade of that tree, I can spend time in peace and happiness, I will see you all in peace and happiness, able to do anything. I may live to see the progress of this nation, this society; that is my desire.

74. Aughars are not *tantrics*. They do not believe in *tantra*, they do not believe in absurd gods and goddesses. They believe in devotion and faith, they believe in themselves, not in something external. That is why the practitioners of the *varna* system watch Aughars with cruel eyes and, even today, spread false rumours about them.

75. This (Aughar) is not a singular path, or sect, or position. It can have every kind of seeker at this stage, and there is no lack of such seekers.

76. When people reach the stage of the Aghoreshwar, their language becomes different from the 'yes' and 'no' of the world. They are known as unattached to the substance and cause of the world. This is the stage that is known as the superconscious stage (*samadhi*).

77. When you speak someone's name, the name ends. When you see someone's form, the form ends. But we are eternal: we are empty of life-and-death definitions and perceptions. The seeker who knows this moves beyond divine illusion and the physical world, and reaches the world of light, the world of the Aghoreshwar.

78. The disciple who believes in me, the Aghoreshwar, is worthy of the grace of Mahakapalik Aghoreshwar... He is a jewel amongst Aughar seekers; he is a precious gem of the Aghoreshwar.

79. I, the Aghoreshwar-as-life-energy, I am known as speech (*swar*), breath (*vayu*), life-divinity (*pran-devata*), life-force (*param shakti*), fixed-within-experience (*anubhut sthir*), a unique element of life (*pran vishesh*), the unfathomable (*aparagamya*), the supreme soul (*param atma*), the Aghoreshwar.

80. ...I became infallible; I became of unfallen seed (*Urdhvareta*), I began moving upwards... All the senses vanished into themselves. A circle appeared before my eyes. In the circle I saw green, red, yellow, white, black, magenta, blue, and saffron colours. Then there were eight circles and the colours changed into an eight-petalled lotus. I saw my dear life-energy arise in my consciousness.

81. Incarnations (of gods) have been only amongst the Hindus, and those incarnations stay within their social boundaries. But there are people who have broken these limits, who have risen above these limits, such as the saints, the seekers, the great souls, the Awadhut, the Paramahansa, the Mahatma, the Buddha. The Buddha is not addressed as *Bhagwan* (God). That is because he provides a new direction. He provides a new system — suitable to the conditions of the time, the period, the place and the circumstances. What he says is his sacred word.

82. Those who stay away from hatred, from jealousy, from people who spew such venom, belong to a different house (Aughar). Their daily worship is their own worship. Their worship inspires them for success.

83. The simple, innocent Aughar! It is in his nature to go into despised places. Perhaps these places are lacking in hatred.

84. The great soul, the Aughar, is tied neither by any custom or tradition, nor by any system, nor is he fettered in any other way. He differentiates himself from such bonds; he is separate from them. He says, "Be kind to yourself. I too feel kindness toward you. Be kind to yourself and get out of this muck."

85. One whose mind rises above somnolence does not remain dormant; he becomes supremely conscious. He sees through everything. He sees this side [of the world], and that side [of creation], as well. Stability, humility, patience are found in him. He stays far away from hatred. He is known as *aghori*.

86. Aghor is without hate. He never accepts the poison of hate. He cleanses the poison of hate. He, too, suffers sorrow in this world. In this world, living in the body, he suffers those things that all human beings suffer. Passing slowly through troubles, he will appear to be screaming, moaning, he will appear to be suffering. But, like the great serpent [of ancient scriptures], he drinks the *amrita* (ambrosia) slowly. He swallows it. He gets the help of good souls. They help him.

87. In the morning and through the evening we deal with our own excrement. When we go to the toilet, we wash our hand. Afterward we may even touch our face with that hand. Who says we do not deal with excrement? Who, then, is not *aghori*? Who does not take the form of Aghor, then? We all do, in the morning and in the evening.

88. We do not want to weigh down this earth; we want to be light. Our gravity should be such that we feel uplifted. For example, notice Aughar saints walking during their ascetic practices: their feet do not touch the ground. They walk above the ground; they appear to be uplifted. If you see them going to their place of worship or practice, you will find this to be true.

89. I, myself, have beautified beauty. Nothing else is important in life. Our 'unrewarded' life is like a glorious monument.

90. Sri Sarveshwari Samooh is my yogic creation. Sarveshwari is my soul.

91. The person who looks after a sick person selflessly, who gives him food and medicine on time, his work is like the worship we Aghoreshwars do. He is a person dear to us Aghoreshwars. He has the grace Aghoreshwars. He has an opportunity to be with God Kapaleshwar himself.

92. Many seekers have to go to the shelter of the Aughars. They please these Aughar-Aghoreshwars with their respect, honour and love. They beg them to have clemency towards those who have become a target of Aghoreshwar's anger.

93. Look at that Awadhut: he has transcended all rules.

94. Definition of *awadhut* :
A = *Avinashi* (Indestructible)
Wa = *Sarwottam* (Supreme)
Dhu = Beyond *vidhi-nishedha* (dualities of do's and don'ts)
Ta = *Sat-chit-anand* (Truth-Consciousness-Joy).

95. One who douses hate and poison is known as an Aghor.

96. Adoration to Aghoreshwar! I salute the great Aghor, master of the throne of knowledge, of the seat of Aghor (*Aghorpeeth*).

97. Before coming on earth
to ourselves we made a promise.
That same promise, people
know as Aghor, today.

98. You must be knowing *vamachar* (the left-handed practice). *Vama* is a part of the dear one. Realized saints like Dattatreya, Abhinavagupta, Maharaja Harshavardhan's father Pushyamitra's guru Aghorbhairavacharya, Kaluram and Kinaram achieved success by walking the straight path. Walking on a crooked path, you can break your limbs.

99. The personal wealth of Aughars who observe moderation in their food and drink is to hurt no one by word or action, to remain self-controlled through their discipline, to seek solitude in their own room on their own bed, and to practice the highest state of consciousness.

100. The point where Aghorbhairavacharya stopped is the point from which Aghoreshwar Kinaram carried the tradition forward. The knowledge expressed by the Awadhuts will be an example for thousands of years. There are many stories of Aughar-Mahatmas found only in the oral tradition. Because of the freely roaming nature of these saints, their stories were not collected and written down. The *samadhi* of our revered Rajeshwar Ramji belongs to the same tradition.

101. Aghor nature: We are born from mud [the Aghor nature] and, after death, we merge back into it. Every person harbours the seeds of Aghor nature which, finding a favourable time and place, grow as the flower of the lotus grows from the mud.

102. O Aghoreshwar, it is your wealth to wisely spread, as far as you can, the light of the name-contemplation of your guru, his virtues, the knowledge of his daily activities, and the treasure of his peaceful, comprehensive life. Go. Travel everywhere, talk to

those who have been deprived of the Aghoreshwar's treasures due to their bad behaviour, about the awareness of his sweet words and virtues which light the path to spirituality, simplicity, and comprehensive vision. Inspire them to walk on this path and beautify themselves with this treasure. There is no greater wealth than this; there is no greater light than this. Lacking the treasure of this light, materialistic people — a materialistic society — burns more than do normal people or a normal society.

103. Human beings find friends, well-wishers and lovers according to their tastes. I will not be able to be so. I will remain like a destitute person. In the heart of this destitute person is a small corner where he can exist sufficiently. That is where I will light my spiritual fire.

104. Aghoreshwar seekers regard alcohol, lies, thievery, and weaknesses as they do excrement. They say that, by indulging in them, they can be attacked by an army of carnal desires. Therefore, you should stay away from them.

105. To get rid of the stiffness of the body and its pain, Aughars produce vibrations and electricity from their body and purify the atmosphere. They like to see children, youths, the old, the trees and vines, the nation all smiling in their healthy, united, non-destructive, trouble-free experiences. This is the glory of their difficult, austere practices.

106. Aghor austere practices: austerity and Aghor are complements of each other. On coming face to face with Aghor austerities, even Brahma, Vishnu and Shiva, even the divinities become willing to give everything they have. Austere practices or Aghor can be adopted by divinities, demons, humans, and spirits. Anyone can adopt them, and when one does, the entity called 'God' is obliged to fulfil one's desires. Brahma, Vishnu, and Shiva all bow before Aghor practices. They are ready to serve the Aghor. The treatise on *bhakti* also says this.

107. An Aughar is a sculptor. He sculpts the shape of his desires as parents shape their children. He moulds his disciples to be like himself, and fills them with colours. He is an accomplished sculptor. Parents may not know if their child will turn out as they wish, or not. But if disciples have good cultural-spiritual backgrounds, they become like the Aughar-sculptor himself.

108. The situation, the progress that you see today did not happen by itself. I did hard physical labour for twelve hours every day. In the remaining time I thought about other work, tree-planting and many other projects. I continuously think about works of social welfare. Thus, we have the situation that we have now.

CHARACTER

People are known through their character, reflected in their personality. A strong character does not waver when faced with problems; it is stable. It always maintains self-control, and works for the good of all who come into contact with that person.

1 To hate yourself, to lack faith in yourself, to lack control over your behaviour, to lack good conduct, these lead to a lack of inner strength. Good conduct is nothing other than friendliness. Good conduct itself is a friend.

2. To make a decision impulsively denotes weakness.

3. Become humble. Speak sweet words to all beings.

4. Pull yourself together. Don't harbour instability, futile criticism or incessant strife.

5. Go to your own refuge. Nothing can be found in someone else's refuge.

6. One who shows mercy to himself, who goes to his own refuge, who protects himself, he cannot be expected to do any bad deeds.

7. A life of self-control provides happiness and peace. A life of self-control generates great insight.

8. Evil purpose lives in bad actions.

9. O human being! Why do you fear sorrow? Sorrow is merely a shadow. Everyone who is alive has sorrow. Sorrow is a crucial link in your life; in the absence of sorrow, your life would not

be clear to you. Keep smiling, and with that smile, keep battling sorrow. This is your life. Sorrow is more, happiness is less. Being without clothes is a sorrow, being vulnerable is a sorrow; disease is a sorrow, hunger is a sorrow. All these are sorrows.

10. Become a saint with your heart, mind and actions. Do not become a saint of whom advantage can be taken. Saintliness must have the power to protect itself. Be mindful of this.

11. A saint can only give you medicine. He cannot regulate your diet or effect the lifestyle changes that you must make.

12. One whose life rests on a foundation of comprehensive consciousness, comprehensive vision, comprehensive knowledge and a stable mind is not hurt by invectives.

13. O seeker! Never feel bad in your heart, thinking you were insulted, mistreated, or ridiculed.

14. A weak person is easily excitable.

15. One who relinquishes desire, expectation and attachment is an able person, a superhero.

16. Do not become anything. Just become human.

17. The saintliness of a saint is reflected in his conduct, not in his knowledge. In the conduct and consciousness of an enlightened person immeasurable wealth, prestige, peace and happiness are found. This is known as true action.

18. A virtuous person has his own strength, his own valour.

19. O seeker, are you afraid of circumstances? Become fearless, become quiet; allow even the remnants of fear to dissipate without leaving a trace.

20. Egotism signifies artificiality and crookedness.

21. O seeker! The only thing within our right is to remain the same for everyone — like the sky.

22. Do not become a wild idiot owl; become like the nightingale, a sweet and innocent forest dweller.

23. Retaining your semen provides you with strength, energy, lustre and longevity. Purify the body. One who saves himself from bad actions and intoxicating substances escapes crookedness and poverty.

24. Great lustre, great light, comes from good conduct.

25. One who sees in himself the smallest fault is a saint. One who does not recognize in himself the biggest fault is a demon.

26. Aughar seekers who are just pretending to be so talk much on any subject.

27. One who cheats himself cheats everybody.

28. While knowing, become like a not-knowing person; while understanding, live as if you don't understand.

29. Even from a person considered bad, learn what is good in him.

30. O seeker! Even in this world of illusions, where you see the deeds of others, their shortcomings and virtues, don't let your voice express an opinion.

31. The question arises — what is the motive behind sympathizing with other people and helping those in need?

32. O seeker! Live, do, behave in such a way that you cheat no one. Even if some one cheats you, do not cheat anyone. Let no one tie you down with the chains of name and form. Let no one set limits for you or measure you. Become limitless, immeasurable.

33. The truly wise one sees God and Guru everywhere. His sight is comprehensive. He instantly achieves super-conscious ecstasy, something that is very difficult to achieve.

34. O seeker! One who sees me everywhere, who sees God everywhere, he sees the messengers of God — earth, air, sky and the directions — everywhere, he is enlightened, he has comprehensive knowledge. In this state there is no suffering; one lacks any sense of pain.

35. You don't need Rama. You need Rama's conduct. His conduct and character *are* the presence of Rama.

36. A person whose life is lived with forbearance is like one who lives on even ground. Here virtues and the seeds of dharma germinate. Here Vagishwari, the essence of humanness, stays within one like water stays in cultivated ground.

37. One who digests sorrows is known as a yogi. However, disenchantment is not good in every situation. The ability to attract (good people and ideas) gives value to life.

38. How bright, how clean our future becomes when we clean our heart!

39. O human, only the night gets to perceive your true good character. The day, blind since birth, does not know it. It is only you who do not think the day to have been blind from birth — that is why you pretend to be a speaker of truth during the day [in your daily activities].

40. Be careful of the animals that graze away at your virtues. One who swears to speak the truth all the time is the biggest liar.

41. Rich in virtues is only he who is desire-free. One who has no needs is very wealthy.

42. Keep an auspicious eye everywhere. Relinquish the sinister eye. The sinister eye is unethical. The auspicious eye is ever-new.

43. Virtues and good conduct are stable and everlasting. Few people find and keep them; fewer tame them.

44. Empty your mind, bring your restless heart home, sit in solitude, concentrate, think about supreme consciousness. You will derive food for thought, perceive ways of living, and derive contentment and satisfaction. This is known as *sanyam* (self-control).

45. By practicing self-restraint, you learn self discipline, as well as a higher system of knowledge which inspires many people of the earth to favour you.

46. The wandering saint who lives on alms makes a big contribution to society by not adding to the population. He helps keeps society free from population pollution. He does not run away from society. He sweeps for people, he cleans and maintains cleanliness, he advises and inspires people. He guides people in the right direction, works toward their mental growth, spreads peace and provides a way for the lost to live their lives.

47. The day you begin to feel that prestige, praise and eulogies are like poison, that day your understanding will become mature. Keeping these things away will help you keep walking on your path.

48. Despite being endowed with treasures, in the absence of any *bhava* (feeling), humans drown in the ocean of life. Some are unable to cross this ocean because of their disrespect toward saints, Mahatmas and good people.

49. If our guru or respected elders are brusque with us, we should search within ourselves to see if we were influenced by bad company or bad actions, by bad literature, advice, rumours or hearsay.

50. By deception and treachery, evil forces lead you astray. Demons act sweeter than your parents, relatives and friends. Be careful with demons. Stay within the sphere of your own temperament. If your desires transgress beyond this, nobody will be able to save you.

51. Never criticize the way someone makes a living, whether he is a butcher, or keeper of animals. Even a butcher, if he has *bhava* (feeling), if he has a goal, he is closer to the Divine than the critic who has no *bhava* (feeling), who has no goal. If the butcher's attention is towards his goal while cutting meat, this attention itself is his worship and his prayer.

52. A saint should never be insulted under any circumstances.

53. What you do daily, what happens within you, depends upon your intentions and determination. With what kind of purpose do you get up in the morning? With what kind of people do you meet and how long do you stay with them? What do you talk about and for how long? These things have a positive or negative effect on you. Keep your feelings and emotions under control. If you do not exercise control, if you indulge in excesses, you may experience obstacles to your practices and prayers. You can even lose yourself.

54. Shape your style of living according to your own natural style. Mould it according to the form of your guru. Mould it according to the form of your dear divinity. If your methods are not right, what will you be able to do? If your style is actually not your style, this adopted style may cause you to squander your life. If your style is wrong, you will not be able to achieve anything. Then you may curse your guru and the ways he has taught you. Upon cursing, you will be condemned not once but a hundred times. Then, it is difficult to say what fate you will find or where you will end up.

55. A saint lends his voice to the voices of others. He leads them in the right direction.

56. One who performs misdeeds in the garb of a saint, who deceives others in the name of gods and goddesses, who does not control his tongue and speech, who dirties his hands with bad actions — to whichever market he may go, he is easily measured and evaluated, as are those policemen without honour who are bribed with two or three rupees.

57. Do not perform a fast (*vrat karana*). In fact, make a resolve (*vrat lena*) to reach your goal. If you fast, your mind, heart and senses may become restless. Then, instead of relinquishing illusions, becoming stable and humble, you exhibit foolishness. That is why, instead, you should definitely resolve [to work steadily towards your goal].

58. Without discipline, you can destroy yourself. In the absence of self-discipline, and because of your moon-like waxing and waning temperament, your divinity is unable to do anything favourable for you even if it wants to. That divinity [like a tailor] is not able to sew the shirt [of good life] of a perfect cut just for you. Your mental state keeps waxing and waning like the moon, yet you ask your divinity [the tailor] to sew a nice shirt for you which is neither big nor small, neither tight nor loose. This is an improper

and impossible thing. With this mental condition you try to worship that princess residing in a fortress, *Durga*, who is herself a spark of energy, a part of cosmic energy itself. If you worship her with this mental state you will not achieve the desired effect.

59. Save yourself from sin-mixed-virtue. If you believe in performing sin-mixed-virtue, it will result in suffering for the people of your village, your society and your nation. Instead of the fraternal love between Ram and Bharat (characters from the epic *Ramayana*), it will propagate the bitterness of quarrelsome brothers such as Ravana and Vibhishana, or of Bali and Sugriv (other characters from the *Ramayana*).

60. Parents who want good children should stay away from indulgences and intoxication. If they don't, then their children, inheriting these undesirable tendencies, will be a deadweight for themselves as well as for society and the nation.

61. In today's universities it is not necessarily true that scholars are of good character.

62. If you do something with impatience, you may become the victim of misfortune. If this happens, neither you, nor society, nor the nation will escape its consequences. Impatience is always prohibited. With impatience, you cannot find a large, lost mountain. With patience, you can find even a small, lost needle.

63. Probably, you are not able to hear my words in the right way. Or, if you are able to hear, probably you are unable to comprehend. Or, if you are able to comprehend, you probably cannot act on them. Furthermore, even if you are able to act on them, can you do so in the way it should be done? Probably, this is the reason you persist in being deprived of everything.

64. I know you will interpret the meaning of what I say according to your own way of thinking.

65. To contact the divinities of earth and heaven, we have to lead a disciplined life. We have to understand the meaning of "no devotion without tact, no liberation without devotion".

66. Due to your excessive cleverness, you have nothing left. You exercise your cunning everywhere. Where you should act clever, you act stupid; where you should act stupid, you act clever. Because of this, you invite every sorrow, and wear it with pride.

67. Worship creative energy, not things. Achieve absolute concentration and absorption.

68. To ignore the faults in others is greatness.

69. There is reverence in seriousness.

70. One whose mind is stable, who is self-disciplined, who has no desires and wants, who has transcended good and bad, he is ever-conscious and fearless. Do it, seeker.

71. Mother and father, friends and relatives can do good for you. But that good is not as good as the good action of those whose minds move in their own direction, who keep their minds within themselves. Great beings determined to achieve their object are to be saluted. They are to be revered.

72. If you have to choose between wealth and duty, choose duty. If you have to choose between sons and disciples, (the example we have is that) Buddha and Nanak (first Sikh Guru) chose their disciples. Their sons later embraced their duty and achieved renown.

73. The wealthy person who makes thousands of sacrifices gains less merit than the person who sacrifices his attachments, his senses, his ego.

74. At the very least, make a compromise with yourself and have patience.

75. It is easy to do that which is bad for us. It is very difficult to do that which is good for us. That is why this life should not be [lived] for ourselves [alone], but for every person. Such a life is a real life. Such a person is alive. The life he has lived never dies. It never becomes old. It is free from disease and from rebirth.

76. The Goddess of Victory cannot be tied by garlands of flowers. Nor can you bind her with good words or wealth. Only Self-absorbed, unsaid, unuttered thoughts are acceptable to her.

77. The best way to live is to live attentively. One who lives with attention knows how to act, not just talk. Such a one is a wholesome person.

78. One who goes to his own refuge is happy, for his refuge is an actual refuge.

79. If the king is pleased, (he) gives land and elephants.
If a businessman is pleased, (he) gives a few pennies.
If women are pleased, (they) give creative essence.
If guru is pleased, (he) gives closeness-to-the-heart-of-beings.

80. O seeker, one who owns nothing has no problems.

81. Whatever one says or thinks about a saint, the saint is not affected by it. Saints are not representatives of any God. They are messengers of themselves. Known to be *awadhut*, they are beyond duality.

82. A great war goes on in life. We have to win this battle against those who are attacking us with many tricks and all kind of cleverness. These wagers of war are tricksters; they are cunning.

But if we remain guileless in front of them, they will be defeated.

83. Saints are philanthropic. Unlike lawyers, doctors and other professionals, they do not charge a fee. Determined and dedicated to service, often without recognition, they keep doing philanthropic work.

84. Don't look at or listen to anything with suspicion.

85. It is good to have an identity of your own. If you don't have an identity, how will people know if you are there, whether you are a human or a beast, what your character is like? If identity with your family, home, country, region, or friends does not rise in you, you remain weak.

86. Whatever has happened within you, investigate that! Whatever is happening in you and whatever is about to happen, let those things manifest. Don't put prohibitions on them, for they will be your history.

87. People who are light will be blown away. People with some weight, who are genuine — cultivate them with care. Protect them, polish them: they are the ones who will provide life to the new generations.

88. There are many among the neglected who are worthy of praise. The day you begin to praise them, that day will you begin the praise of divinity. The day you begin to praise excrement, that day you will become worthy of praising sandalwood and vermilion. As long as you praise one thing and neglect another, your mind and heart will remain polluted with duality. Duality leads to regression.

89. With saints, sadhus, seekers and special guests sitting with them, we can touch them and derive sweetness, know things

in a new way, find new ways of seeing. Thus, we achieve peace and happiness. Peace and happiness brings us face to face with everything — that is, The Unknown.

90. Austerity is mental. The physical practice of austerity is nothing. Only the practice of keeping a disciplined mind has meaning.

91. Filth and excrement has its own importance. When in its proper place, it should even be revered. Excrement and garbage, as fertilizer, provides food and water for plants and trees. Have respect, love and praise for everything.

92. A friend should be like the earth, which moves around the sun seeking light for its friends. Receiving light, the inhabitants of the earth become happy, peaceful and capable of performing good actions.

93. Friends do not encourage one in bad deeds, because bad deeds lead to ill-health, weakening of the mind, and troubles.

94. Instead of meditating, pay attention to your behaviour. It is the greatest prayer. To be always aware of our behaviour is beneficial for us and for others, too. It demonstrates great friendship toward ourselves.

95. When moral behaviour is needed and discipline has to be maintained, there saintly behaviour is not needed. There, saintliness will not be useful. Relinquish the feeling of harming anyone from your heart, follow the principle of "Love in your heart but harsh words in your mouth". Keep love in your heart, but use words harsh enough to turn back the wayward person. A polite voice may be dangerous and lead to a bad situation.

96. Pure food and pure water deeply influence the character and behaviour of a person. If you partake of the wealth acquired

by the wrong people by the wrong means, it will affect you badly. It is said, "Like the food, so the heart and mind".

97. Pictures influence thinking, and thinking influences the character and behaviour of a person.

98. With forbearance, one will exhibit good behaviour even in trying circumstances, and understand the difference between good behaviour and unrestrained behaviour. One should please the Guru and the Dear Divinity, and not worry about rotting and decaying people. Take the support of good behaviour and proceed toward good actions.

99. Humility makes a person great if he has no wickedness in him.

100. The company of untrue human beings and their narrow-mindedness, as well as their vibrations and polluted aura, contaminate one's mind and heart and intellect.

101. The word '*thir*' (stable) is used for Mahatmas, saints, good people, Awadhuts, Auliyas, seekers and unattached people. They all share the characteristic of stability. Instability does not visit them. The instability and rushing around that exists in our lives does not exist in their lives. The instability and rushing around in our lives is related to being in the company of tail-less animals — and their beastly thoughts, feelings, characters, actions — who only in form resemble human beings.

102. Everything from sweets to invectives, stones, bestial words and behaviour, are flung upon saints and Mahatmas, but they overlook them. If they react to them, they will not be able to remain '*thir*' (stable).

103. Within those who are contented arises the feeling of: "O my divinity within me! If I am pure and peaceful do not do things

according to my desire, but according to your desire, so that it brings more goodness and peace to me." People like this, even those doing the most menial jobs, receive the objects of their desires, their desires are fulfilled. Things which had seemed so distant, begin to happen.

104. All great saints have battled with their own beastly inclinations rather than with any other person.

105. By itself, wealth can bring great sorrow which may also afflict others. It can force you to do many bad deeds. But if you possess the wealth imbued by God, then even as a simple householder, a humble person, you become like a great pipal (*ficus religiosa*) or banyan tree which, germinating from tiny seeds, become places of refuge for many beings. They become providers of coolness, happiness and peace. In a blind quest for wealth and prestige, do not become like the tall coconuts and palms which, arising from huge seeds, do not provide shade for anyone. They do not provide happiness, coolness or peace. Even birds do not nest in them. Occasionally, vultures perch upon them. With God-imbued wealth you will be like the small streams and ponds whose water is sweet, quenching the thirst of both big and small creatures. Despite being but a simple householder, you can take care of family, friends, relatives, saints, seekers, Mahatmas, great people, and beggars.

106. Beware of people with doubtful backgrounds. They can cheat you or take you onto a doubtful path.

107. What does a saint do? Why does he ask his disciples to wander? Where will they wander? Will they beg to survive? No, no! You will not beg. Anybody can give you a little food. People throw food in front of dogs just like that. Why won't they throw food in front of you, too? Yes, go wander. See what difficult situations human beings go through. Observe these! Look at them! Learn from them! Wander! Do not go about

teaching! You do not have the right to teach, and those people are not ready to learn. They will make a fool of you. Teach only the person who likes to be taught.

109. Never call from behind respected elders or soldiers fighting on a battlefield. If a great saint is passing, instead of calling him from behind, go in front of him humbly and then say something. He will respond with a silent cry in his heart. He will not say anything. He will not produce a sound. The person who does not produce a sound is the person who truly gives you something. If he produces a sound, then you know he is not giving you anything. He is simply beating on you as a hollow drum.

Sentiment

The sentiment with which we live lights our life. If we live with a sentiment of happiness, all those who are around us also become affected by it. If we live with sorrow, we spread sorrow. In effect, when we are happy, it is the divine Mother's grace. This is especially so because true happiness is a state beyond pleasure and pain, riches or poverty, strength or weakness.

1. If your inner disposition is bound by emotions of hesitation or shyness, do not consider this a weakness. These emotions have a separate place of their own.

2. Our happiness is the happiness of the Divine Mother. A heart above pleasure and pain indicates her closeness.

3. Irritations are vibrations from the dancing steps of Pranamayi (Mother as life-force) residing in our heart.

4. The Divine Mother is our faith and devotion.

5. Faith is wealth. Faith is unfailing wealth. It can be neither snatched away nor nationalized.

6. It is necessary to give lasting stability to your faith.

7. Without faith, beliefs cannot be generated.

8. Where emotions have never appeared, you will find no trace of emotionlessness. Non-emotion is the expression of absolute emotion.

9. In a desire-free heart, attachment does not arise.

10. Your tendency to seek to be worshipped can cause your destruction. This can lead to ignominy, and the rise of egotism and false pride.

11. Forget distinctions of big or small, high or low. Keep walking your path of duty laughing, playing, talking, and meeting with everyone.

12. Never give feelings of respect and disrespect, insult or praise any place in your heart. These feelings make life one-sided.

13. Fear only yourself; do not fear anyone else. This will take you to greatness. You do not have a right to worship anyone else. You have a right to worship only yourself. Worship yourself. You will become complete, absolute. Achieving the absolute state, you will achieve the goal of "welfare to all, happiness to all".

14. You are 'self-born'. The day you feel 'self-born' in your character, practice it in your behaviour, from that day you will become free — free of life as well death. Free of the dissension of profit and loss. You will no longer be a person where attachments seek shelter.

15. The person who feels guilty and shows remorse on doing something wrong has a simple temperament. That person will move toward the state of *samadhi* (absolute consciousness) easily.

16. Three fires should be given up: the fire of desire, the fire of jealousy, the fire of attachment.

17. Do not be angry at an angry person.

18. Go to your own refuge. Give up the colour, form and nature of your past actions and your caste. Do not remain attached to them. Only then can you change your true form; only then

can you change your colour and nature. This is possible only when you go to your own refuge.

19. What are the contaminants of the mind? i) Greed, ii) Hostility, iii) Anger, iv) Feuding, v) Miserliness, vi) Hard-heartedness, vii) Envy, viii) Jealousy, ix) Illusion, x) *Sathya*, xi) Stupidity, xii) Violence, xiii) Praise, xiv) Prestige and xv) Negligence; these are the contaminants of the mind.

20. Intoxication is another name for distortion.

21. Learn to remain within yourself. Truth lies only within.

22. Do not give a place to eagerness in your life.

23. That feeling is pure and wholesome which resonates with auspicious thoughts about the Divine Mother and the guru.

24. When your mind becomes like a roasted seed, understand you are in God's lap.

25. A heart without longing is unmovable; a rock indicating the strength of the soul and supreme joy.

26. Non-attachment exists only where there is no desire or jealousy, where even the concepts of heaven and hell do not exist, where no distinctions of 'we' or 'ours' remain. Achieving this state, vibrations no longer arise in you. When no vibration arises in you, you can see the world stripped of its illusory form. This is true knowledge.

27. Inside the mind hides affection. Remember this — the more your affection rises secretly, in solitude, the stronger it will be.

28. Physical love is desire and attachment. Real love exists by destroying that attachment. Spiritual love is real love. Seek

shelter with the person who is a master of real love. He will show you an all encompassing form of love that lies within your heart.

29. Search without egotism. You will find love. The day you find the master of love within your heart, you will know that love is God.

30. One who has no love for living beings cannot have love for a stone idol in a temple, or the formless God of a mosque.

31. Reverence and love are as different from each other as are the ocean and the Himalayan mountains.

32. With effort, courage, patience, wherever you live, keep a feeling of benevolence for village, country, state and nation. Oppose the unjust, the cruel and those of lowly deeds.

33. Without goodness in your heart and in your behaviour, your talents shall be scorched. If your heart falls, you become hopeless, and your mind and heart become discouraged.

34. Those who repent on making a mistake, that very moment their misdeeds are expiated.

35. In return for beneficence you give gratefulness, not sermons.

36. A generous heart is always respected and always will be.

37. Stay away from jealousy. Jealousy makes life egotistical.

38. Don't have blind faith in me. Blind faith produces separation.

39. Once doubt taints a person's heart, he lives a life of helplessness and resignation, like a person who falls into a well in the wilderness, and he keeps screaming for help, but nobody comes.

40. Don't be happy and encouraged by sweet words, nor sad and discouraged by harsh words.

41. One who learns from his guru with humility in his heart and mind, through humble actions, knows; knowing, he becomes enthusiastic about his life and duties. He becomes a source of inspiration for others.

42. One who is not swayed from a good resolution, who becomes neither afraid nor doubtful, he will be successful.

43. Humility toward the guru embodies compassion, kindness, and friendliness.

44. Poison, faith and the world — these three words have three meanings respectively: morning, afternoon and evening. In the evening desire burns women; in the morning it burns men.

45. Weigh the feelings of humanity neither against money nor against scholarship. Nor can you weigh them with eloquent words.

46. Remain satisfied within yourself, and keep others satisfied, too.

47. Because of many illusions, at times we find our faith building up and, at other times, we find it breaking down.

48. Hope is also a part of the life of human beings. I hope the best for you, and you have hopes from me.

49. Mental stress is demonic in character and causes cruel behaviour. Free your mind of stress, find happiness in your reflections, find affection, find love, foster a feeling of respect towards everyone. These are the virtues we need. I hope you have an abundance of these virtues in you.

50. Human beings live in fear because of animosities and jealousies. Afraid of their friends and relatives, their wife and children, their neighbours and acquaintances, their lives are afflicted by fear. Pray that they may be relieved of fear, that they may become fearless.

51. The belief that lies within us manifests in the devotion, faith and perseverance with which we worship. It is our dearest friend.

52. One whose heart and mind are unstable keeps wandering. Without stability, he does not understand what he is or what he is not. Because of this lack of understanding, he becomes angry at many people. He holds no affection toward his well-wishers or friends. He gets tangled within himself as well, and he becomes angry and displeased with himself.

53. Self-confidence awakens when our weaknesses disappear.

54. Those full of false pride in the name of Aughar Aghoreshwar give rise to distortions. They have fallen from their position.

55. Don't let faith get stuck in a place full of bad company. Think before putting your faith and trust in the hands of an untrustworthy person.

56. Your faith and devotion towards Devi, Bhagawati, Bhagwan, Bhawani, is not separate from you. Faith and devotion are, themselves, the form you worship. They rise in you and direct your devotion.

57. Perform service towards all. Do not exact service from anyone; do not let anyone's head bow before you. Bow your own head before others. Let this be your feeling and your duty.

58. You have been with me through the ages. In this period, too,

you are present, touching me with your good feelings and your expressed but unspoken thoughts.

59. Do not do anything. Just straighten your temperament a little. Make your mind realize that devotion and faith are with you, and that faith and devotion for the Divine Mother has great strength. Your belief has a very long reach.

60. If I see God in you, how can I have pride that I am a big man? This life is not made for such egotism.

61. A person may think that he is clever, wise, and has great understanding, but this is why he knows nothing. He has become so wise in his own eyes that he has more wisdom than Wisdom itself.

62. Many things generate happiness. But they are artificial, and artificial happiness is like a short-term guest. Troubles and sorrows have no form. Troubles and sorrows do not take the form of our friends and relatives. They arrive like guests. When they come to visit we have to put up with much vexation to take care of them. To save ourselves from such guests is a virtuous act.

63. At times the mind deviates from the good. Or, bad feelings arise. When these feelings arise, then everything — all our prayers, worship, meditation, reflection, and all our reverence — everything seems like poison to us. We become dull. We practice unwanted behaviour.

64. There are twelve hours of night and twelve hours of day, so half our life is spent in darkness. In the dark state, one is frightened and unable to achieve anything. But for one in whose life even a little bit of light exists, it is possible for him to enjoy at least twelve hours of light. And, for the night's twelve hours, with electricity, with perfumed oil lamps, the

darkness can be cut apart and thrown away. One can live a free life. As long as one lives on the earth, one lives well. As long as the merit of one's good deeds last, one enjoys life.

65. In our lives, many a time we see darkness at every step. At every step we feel: What will happen now? How will things work out? What will happen after this? Now what will happen? Oh seeker! We have given everything into the hands of an omnipresent being. That omnipresent being, that unknown God, will do something for us, does do things for us. Have absolute faith. That faith is our devotion, our God, our Mother Goddess, our divinity. When we help ourselves, that being helps us.

66. Many kinds of feelings arise in men and women, many kinds of desires. Those feelings and desires bring agony to their home, to their family.

67. We pray that the divine spouse's health, mental condition, heart and mind be good. That such a one not be afflicted, again and again, with carnal desire, with desires that kill us, that cause our health to deteriorate, that cause family and friends to cry. The cry of friends and family can turn family and society upside down.

68. Our thoughts are in conflict with themselves. When this conflict dies down, our heart and mind become calm and quiet and we understand that we are close to the Divine Mother, Bhawani, Uma Gauri.

69. Do all things in a simple, straight, natural way. Whatever work comes to us as the inspiration of God, the Supreme Soul, the master of all, the Divine Mother, the kind Mother, let us complete this work well. If we add anything of our own, it will be tainted with ego.

70. Sin is something that pollutes our heart and mind.

71. When good days arrive and saints bestow their grace on you, all those wrongs you did but for which you understood your mistake, these will turn out right for you. When bad days arrive, rights turn into wrongs.

72. Our mind is the cause of bondage, as well as the provider of liberation for us.

73. Faith is like a banyan tree, a wish-fulfilling tree. Living under such a tree, what you visualize in the morning or evening, and while you walk about, will have an effect on you.

74. How one sees one's self, this is how one becomes. If one says: "I am dirty. I am dirt", one sees dirt everywhere. If one thinks: "I am pure. I am conscious", one becomes so.

75. Create good feelings about yourself. Feel that you are pure, wise, knowledgeable, deep, with equal vision and far from ignorance. Feel that you will remain far from ignorance. God, we need your help! Divine Mother, creative energy, we need your help! When we get help from you, only then will we succeed.

76. One's mood upon arising can determine how one's day is spent. If we wake up with rancour, then our day is spent in rancour. One trouble after another follows us. Even if troubles don't happen, our heart and mind suffer from worry — "What will happen? What should I do?" — and we are disoriented.

77. The wilderness of our mind is like a forest. Grass and weeds take root. Many useless things grow there. Some take the form of big trees. People lose their way in the forest and become lost in the jungles of the mind. Lost in the jungles of the mind, life becomes feeble.

78. A blessing means that whatever I say should have a good effect

on your mind — and its effect should not be limited just to you. Let it touch your inner soul, then give it a practical form.

79. Think favourably about yourself and those under your care, those dependent on you. The day you begin to think favourably about them and don't utter inauspicious words to them, bad things will no longer happen.

80. The entity we meditate on creates tests for us. Our hearts feel strange. Our minds feel strange. We are inspired toward devotionlessness. Because of this, we feel badly toward the entity. Then we lose everything. We cannot do anything. First we must say to that God: "O God, O Mother, let the knowledge acquired from my guru always be with me. Let me have faith in it and devotion toward him."

81. With devotion, your mantra bears fruit. With faith, your mantra bears fruit. If you do not take a mantra, if you do not take initiation, your body remains impure. One's children and grandchildren are born without spiritual refinement.

82. Do not let your faith break over small things. If your faith breaks, all the days spent doing *japa*, worship, virtuous actions — all will go to waste. So do not let your faith break over small things.

83. Necessarily, a disciple has ignorance.

84. The Divine Mother is known only through your devotion. She is worshipped only through your devotion. She is seen only through your devotion. If one lacks devotion, she will not be there at all.

85. Even the life created by a mixture of the impossible and possible does not affect one's heart and mind to alter one's future to be wholesome. Grandmother! Please untie the language-generated

literary knots of our hearts. Your grace is what we need now, Grandmother! You are the goddess of knowledge, are you not?

86. If you acquire even a poppy seed's worth of faith in my words, you will be able to ask a mountain to move from here to there and from there to here and it will not seem strange to you.

87. Sin and virtue are only ideas of the mind. Keep a divine attitude in your soul.

88. What is sorrow? Non-fulfillment of our desires.

89. Patient people live forever. Impatient people burn up like dry sticks.

90. However bad a person is, however bad his thinking may be, that person is bad only up to the time he expiates his deeds, and not after expiation.

91. Jealousy, hatred and competition devour human beings. They indicate weakness.

92. The manifestations of stress and strain in the mind are indications of human weaknesses. Stress leads to failure.

93. One who does not deprive others of his sweet smile also does not give rise to envy, jealousy and hatred.

94. The person who tricks sorrow is a Mahapurush. The sorrow one acquires makes one humble.

95. If you see compassion in someone, the person is a true human being.

96. An untrue person is one who repeats somebody else's bad traits, criticizes repeatedly, and tries to cover up his own bad charac-

teristics. He is not worthy of companionship. He is a vessel full of despicable thoughts.

97. A deceitful person is like a white grave which looks beautiful from the outside, but inside it is full of the stench of a corpse.

98. If a person's mind is not in harmony with his heart, then such a heartless person is like a beast.

99. The difference between animals and humans is that humans can change their temper, thoughts, and ways of thinking. This is not possible for animals.

100. One who is attached to and controlled by desires performs bad actions with his body and his mind. Having performed negative actions, when such a person leaves his body, he achieves a bad state and is reborn in hell.

101. If an action makes you feel guilty, even if it is a familiar and interesting action, give it up.

102. If on doing something you are pleased, there lies your true duty.

103. For courageous people even the impossible is possible.

104. Love everyone, trust only a few. Beware, do not hurt anyone.

105. Have respect and devotion toward all, but love can be had only from your lover.

106. The more people who are dear to you, the more sorrow you will have. The less people who are dear to you, the less sorrow you will have.

107. I know only this much about your mind that you impute many meanings to one thing, and you have many ways of thinking. Because of this your life becomes distorted, and you become angry at yourself.

108. What you look for in temples and rocks [i.e. stone-idols of deities to worship] lies not in rocks and boulders, but in a state of ecstasy within [known as *samadhi* consciousness]. This, which you shan't find in the scriptures or in the Puranas, which you shan't ever find in any rock, you will find in *samadhi chitta*. When your mind is stable, you will have a divine vision.

Ritual Action

There are many ways to propitiate the God or Goddess whom one worships. To worship them properly, one also has to be in the right mental and physical state. For example, it is not good to meditate when one is feeling particularly sad or agitated. So as well, there are some basic rituals associated with worshiping God within yourself, through meditation. These include the knowledge of self-purification, securing the directions, breathing exercises, and chanting the mantra given by the Guru.

1. Become neither God nor a representative of God. Represent yourself. Otherwise, you may be separated from yourself. One who worships himself deserves kindness. He is kind to himself. He saves himself from falling low, from troubles, from illusion, from imagining an unreal life. That person is a human being. There are many people who live as animals among human beings.

2. Knowledge alone does not lead to salvation. Action is primary — then with the strength of knowledge, we can fly as a bird with both wings in the sky of salvation. We need both wings to fly — the wing of knowledge and the wing of action.

3. Determination is the basic mantra of self-knowledge. It is essential to meditate on the Self.

4. "O my Self, I promise you, I will behave nicely with you, I will never beguile you, I will never let you fall. This I vow to do. This, I promise you."

5. Without a cleansing of the Self, amassing inner strength is useless. To harbour desires in your heart is to turn away from your Self.

6. If you stay in a quiet, peaceful state for even two or three minutes, you will realize a new life. You will experience a new spirit.

7. By practice, even that which is hidden becomes visible. It, then, becomes conscious, healthy and strong.

8. To realize your past glory [of your own Self], you should practice the five-fold path, the five-fold path that produces vision and intellect.

9. By deep meditation you can achieve knowledge of the one true entity in the cosmos.

10. **Daily Practices:**
The time for daily practices begins early in the morning in the 'divine period' [*Brahma muhurta*, an hour and thirty-six minutes before sunrise]. As you get up, remember God, look at the palms of both hands, say the mantra:

कराग्रे वसते लक्ष्मी, कर मध्ये सरस्वती
कर मूले स्थितो ब्रह्म, प्रभाते कर दर्शनम् ।।

"Lakshmi (the goddess of wealth) lives in the front of my hand
Saraswati (the goddess of knowledge) lives in the middle
At the root resides Brahma (creator of the universe)
At dawn, thus, I see them."

Then, before stepping on the ground, pray to mother earth:

समुद्रं वसने देवि
प्रवर्त स्तन मण्डले
विष्णु पत्नी, नमस्तुभ्य
पादस्पर्श क्षमस्व मे ।।

"The oceans are your clothing, O mother
The mountains are your breasts

Wife of Vishnu, I beg you
Forgive me, I touch you with my feet."

Then complete your toilet, shower and put on clean clothes. Alone, at your place of worship, sit on an *asana* facing east. Keep water for self-purification in a copper vessel on your right hand side.

11. Upon arising, setting your feet on the earth, touching your face with the palms of both hands — which serve as symbols of action — say to yourself, "Today may I achieve creative strength, without the support of which I am deprived of success". Then touch your eyebrows, for the father of Janak, 'Nimi', our predecessor, is present in your eyebrows. If your hands are clean — if they are not bloody — then touching your eyebrows will give you strength, and a feeling of oneness.

12. To defeat an enemy: in the morning take three steps forward and three steps back, press your feet hard against the ground, then take a step and walk. By doing this, you will defeat the bad soul that has attached itself to you. This is also knowledge. You should learn this, too.

13. It is not proper to meditate if you are troubled and ill at ease.

14. By getting away from fear, regarding everything as a miracle of God's power, you will awaken pure feelings in yourself. Awake your faith, practice it, be with God.

15. When you pray to God, hold your breath for a moment, bring a feeling of restfulness into your heart. Don't harbour desires. Keep your mind and heart happy. You will then be experienced in doing everything. You will remain cheerful. As far as your faith holds, you will achieve success.

16. Empty your mind, lighten your heart, loosen your body, close your eyes for a moment. Do not close your eyes to put yourself

in darkness. Close your eyes to turn your 'out-sight' inward. See with 'in-sight' your inner depths. See what is happening there, what is not happening there. Look for the supreme truth.

17. Perform *pranav* (chanting of the mantra *Om*). Then empty your mind, make your heart light. Sit straight and do not perform any action. No action at all. Do not think of anything or anyone. Do not perform *japa*. Absolutely thoughtless, do not remember even the Supreme Unknown.

18. Live in a state of 'vibrationlessness', a state where no thought vibrations rise in your heart or mind, where no attachments grow in it. Whether standing or sitting in the lotus position, be mindful of your mantra. Let the vibrations of *pranav* emanate from every pore of your body. Maintain a conscious experience of it. This is called 'kindness'. This is the 'strength of the soul'.

19. Close your eyes, close your ears, stop your breath, make your body as inactive as a log, experience yourself. There will be no vibrations.

20. We sit on an *asana* (the seat of meditation). By sitting on the *asana*, we take control of our body. Taking control of this inert body we perform our practices. What practices do we perform? We wake ourselves up. But only a person who is actually sleeping can be awakened. You cannot wake a person who is pretending to be asleep.

21. Continue your prayers even while completing your toilet and you will achieve peace. This is *aughar* knowledge. Pray while performing your toilet; see how much peace you feel. You will feel more peaceful than if you had prayed in a temple. Peace depends on how you focus your mind, how determined you are, how you look for your divinity. The creative power is everywhere.

22. Pay attention to your Self, where everything is found, where nothing is lacking. While performing actions, remain unattached. Even if others see you as running after action, be still and unattached inside. Search in the forest of your mind in a state between the states of being focused and unfocused.

23. Why don't you observe, analyze and ponder over all that is happening within you every day? Why don't you accept that eagerly? Why don't you make it your own? It will, in a very short time, take you towards the Absolute Unlimited, towards that which has no limits at all.

24. When you remember Maheshwar Shiva while walking or doing other things, Rama roams within you. When you remember Rama, you rise above body-consciousness and enter Shiva-consciousness. '*So'ham*', the divine knowledge, automatically comes within your consciousness.

25. The joy of living in solitude with discipline is far greater than the joy derived from gems bought by wealth.

26. O Sudharma! In my realized state I saw many circles and colours. If one makes circles on his clothes, or on the ground, or on his flag or icon, and colours them in as many colours as I saw, and in the same sequence as I saw them, and then meditates on my realized state and invokes me, then he can achieve a lot. At that time I was fourteen or fifteen years old. If one meditates on my form at that age, meditates on my condition at that age, meditates on the characteristics and functions of that age, he can achieve a lot.

27. Great souls and *munis* used four major kinds of spiritual powers in ancient times. What are those four spiritual powers, and a fifth one too?
1) Retention of semen, 2) stopping one's desires, 3) living with one's own life-force (*prana*), 4) following the arduous

way of the example set by one's guru, and 5) living an ideal life. One who is engrossed in his mantra, diligent in his spiritual practices and engrossed in action without laziness can achieve these five spiritual powers very easily.

28. A divine entity generated by mantra, rituals and herbs is not a divinity that will do good for us. It will inspire us towards materialism. It will prevent us from going to our own refuge, to the refuge of our soul. The divinity generated by mantra, rituals, and herbs cannot benefit our pure body, the body in which resides our magnetic attraction, our conscious self, our joy and happiness.

29. Sit with a straight body and with your memory in front of you.

30. In this age of science we know that sound spreads through the whole solar system instantaneously. Consider mantra-knowledge, posture-knowledge, ritual and *yantra*-knowledge to be similar to such instantaneous communication. Look into it for yourself, in reality.

31. The use of alcohol is not for everybody. Its use is only for those who have found a *sadguru*. Alcohol prevents the seeker from being sucked into the attraction of this world.

32. Buddha, before gaining Buddha-hood, performed Aghor practices. Sujata helped him in his practices. Buddha was beyond the do's and don'ts of the world. Only by keeping a constant practice can one move ahead on one's path.

33. Silence is the best *japa*.

34. In worship and prayer, you should know which foot to keep on top, how to start the sound (of the mantra Om) from the navel, how to behave with the mantra who is a friend. Learn

to gauge if the vibrations in your heart, if the emanations are of the right kind. Know when and to whom to offer fruits and flowers. Guru should be worshipped with white flowers. For peace and stability in your heart, offer soft, blue flowers at the feet of the Divine Mother. So that your actions may be auspicious, worship with yellow or yellow-white flowers. If you have no flowers, worship with the five basic elements — everything is composed of five basic elements. The method of how to do so is described in the *Safal Yoni:* Consider the earth to be perfume, the sky flowers, the wind incense, the sun a lamp, and water, food. Offer them to your dear divinity with all your heart, mind and soul.

35. If one worships the Divine Mother with gold and silver, one will be born poor in the next life. One who worships the Divine Mother with flowers, fruits, and grasses, if he takes rebirth, will become wealthy, prosperous and happy.

36. When you meditate, let the mantra resonate in your *pran*. When energy wakes in your *pran*, the seeds of divine characteristics will be sown. Let *japa* resonate in your heart. You can even say the mantra aloud. With enough practice, a time will come when you will not need to say it aloud. With your mouth closed, the whole process will begin: from head to toe, your body's pores will begin to resonate with the sound of the mantra. Hear the resonance. Feel the joy of the waves produced by it.

37. When you sit on your *asana* to do *japa*, touch the earth with one of your hands, because one derives strength from the earth. If you do *japa* with your right hand, touch the earth with your left. Also when you get up after sleeping, salute the earth. The earth is the mother. She harbours strength and energy.

38. When you sit on your *asana*, keep your arms and legs in the appropriate posture (*mudra*). This generates a power of

attraction within you. Let your thinking deepen. Quiet your mind, discipline your senses, then meditate.

39. Sacrifice and *yantra* are necessary to generate energy. Don't be afraid of the obstacles that arise when you start your prayers and meditation. Don't be angered by them. Sacrifice them.

40. Shivaratri is the day to worship the Self. The third eye of this *Mahadev-yantra* takes you toward the sky. It makes you aware of the ephemeral nature of the world. You will experience a desire-free heart where exist neither time nor action, nor do's and don'ts. True Shivaratri practice requires a knowledge of the right sequences and their quantities.

41. Purify the *asana* by sprinkling water on it. After purification, put your right foot on the *asana* first, then your left foot. Sit facing east, north or west with a peaceful heart and mind.

42. Seated on your *asana*, do the *digbandhan*, the act of 'tying the directions'. For *digbandhan*, Aughars have many mantras. One can say aloud: "*Shri Guru Padukaye Namah*"; "*Shri Adiguru Padukaye Namah*" or "*Mahakali, Mahalakshmi, Mahasaraswati Devataye Namah*", and then clap. Bad souls run from the sound of clapping. Then we perform *achamani* by dropping water on the right palm three times with a spoon or mango leaf while saying "*Om Tatsat*", drinking the water each time. This is known as *bhutashuddhi*, "the purification of the past". By performing this ritual we are asking God to burn up the bad effects of our past misdeeds.

43. After *achamani* we perform *pranayama*. In *pranayama*, breathe in through the left nostril, hold your breath, then exhale through the right nostril. This succession of inhaling, retaining, releasing should have a 1:3:2 ratio — that is, hold your breath for thrice as long as it takes to inhale, and breathe out for twice as long a duration as when you breathe in. Count

this silently, or recite the *guru-mantra* silently in the same 1:3:2 ratios as you perform *pranayama*. Practicing *pranayama*, our channels become pure. This exercise, a part of purification, makes our body light and energetic. It also makes our ideas and feelings bright and divine.

44. When doing *pranayama* (purification by air), the life-force comes in with the air. Breathe in through the left nostril and slowly breathe out through the right. Do this three times. It takes only a little time. Hold it for thrice the time it takes to breathe in, and release it in twice the time it takes to breathe in.

45. If you perform *pranayama* and *pranav* moderately and regularly, your mental weakness and physical laxity will disappear. Twenty-four times, draw your breath in through the left nostril, hold it for twice as long as it took to draw it in, and then release it through your right nostril. Slowly increase the length of this practice. In twelve hours do it three times. With concentration, in a state of soundless, thoughtless solitude, do this at dawn and at dusk. If you persevere in this practice, the latent rays of light in your body will become stronger, brighter. They will become flames of enthusiasm and inspiration for you.

46. Do *pranav* for at least twenty minutes, but no more than thirty. Sitting, without worries, raise the sound of *pranav* from the navel. Take it to the *brahma-randhra*, at the peak of your skull. Do it in a state of wakefulness. It will take you toward a supernatural light whose electrical rays will help you. Do *pranayama* and *pranav* one after the other to perceive their benefit.

47. Worshippers and seekers, perform *pranayama* and *pranav* before and after worshipping the divinity, before meditating on the Guru, before invoking the Aghoreshwar.

48. Before doing *japa* with the *mantra*, perform *achamani*, a purification that is done by taking water in the palm of the hand and invoking the name of the Guru or Divinity. Say, "O Essence, you are true". This purification rite burns the effects of past deeds; all five elements turn into their original essences. Understand this purification so that a sick intellect, distorted perceptions and the understanding within us can be cast away and the doors closed on them. Following this purification rite, take water with the third finger and touch both eyebrows. Then sprinkle drops of water on yourself. Sprinkling this water causes bad souls hovering about to go away. Water is the basis of life for all beings. By using mantra-sanctified water you can also perform other actions. Using mantra-sanctified water, a bad soul posing as a friend within a person will run away and that person's health will improve. He will find *amrita*, the true nectar of life. All this will happen within you, but without a strong will it is distanced from you.

49. So, after purification, while praying, we perform *pranayama*. This purifies our channels so that their flow does not contradict each other. The power in these veins to provide the flow for a good mind and thought — that flow should not be hampered. This flow should make us think nice thoughts and force us to live a knowledgeable life. This flow should enable us to see the divine truth, for which we have a deep desire within. That is why we perform *pranayama*. When the channels inside have been purified, we can see the truth. Then we try to mould that purity into our lives. Performing *japa*, we are able to confer with our senses. With the help of our mantra, we no longer do anything that would generate guilt in us, or which would make us restless and explosive. We are no longer led into terrible mental anguish.

50. To perform *dhyana* is to meditate. What is even better than meditating (performing *dhyana*), is to pay attention, i.e. to practice absolute awareness. If we perform *dhyana*, we imme-

diately face the dilemma of meditating on form or formlessness. But one who pays attention will avoid this dilemma. One who merely performs *dhyana* creates a separation between himself and truth. He places a curtain between the two. Therefore, do not perform *dhyana*, but pay attention. That which is truth will come to light. That which is untruth will fade away.

51. Visualize the Guru sitting on a white lotus wearing white clothes. Sit on an *asana*, become triangular like a *yantra*, get situated within yourself, and feel the vibrations of *mantra-japa*. Watch what shapes form when your breath comes out of your nostrils. Remain vigilant towards sensory or mental attacks. Many hateful things we have heard or seen in the past, have been made to hear and understand, have left their scars on our mind. We must not now let these things create fears and worries in us. When we pay attention to these things, slowly our divinity begins to respond to us. One becomes that divinity. Everything depends on our way of acting, our faith, our belief, our stability.

52. Meditate on that divinity within which has no colour, form, or shape. Meditate on the unthinkable one who does not enter your thoughts easily. Meditate on divine consciousness, the divine light from which we arise and into which we disappear. Meditate on your own form. Mediate on one who is dear to you. That One is your divinity. Meditate on the Guru wearing white clothes. Meditate on him wearing red, yellow or green clothes. Just as a train stops on being signalled by a red flag and moves again on seeing a green one, each colour signals its message. The Guru wearing yellow signals auspicious acts, red signals the defeat of an enemy, green signals happiness and prosperity.

53. Pay more attention during meditation; mind and consciousness should be totally focused. All ten senses, every faculty should be focused, lying latent within.

54. When we meditate — after emptying our minds of everything, without any worries, without any desires or attachments in our hearts, without anything coming into our thoughts, without any feelings of jealousy arising — then we can clearly see that soul, that *atma* who, to see, we have wandered for a long time, to many places.

55. Even if we have little to live by, if we focus on experiencing joy and wealth, if we control our senses and concentrate them inwardly, then the soul or *atma*, who we address as God or Goddess, will provide clear experiences from within.

56. Experiences from within are possible, but happen only when we have stopped the wanderings and desires of our senses. Meditate in solitude for ten minutes to half an hour. Then, when you think about someone or something, you will see it clearly.

57. By concentrating and becoming peaceful in our heart and mind through *pranayama* and *pranav*, creative energy spreads its light in every direction. It becomes a synonym for the unfathomable wealth of joy, enthusiasm and healthfulness.

58. So, we purify the past (*bhutashuddhi*), we purify the life-force (*pranshuddhi*), and then we perform *achamani*. We perform *achamani* by saying:

Atmatattvam Shodhayami Swaha
(I am investigating the Self-element)
Pranatattvam Shodhayami Swaha
(I am investigating the *prana*-element)
Viryatattvam Shodhayami Swaha
(I am investigating the semen-element)
Gurutattvam Shodhayami Swaha
(I am investigating the Guru-element)
Shivatattvam Shodhayami Swaha
(I am investigating the Shiva-element)

Shaktitattvam Shodhayami Swaha
(I am investigating the Shakti-element)
There is no rule about when to do this. There is no rule of serialization. You can perform it before or after other actions.

59. After performing *tarpan* (water sacrifice) we kiss the *mala* and stroke it with our fingers. This is called doing *japa*. *Japa* with the *mala* prevents the mind from running away with us. It brings the mind back to itself. It does not matter if you say *japa* aloud or not, but keep it continuous. Let the constriction in your larynx and the constant memory of what you are doing remain unbroken.

60. After *achamani*, perform *digbandhan* (securing the directions). After *digbandhan*, perform *japa*. We do *japa* in whatever way the Guru has told us to. One need not think about it, because the Guru, when he gave it, knew one's condition and mental state. Remember the Gita: "*Yagyanam Japo Yagya*" (the best among *yagyas* is *japa yagya*). During *mantra-japa* many seekers hold the *mala* in their right hand and touch the earth with their left hand. It will be good if married people visualize their creative energy on their left side. If their creative energy is not cruel, but pleasant, cool and normal, then it will be beneficial. In *japa*, never use the finger used for pointing out the faults in others (the finger next to the thumb). When performing *japa*, turn back the direction of stroking the beads when you reach the *mala*'s apex. In *japa*, the direction is always reversed upon reaching the apex.

61. Start your *japa*. A *mala* has 108 beads. Eight beads represent what we owe to our Guru, father, divinity, mother, to the ruler of our country, the lineage and family in which we were born, and the person who gives us our food. The *japa* value of eight beads is distributed among these people. Then we count the 100 beads that are left. Then we count whatever promises we have made to ourselves — whether we do it

10,000 or a 100,000 times, we do it. On completion, we sacrifice in *hawan* one tenth of all the times we have done *japa*. This action is known as *purashcharan*. To perform this *hawan* of one tenth of our *japa*, we may not have enough materials. It may also take too much time. So we do *japa* for that one tenth again. If we do not have enough materials, then we sacrifice in *hawan* one tenth of this one tenth. We do this not to make trouble, nor to perform undue actions of attraction, repulsion or aggravation, but for joy and peace. In a place where *hawan* is not possible, we perform *tarpan* with rice, *ghee* and *gur* (molasses). We perform *tarpan* in water.

62. Perform *hawan* after performing *japa* with the divine *mantra* given to us by our Guru. During *hawan*, perform *ahuti* (putting blessed materials in the sacred fire) carefully with three fingers of the right hand. Exclude the finger that points faults in others. Be careful to *offer*, not to *throw* the blessed materials into the fire. For Swaha, the wife of Agni (fire), say '*Swaha*' each time you put materials in the sacred fire. This act is not performed with just one hand. The left hand should touch the right elbow while the right hand performs *ahuti*. A person with only one hand should mentally keep his other hand at the right elbow. Handicapped people should not perform *ahuti* because it does involve fire, but if they have faith, they can do it. There is no stricture against it. After performing *japa* with the mantra given to us by the Guru, we recite a prayer for peace:

Akash shanti	(peace to the sky)
Prithvi shanti	(peace to the earth)
Charon dishayen shanti	(peace to the four directions)
Nadi shanti	(peace to the rivers)
Parvat shanti	(peace to the mountains)
Vanaspati shanti	(peace to all vegetation) etc.

Then we perform *ahuti* for each thing we mention. Thereafter, we pacify the restless souls of the village, town and region by *japa* and *ahuti* for each. We add '*Swaha*' after mentioning each thing. If we are poor and cannot afford the materials, then we can perform *ahuti* in the fire with flowers, or, with water we can perform *tarpan*. If we live in a city or in a place where we can't light a fire, then we can just perform *tarpan* with flowers, rice and water. If we are bathing in a pool or at a well, we can perform *tarpan* for our forefathers, divinities, and all souls. We can perform *tarpan* with rice, flowers, *dub* grass or whatever is available. This is not a death-ritual *tarpan*. The purpose of this *tarpan* is to have a quiet and peaceful mind and heart. Adverse vibrations from cosmic entities attacking us should now stop. By doing this, the shadow of a bad soul that has fallen on us, or who is about to fall on us, will dissipate and disappear.

63. After completing all these actions, take a little water in the palm of the hand, purify it with the *guru-mantra*, or with a divine mantra, and drink it. The meaning of drinking this water is that one offers to one's Guru or divinity whatever one has done until today. The *punya* (merit of good *karma*) that will be achieved by doing this, is offered to them again. Whatever is left after that, even that is offered to them again. Whatever is left over of the left-over of the offering, may that be for me.

64. Far as the question of flowers etc. is concerned, you pluck them to offer to your guru; you can say "*Shri Guru Charan Padukaya, Patram Pushpam Samarpayami*" (I offer these flowers and leaves to the feet of my guru) and give them into his hands. If you do not want to pluck flowers, do not want to take it away from someone, do not want to influence your guru with something that belongs to somebody else, then say mentally: "I have this body, raggedly old body, this I offer to you. O Divine Mother, give me the right wisdom; give me good inspiration." Whatever flowers and leaves you have, offer them. At that time, your gesture should not be that of throwing it at them, but of offering it to them.

65. Your mental state while acquiring and offering rice, leaves, flowers and other things to your divinity is important. While collecting flowers, become so absorbed in doing so that even the cacophony of a passing army would not disturb you. Only then will you know the divinity of the mantra, the benefit and virtue of offering flowers to your divinity. But if your mental state is turbulent, if you are thinking about the deeds and misdeeds of people while collecting flowers, then you are not picking flowers, you are collecting little pouches of poison for yourself. You are collecting garbage that you will then throw on your divinity. That is why when collecting and offering flowers to your Guru you should be completely absorbed in these actions.

66. As part of this practice, we also break a stick of wood. Why do we break a stick of wood? By doing this we are symbolically making a sacrifice, we are defeating our enemies, we are making a vow.

67. By breaking a stick of wood, we make a vow. That vow makes us strong, makes us see things beautifully and auspiciously. It makes us sweet. It makes our voice beautiful; it makes our face and expression beautiful. It bestows unlimited joy and happiness on us!

68. Without practice, even the best knowledge turns into poison. That is why this one moment of practice each day in the course of twenty four hours gives us the capacity to work for a hundred years, and to become successful in our undertakings.

69. Friends, who do you have a right to worship? Until now you have not worshipped yourself, you have not become aware of yourself; you have been very harsh towards yourself. And, neglecting yourself, you have worshiped others! That is an insult to the pure soul residing in your body, residing in the temple of your heart, the pure soul available to you as yourself.

70. If we keep worshipping and practicing without finding out which mantra we have a right to use, which divinity we have a right to seek, who we have a right to worship, then our practice remains ineffective.

71. Proceed toward solitude. In solitude, search for that concentration which encloses everything. Concentration is a great power; it is a great energy.

72. The *kalash* (pitcher of water) of *Navaratri* is important. We cherish this *kalash*. We honour it, we offer flowers and garlands to it, we perform *arati* (adoration with kindled lamps) to it, we worship it because the *pran*, life-force, which has been established in that pitcher is one's own *pran*. Without life-energy, human beings become lifeless.

73. For the nine days of Navaratri, for these nine days, with a stable mind and heart, with pleasant feelings and thoughts, let us watch what happens within us. Let us understand what happens within this body-*yantra* of ours. Once you know this *yantra*, understand it, hear it, nothing will be difficult for you. Everything will be available to you. Everything exists within this world.

74. For these nine days of worship we should smear *vibhuti* (ashes) on our body. Our body becomes a cremation ground, to which divinities come only because of these ashes. Because of these ashes great souls come. By smearing these ashes, by remembering these ashes, our cremation-ground-like body begins to seem pure and auspicious. It then looks beautiful, clean, and untainted. *Vibhuti* is the name of prosperity and glory. You wear this prosperity and glory. The day you become nothing, turn to ashes, that day your prosperity and glory becomes everything and disappears in this country's soil. You then exist everywhere, in every particle. If you do not have *vibhuti* (ashes), then think of water as *vibhuti* and put a little on your forehead.

The lines made by *vibhuti* can erase the lines of death from your forehead; death, with whom you fight every day. *Vibhuti* is a great shield of protection against negative things. But you belong to a new age; perhaps you don't believe in this.

75. When you get up in the morning, rub both hands on your face with the supplication, "O God, O Supreme Soul, O brightest light, O ray of hope, today please help me meet good people, let the one under whom I live be pleased with me, let me earn my livelihood without trouble."

76. In the same way, in the evening, before going to bed, rub both hands on your face. We say to God: "Now let me sleep without thorns, without troubles, in peace. Let no wild animal or being, no problems or difficulties bother me. I want to live in peace." Then our night will be spent in peace.

77. Your Guru asks you to carefully keep the mantra and cherish the divinity dear to you. Keep them with the care a bird keeps her eggs. At first it is a little uncomfortable, but that will go away if what you cherish is pleased with you.

78. Sitting in front of the Divine Mother, connect with thought and concentration. In that connection, be mindful of the shapes your breath takes. When concentrating, do not perform *japa* or any other kind of meditation. Stay focused on your breath and the connection. This is known as *swar-sadhana* (breath practice).

79. Circumambulating a statue of Lord Ganesha in which the life-force has been established by a saint, a realized person, or a great soul, this bestows the same fruits as circumambulating an image of the ever-giving Lord Shiva. It also bestows the fruits from other kind souls, virtues, good characteristics, and the fruits one receives from visiting the most sacred places on earth. This is the merit gained by circumambulating an image

of Lord Ganesha. But if you perform circumambulation of a statue in which the life-force has been established by a smuggler, or by a person of negative thoughts and feelings, this can hurt you. Better than doing the latter, would be to make a Ganesha idol of cow dung and circumambulate that.

80. Friends! If you think you have the right to venture into the fields of divinities and their manifestations, religion and duty, rules and laws of the country, as well as their customs and constitutions, then you must also accept and follow the standards and guidelines of each. This acceptance is also a worship of yourself. To follow standards and guidelines is a form of worship.

81. This word that emanates by itself from within you, emanates by itself from your pores, is not to be spoken aloud. The word is happening. It happens within by itself. Without our thinking of it or focusing on it, it happens by itself. Our senses are being disciplined. Keep your attention focused on that.

82. Make the mantra that is dear to the divinity so conscious and powerful, your soul-self so conscious and awake, that you understand everything. Understand who is going on that path, who is coming on that path, who wants to talk to you and who you want to meet.

83. If you want to send a message to someone in a foreign country far away, then become very quiet, close your eyes. From deep within your heart focus on that village or town, that country, its soil, then send your message to that place as you send a message over the telephone. When you do this, the person you send it to — be this your mother, sister, or some other well-wisher — will receive and be affected by the vibrations. They'll feel a vibration; a shiver will run through their body. If the recipient is a mother, she will open her eyes and wonder: why did I see my son's face last night? How did it come to me?

84. We beg everywhere. Who gives anything without being asked? And, as beggars, we will receive both invectives and good words; sticks as well as sweets. Be ready to accept everything. It should not be that we are ready to accept sweets, but that we run away when we get a stick. It should not be that we feel good when we get the sweets, but not good when get the stick.

85. Don't reveal your mantra, your knowledge, your divinity to anyone unless they ask about it. Especially, don't speak about your Guru.

86. It is important to light lamps and incense and perform *arati* (oil-lamp adoration) in the evening, because everybody wants to leave darkness behind and move toward light. They pray, "O God! Light a lamp to dissipate the darkness in our hearts that we may be rid of it, that we may be able to help others to develop virtues and good thoughts, good behaviour and to practice good deeds". At evening time we perform *puja-arati* so that, turning away from negative souls, we may befriend good souls. These good souls remind us of our progeny and our ancestors. And, if any negative souls have attached themselves to these good souls, the good souls may, by the light, be able to rid themselves of the bad souls.

87. We think mantra is something different, the word is something different, the letter is something different, divinity is something different, and that the Divine Mother is something different. We think, like in a cartoon, that the gods have four hands, ride tigers, ride elephant, ride horses. Friends, it is not so.

88. Friends, one who meditates on an aggressive mantra, his temperament becomes aggressive. One who meditates on a hard mantra, his temperament becomes hard. One who meditates on a mantra, a certain divinity — according to the

rules and procedures of meditation, *japa*, worship — he begins to meditate automatically and becomes like the divinity of the mantra. The one who you invoke comes close to you. When the divinity comes close, you begin to fidget and become restless. With *mantra-japa* you should also have a *yantra*. If you do not have a *yantra* (instrument), then reciting the *mantra* is just like going bang-bang-bang. Then, the divinity does not come close. She looks at us and turns back. She says we are not ready for her, that it would be foolish to go to such a person. She wonders why he is calling her if he does not have the stability to receive her? Even if we do have an appropriate *yantra*, and that *yantra* remains in good condition, still she may not come all at once. She stops and smells the air, to check if the *yantra* is ready. So, we need right vision, right hearing, and right sense of smell. Even the seeker needs to be able to gauge smell. And we also need right speech, the pure speech.

89. Our speech should be pure so that the *japa* sounds, voiced at the right volume, sounds appropriate to the divinity. Thus our voice will find its object, and the divinity, attracted by it, will turn to us. If it turns to us and our *yantra* is not in appropriate condition, instead of helping us, it can smash us to the ground. It can also kill us or make us insane. We can get hurt, become confused, aggressive, and do negative things. This will be our complete failure.

90. If we do not practice, our inner being becomes lazy. Without practice laziness, sleep and yawning eat away our life, and take us closer to death. But if we practice our life remains active, beneficial.

91. We should teach the devoted people in our ashrams and their children how to do *hawan* (fire *puja*), *japa*, *tarpan* and how to worship various divinities. Do this at least once a week. Also, tell them about saints and great souls who have been great householders.

92. Once a soul is weakened, many take advantage of it. This is a *tantra* (a body of knowledge which can be used either positively or negatively.) You have to understand tantra in this sense only. Tantra does not mean magic and sorcery. You will have to understand worship and prayer in this sense, too.

93. To be protected against attack, before worshipping or meditating, purify your place of sitting with water and by spreading grass or a similar cover, and then your *asana*. Thus you tie your *asana* to the earth and the four directions with your mantra and by sprinkling sanctified water. It is necessary to do this to escape the *brahmarakshas*, and other temperamental, cranky, malicious, negative souls who attack us from the earth, the sky, and from the depths of the netherworld. Do not perform your practice just anywhere, nor when sitting on bare ground, nor on newspaper spread on the ground.

94. During meditation, be aware of everything you do. Do not perform actions that weaken you. Stay away from unnecessary talk. It can generate self-alienation and insecurity. Your divinity, your dear one, is standing close to you. She asks you to come forward. She says: "If you take one step forward I will come five steps to meet you". But afflicted by laziness, the effects of the environment and illusions, you remain deprived of your divinity.

95. By becoming stable, the worship and meditation you perform will lead to knowledge of many kinds. You are performing five to seven different kinds of practices. If even one of them comes to fruition your life will be transformed and become very beautiful. If, when leaving this place, you are not afflicted by negative company, nor accosted by negative souls, nor thrust into negative situations, nor affected by family members with demonic dispositions, you will refrain from abhorrent deeds and your life will remain good. What little you have will seem like a lot to you.

96. On *Dashahra* (the tenth day at the culmination of *Navaratri puja*), sacrifice the animal tendencies within you before the Divine Mother. By not doing this, you send her away. But if you make the sacrifice, you will rise above your beastly state to a good place. You will become a divine person. Even today, you can sacrifice the beast in you and rise to that position.

97. O bachelors! If you worship the seven sisters — the seven forms of the Divine Mother — as your dear divinity, you will regain lost prestige and lost opportunities without difficulty. O bachelors, to worship these seven divinities with *Akshobhya Bhairava* (a fearless form of Shiva) is a great worship. To do auspicious actions, worship with yellow flowers; for peace worship with blue and pink flowers; for defeating an enemy, worship with red flowers. To conquer your senses, consume porridge that has been offered to the seven sisters. Keep the porridge from the gaze of greedy landowners; even before the worship, stay away from landlords. Just to see them or be touched by their shadows may affect you negatively. You can worship by making sacrifices to the seven sisters. These offerings are consumed by the worshipper who will then move fearlessly upon this earth free of all afflictions.

98. What are *bhajan*s (devotional songs)? When feelings of duality do not touch the mind, when we don't criticize respectable people, this is *bhajan* [as good thoughts]. Hymns and worship do not have anything to do with food and drink.

99. What is worship? It is the adoration of an object of worship. What is an object of adoration? Our own desires and feelings are objects of adoration. To worship desires and feelings, people make offerings of wine, meat, goat, rice, lentils and money to divinities. One offers flowers, and another offers something else. The divinity remains unmoved. We see this in its statue. Understand this sign. Calm down the eagerness and restlessness that arises in you to be like that unmoved

divinity. Eagerness and restlessness is not divine consciousness. Eagerness and restlessness push you into a hellhole where only cruelty resides.

100. The stance or posture you take during the day fades into the earth and sky. It is seen by your Unknown Friend like you see things on television. Nothing you do is secret from the Great Unknown. In all conditions and circumstances, you need to be conscious and vigilant regarding your self and your actions. Know how to behave in front of your parents, your Guru, great souls and good people. Know what posture to take, what adornments to wear. Learn how to live in your home, village or city, in private and in public. Pay attention to these things, for they are not hidden from your Unknown Friend.

101. *Mantra*, *maithun* (sex), and *mudra* (posture): these three are to be kept private. The better you keep them to yourself, the more you gain respect in society. The scriptures extol the virtue of keeping these to yourself.

102. If we don't follow the practices recommended to us by our Guru in the proper disciplined and measured way, we will not see our own nature in our Guru's nature. When we sit down to worship and meditate we should relinquish worries, give up restlessness, draw ourselves in as a tortoise draws its limbs into its shell. Only our mantra should vibrate — sending a shiver into every pore of our body. Thus will we begin to achieve a state of *samadhi.* In that state nothing else will arise. If you do your practice, the day is not far away when you will see the form of the Divine Mother in the words that come from your mouth — the form you want to see as something different.

103. Teach these practices to at least ten people. Teach the mantra. Teach them the methods of performing *tarpan*, vow (*sankalp*) and *hawan*. Teach them how to use mantra for different pur-

poses. Teach them how to perform *japa* by taking the shape of a triangle while sitting on an *asana*. Tell them their own body is a *yantra*. In this triangular *yantra* we establish ourselves and remember our divinity within ourselves. Tell them the importance of seeing your own nature in your Guru's nature. Observe the postures and expressions of your Guru while doing things, and do things in this way in your own life.

104. When first learned these things sometimes my hair stood on end. At times I would see emanations from each hair follicle of my body. I would see one-lettered mantra coming from my pores. I observed the vibrations of those emanating mantras. I observed my breath and the forms that rose in it. I observed the length and shortness of my breath. I observed how I saw my Guru when I closed my eyes — what clothes he appeared in, and if his posture was that of fearlessness, to teach us fearlessness, or the posture of giving. Pray to God to become fearless, and that everyone may become fearless.

105. While saying prayers keep your back straight, your head high, your nose forward; keep your focus between your eyebrows, your chest upright. Sit in the lotus posture, inhale fully, exhale fully, and don't let any thought enter your mind until your soul is clean and purified, until you achieve the object of your meditation. But you are unable to do this. As soon as you sit, your body begins to fidget. You remember negative things or, if not negative, then neither good nor bad, but disturbing thoughts come to mind. You experience either greed or attachment or strange forms and strange vibrations. Then you keep yourself immersed in these vibrations.

106. *Tapasya* (austere practice) is nothing but to live free of the fetters of the mind, where we physically discipline the body but meditate with the mind. If our mind is restless, it will really not matter however much we might discipline our body. That is, in fact, a sin towards the body. But if our mind

becomes clean and pure, then our practice gets fulfilled. One who practices this way is a real seeker. Many divinities have been seen bowing before such a person.

107. During prayer we hold our joined hands near our heart. We hold them near our mind. This is done to achieve closeness between our heart and mind.

108. When we do virtuous deeds with good thoughts and wholesome feelings, troubles arise. Don't let the mind go toward them. Seekers and *mantra*-meditators experience lots of such difficulties. For example, in a cremation ground, a wild buffalo will appear to stomp in front of the seeker or a sea of fire will rise in front of him or it will appear as if a river is bearing down on him or that the land is breaking away and will fall into the ocean with him. If, at that moment, the seeker loses control or runs he may go mad or from then on lead a sorrowful life, or have a life loaded with insults. So, if those people who want to achieve the power and knowledge of mantra have not prepared themselves to receive it, if they make a mistake, then they may become victims of such an accident. It is because of their mental weakness that we see people having accidents every day.

Human Beings

What does it really mean to be a human being? People the world over want to become Christians, or Hindus, or Muslims, or Buddhists, or even rich or popular and the whole gamut of such labels. But are we ready to become a good human being? And if we are, then what does it mean to become a good human being?

1. True humans do not make rules.

2. The selfish human, thinking only of himself, is not far from bad days.

3. Is it necessary to speak lies even when awake?

4. For decades we have been forced to see things through many different eyes of discrimination.

5. Say the truth; are you not afraid?

6. Will you leave and go away from the one that you used to trust?

7. Five indications of foolishness:
   a) To weigh down the intellect with books.
   b) To believe the maker of the world is God.
   c) To think bathing and ablutions are religious acts.
   d) To be proud of one's birth/caste/class.
   e) To expiate sins by torturing the body.

8. Donkeys, dogs and other animals have character. Human beings should strive for good character, particularly for the benefit of their offspring. Without any virtues, their offspring will be bereft of good character.

9. If you remember your promise to yourself, then you will be a human being.

10. Because of illusions generated by religions, because of the bad actions of human beings, we see distortions in all beings.

11. If, after reflection, a person achieves harmony through an experience of God and is eager to become one with that entity, that person is a saintly person. That person becomes established in his soul. To do so, he must possess this ability to do so, and not relinquish his place. To be deprived of one's place, to relinquish such a place after achieving it, a person's value may diminish and even cease.

12. People without faith, devotion or belief, people whose conscience becomes feeble, people who have lost the ability to discriminate between right and wrong, people who, angry at themselves, torture themselves — what can one say about them? They can't even forgive themselves.

13. The one for whom we have to do everything, if that entity disappears, then what will we do and for whom?

14. We are an environment unto ourselves. The young men and women who hesitate to add to the population make a great contribution.

15. At night we see things in dreams. When life begins to leave us, tears will fall from our eyes for our obstinate, excessive actions. There will be no happiness, the mind will become boggled, everything will be lost.

16. If you listen to everybody's good and bad but do not reply, then your mind and conscience will praise you, appreciate you, eulogize you, give their love to you.

17. Only pigeons will live in the tall turrets raised by those who have slaughtered souls living in small huts. Those who constructed these turrets are gone. Ghosts and demons dance in them. Humans who attempt to live there live like demons. Their actions are worse than those of the demons.

18. If human beings themselves are not pleased with human beings, how can the gods be pleased with them?

19. The matchbox and the matchstick each have a layer of combustible phosphorous on them. Friction between the two produces fire. In the same way, what the divine entity is, you are. People, in whom negative things arise, once had goodness in them. If today you have goodness in you, then bad things must also rise in you. If you are prone to reactions and arguments, then, like the match-stick, you will ignite and burn. But the day you develop the strength of forbearance you will become like a demigod of a holy place, worthy of being worshipped.

20. Human beings wander aimlessly because they lack *bhava*. Human beings drown in this world as if it were an ocean.

21. When we have developed enough strength to know, understand and do everything, then we may be able to show devotion. This does not happen in just one life. It takes many lifetimes to do it.

22. Where you sit, how you sit, how you stand — these affect your way of hearing, thinking and understanding. Yourself wrong, you impute unnatural meaning to the sayings of saints.

23. The strength of human beings gets dissipated by their narrow-mindedness. They are then unable to retain any good behaviour.

24. Lazy people, whatever form they may be in, are a burden on the earth.

25. A craftsman creates palaces for others but lives in a humble hut. Some craftsmen spend their lives in peace and happiness. Some craftsmen are no less than saints or Mahatmas. A craftsman, aided by his imagination, creates a valuable artefact. Though he may not have been educated at a university, he acquires skill by practicing the traditions of his ancestors. As a craftsman gives shape to his imagination, that artefact may become valuable. A craftsman's mental state affects the good or bad form of the artefact.

26. The children of drug addicts and people given to various kinds of intoxication often are born with physical or mental abnormalities... Take the offspring of Shiva, for example. One has six heads [the God Karttikeya] and the other has the head of an elephant [the God Ganesha].

27. The mental condition of the father affects the character and ability of his offspring, as do the mother's character and temperament.

28. The weaknesses of human beings dull their vision and voice. In that state of befuddlement, they are unable to understand right from wrong. Furthermore, if they do understand anything, they think they are the only ones who understand all. One who understands like this shall be insulted, and will become an object of ignominy.

29. We have been reading books for such a long time, but we haven't understood a thing. If human beings didn't exist, there would be nobody to care for the gods and goddesses. Animals shan't enquire after them. Our presence proves the existence of that [type of] entity. If you yourself were not here, then all this [the visible creation] would disappear. If you don't open a book, the termites will eat it.

30. Today human beings are herded into groups and are told to go to such-and-such a place of pilgrimage and throw stones at it. In many temples dogs cry and jackals raise their howls. If you have true devotion why don't you set those places right?

31. You are human. Your acts should be different. Otherwise, inasmuch as filling your belly is concerned, even birds and animals are able to fill their bellies in some way.

32. Big people are like coconut trees: a person sitting under them finds no shade. I would prefer to live under small bushes where we will find cool shade, and we will feel peaceful.

33. The kind of self-discipline that should exist in our lives, the kind of self-discipline that has been extolled — we are incapable of exercising that self-discipline. So, we become forced to live a greatly intemperate life. We do not have any particular method or way of living our life. When the method of living is unmethodical, we face great difficulties.

34. Angry in one moment and pleased in the next: this is the sort of state we people are in. Now in one moment we pray to God and the Mother Goddess, and the next moment we forget it. Something quite different happens after a moment.

35. Over the course of the whole month, the moon is never complete. Every day it is either waxing or waning. One day it becomes full, and then immediately it spills over into a state of incompleteness. It begins to become small. In the same way, we people also keep waxing and waning within ourselves. We are not able to situate our mind within our heart properly. We leave it to wander in some other forest. The result is that many different kinds of behaviours, thoughts and characters get generated. Many transient thoughts and sentiments which produce sorrow become generated.

36. We think only about others; we rob and steal the useless thoughts of others and, labelling them as our own, we become involved in the nether action of distributing them amongst our friends and relatives to gather praise from them. Exactly the same is the state of our country.

37. We have to think about ourselves, and ask ourselves: Has our Self has been stolen from us? Has our 'individuality' has been taken away from us? Have we have been deceived by someone? The thought of today is different from the thought of yesterday. Our thoughts right now are different from our thoughts of a few moments ago. Some different kinds of vibrations are arising within us and our way of thinking is also changing with it. We are becoming forced into alien thoughts, behaviours, and personae. To observe all this is also an austere spiritual practice which I have learnt from those vultures that sit on very tall palm trees, gazing in every direction in search of their livelihood.

38. A person caught between two minds does not remain either with himself or with the other. He loses everything in that state of being between two minds.

39. The person who has the strength to endure the attacks waged on all sides by guilt, disappointment and sorrow, this person is a real human being. He has an eternal life.

40. Undisciplined people, and those who become frightened on the path, and those who walk a little distance on the path and then turn back saying "it is useless" and who are not afraid of turning back when tired, become goal-less in life. Their whole life is wasted.

41. My advice is, "without tact, there will be no devotion". In any kind of work you need tact; only then can it be done properly. If you have no tact, you merely have devotion; then that can

amount to wielding the stick. It can also mislead you. Your prayers and meditations can turn into invectives as well. If they are thereby tactfully performed, devotion and actions which have been stipulated to be done with tact can lead to success. This is what is also known as *yoga*. Otherwise, go ahead, hit your head, abuse your body; you shan't be able to find that being.

42. You people have the voice of heavenly gods, gods who reside in heaven. If you have a stable mind, if you are completely absorbed in your work, if you are not given to criticizing others or seeking praise for yourself, and if you are not ready either to deceive yourself or to keep yourself in darkness, then you can achieve your desired effect.

43. Because of imaginary demigods and demigoddesses, and due to many an error relating to God or the Divine Mother, we perceive ourselves as groping about in pitch darkness, and even our education and teaching is like that. That is why our lifelong effort trying to reach the reality goes to waste. When we become surrounded on all sides by death, sorrow, troubles, inclement astrological configurations and difficulties, then our throat becomes tight, our eyes flow with tears, our nose runs, phlegm and bile begin to rise and other wind-related troubles make our condition very much like a disorder of the three *gunas* (the three humours). At that time we cannot see the heavenly demigods, nor do we see those other beings bearing heavenly names. At that time everyone can only utter Ah, Ma! and O father! be they alive or not. If they have practiced a lot then maybe they will be able to say Ah, Guru! Ah, Ram! Their condition becomes like that of a parrot caught by a cat. This is the condition we are all in.

44. Only from the human-tree do we find fruits in the form of saints and Mahatmas — fruits which are sought in all the markets of the world.

45. Seeing the way the trees in our gardens seem to be at peace and in happiness, I do not see human beings likewise in any city or town. The reason for this is the short-sighted intellect which closes its eyes and immediately decides to prompt you to live in darkness.

46. We have to worship the God beneath our feet. We have to behave in a normal way with the common people.

47. What God does not do, a saint does. We will attain that position of a saint. That position has been attained not only in our country but also by saints in every country which has had its own pure, clean, all-encompassing and proud culture.

48. Wealth cannot buy happiness. Many rulers and top administrators have given birth to nations, to countries. That is why they will not be everlasting. In time, they will be found to be devoured by time. And then there will be many more to come, and that is also an absolute truth.

49. The merit of one moment spent with a good person is more than the merit achieved through prayer and worship of hundreds of years.

50. The life of a miserly and stingy person is like a stagnant pond which harbours nothing but bugs and dirt. Even when they have nothing, generous and benevolent people inspire people to fulfil the needs of human beings. Their life is like an unfathomable lake whose purity increases every day by leaps and bounds. The miser's life is like that of an unsatisfied ghost that keeps yearning for even a drop of water, and despite being next to a pond, he cannot drink. The generous person's life is like that of a holy ghost who is worshipped everywhere, offered fruits and flowers, who is praised and about whom people sing hymns.

51. One who is great, one who is like a saint providing cool, sweet fruits, one who does not even look at foolish people, he becomes happy in the same way that human beings derive happiness after relieving themselves of their wastes.

52. The company of a foolish person itself is sorrow. The company of a thoughtful person is like a vision of beauty.

53. Close to God is one whose words are true. Who speaks lies, remains afraid.

54. O seeker! It is also an essence of Hindu scriptures that, for example, a traveller from a far-off place is respected and welcomed by relatives and friends, and with great interest they become very keen to listen to those old memories of his which have turned into stories. In the same way, people who have done good deeds in their past lives look at other people very humbly. We will also have to learn to see it that way, seeker.

55. Human beings classify as wrong those people who remain quiet, as well as those who speak much and those who speak too little, too. It is a weakness of human beings; therefore:
Do not be loquacious, nor be too quiet
[Just like] not too much rain, nor too much sunlight.

56. Despite being clean as a gold coin and pure as the Jambudweep, human beings still exhibit their weakness by inflicting criticism on others. Such people are shallow and not fit to be befriended. Even excrement has a place of its own. But these people are even more relinquishable than that. On Jambudweep, in India, nice people are like those rivers that provide liberation, devotion, creative energy as well as livelihood, and are praised by all good people. Such nice people should be saluted.

57. *Vrat* is a matter of making a vow; it is not a matter of mere fasting. A million times better than fasting is to make a vow.

If you merely fast then it is possible that your mind, heart and senses become restless. By doing so, instead of relinquishing illusions and becoming stable, you begin to exhibit foolishness. You begin to give birth to many black thoughts within you.

58. Sons and daughters are born to humans. And progeny are born to birds and animals. If they are real human sons and daughters, then they listen to their parents. They do not ignore them. If they ignore them then they are not sons and daughters, they are merely children. Just like those of birds and animals.

59. You are tricked by yourself at every moment.

60. Without knowing a person's history and character, do not remain in the company of any person, however close may that person be to you. Even if he is a relative of yours, do not be in close contact with him. It is possible he may deceive you. Like a bad omen.

61. Because of the horrible effects of the actions of your past lives you have given up your most valuable wealth at the price of pennies. And you keep giving it up all the time. You have been given the wealth of nice words, the wealth of good character, the wealth of humility, the wealth of wisdom, the wealth of gravity, the wealth of politeness. You have been asked to live in a good way but you did not retain these gems even at the price of pennies. You discarded them simply by saying, "this will not do anything for me". As a result, you wander impoverished. You go and beg in a Mother temple, in a Shiva temple, in a Vishnu temple, that perhaps they may give you something. What can they give you? When you have lost what was your very own, what can they give you? They themselves are very poor. And if at all they have anything, then it is the wealth of demons that they have won in battles from them. If they give that wealth to you, it will destroy your mind.

62. Ambrosia, like milk, is also known as *piyush* in Sanskrit. About this, it is said in Hindu scriptures that Vishnu resides with Lakshmi in the ocean of *ksheer*, where there exists great peace and happiness. The Mother who gives this *ksheer* is brought to you by the *mala* (prayer beads). Humans even regard using the *mala* to be stupid, and they think they won't get anything out of it in life... You should understand the importance of that *mala* which brings the Mother to you. Then, do what you think is right.

63. The cunning of very clever people forces them to speak lies. Only they themselves remain afflicted due to this cunning, suffering by many kinds of disease, sorrow and illusions.

64. You have a place and an importance of your own which you do not know. You are like an invaluable diamond which is not openly shown just anywhere in the market. The day you get to know that real form of yours and realize your own value, then perhaps you will be able to lose yourself. You will not, then, like to be with these negative people who run only after coal and ashes, and in whose hands even a diamond becomes like dust... In the lives of many people many invaluable gems have come, but due to neglect and disrespect they have all turned to dust. And now we are running after coal and ashes. What is all this religious business and duty? It is that same coal and ashes. It is a remnant of that which has burnt up and turned into this form. What is that which has been burnt up? It is that one thing which is ours. That has become burnt up.

65. Even people who carry the message [of God] have had to live lives full of ignominy.

66. We are directionless because we really do not have anything, and how will anything remain with us anyway? We have never done anything for it, nor even have we paid any attention

towards it. Till today we have been living here like savages, lugging around the things of a prehistoric age atop our heads. We have kept our intellect lost in books.

67. All inspiration of God, or of bad actions, is given to us by this mind, and it is also an exemplification of human weakness. A person necessarily has to bear the good or bad fruits of good or bad actions respectively. It is not as if goodness will wipe badness away.

68. Those of the same age and generation as us that we know are not good people, however close may they be to us — leave them, or they will devour us and digest us.

69. You are like a poor seeker, like a pauper, like the dust beneath the feet of the people strolling on the road. But this little grain of dust when it flies into your eyes, it shuts that eye which makes everything visible, and shuts out all that we keep hankering to see all the time. Even that grain of dust has that effect. It is not that, since it is a minuscule particle, everyone can trample it underfoot.

70. When times of trouble arrive, the mind gets disoriented. Even a person like Rama believed in the golden deer and, listening to his wife, he ran after that deer with great eagerness. As a result he had to suffer unfathomable pain.

71. You have nothing to call your own. There is nothing that you can say, you cannot say that this is my wife, these are my children, this is my house and foyer, this is my place of refuge, these are my friends and relatives, this is my city and country, I am from such and such a place or such and such a person is mine. What is really yours is waving right in front of your eyes, like a wick on a stick of dynamite. It is burning, and you can see it burning. Even then, this mind of yours, your eyes, they don't open. You are not able to think what to do.

72. Despite being criticized, neglected, sequestered and insulted by home and family and society, we remain clinging to it in the hope that there must be something here. And what is that? It is a weakness of our mind and heart as well as a betrayal of ourselves. We are hell-bent on being a traitor to ourselves. This is what I call the suicide of a person. Because of this sin we take birth in many different kinds of forms, and die again. It is because of this alluring mirage that we take uncountable births in the forms of birds and animals and other beings, and suffer unfathomable sorrows and pain.

73. By saying only a little you can understand much more. You have a deep insight.

74. Friends! We ourselves have created hell. Because of the effects of keeping negative company, we give birth to hell ourselves. If you keep good company, then in the eyes of both good and bad you will be regarded as good. But if you keep bad company then leave aside the good, you begin to be weighed on the scale of badness, by the bad. This is because that person only can understand your value through his own prism. If he weighs you wrong, then that is the way he weighs things. You should weigh that person by a good standard, and also weigh yourself by a good standard.

75. Friends! 'Friendship' and 'friend' have vast definitions. A friend's pain, for a real friend, is bigger than any other pain in the world. A true friend inspires one only towards good actions. Instead of egging you towards cheap acts, he always inspires you towards profitable deeds.

76. Till the time you acquire authority over yourself you are not even a human being. Even an animal has some authority over itself, but we do not seem to have any right on ourselves.

77. We desire peace, prosperity and happiness, which is possible only by friendship. If you do not have peace then, despite having everything, you are very poor. Food grains, water and money can be found even in the homes of the riff-raff, gangsters, the thieves and prostitutes. If you do not have peace then what is the difference between them and you?

78. The person adorned with all the eight life-rituals who bows at the feet of the Mother and his guru is a very pure and great person, and provides salvation to his past seven generations as well as the future seven generations.

79. When you join the ranks of good people you will yourself become accomplished in social theatrics, the same as actors play their part to attract everyone's attention on stage. But it is also true that you do not have the time to play such theatrics. Also, these theatrics are not the truth, nor should you gravitate towards them. But you should definitely move towards the actual truth.

80. There are many humans who just are incapable of passing their time. Time weighs heavy on their hands. They know very well that life is very short, but even the time of that short life seems unpleasing to them. They have no idea of what to do... Let us use our free time in a good way. Let us try to find the company of the guru and the gods, and in this free time, in the company of great souls, let us produce nice thoughts.

81. We find many people that, after meeting them, we begin to have nice experiences. When a human begins to keep himself in those experiences all the time then he leaves behind the *Gita*, the *Ramayana*, the Quran, the Bible, fasting and worshipping and all such things. His mentality becomes as:

> "No need to fast, no one to salute,
> throw into the water all the books."

82. In the same way that gems and diamonds are very rare, so also saints and Mahatmas are very rare. There is no difference between a saint, a poor guest at the door, and a beggar. They are all the same, and they are all very poor. They are so poor that often they do not even have any words to give you. Even then they keep giving their pure words as blessings to people. They speak nice words. If sometimes they happen to scold you or admonish you out of worry, then know that they have used their tongue to give you something, the same tongue with which they have recited the name of God millions of times. Is this then not their kindness?

83. The whole of human life gets spent in wicked deeds. There are very few people who stay away from these and conduct new research on their life, who live in a new way. It is people like these who understand the reality and also achieve it. Such people are known as high-born people.

84. Those who are high-born, their love, affection and respect is not superficial. It, in fact, is like that chain of iron which cannot be broken. They hold you with their strong chain of affection which does not break their whole life long.

85. Those who are born in a nice lineage, those who are endowed with nice cultural traits, they never give their advice in the ashram or on the occasion of somebody's marriage, or in the planning of somebody else's work. If they can do something they actually do it to help them; otherwise they leave the place quietly.

86. If we rise from the state of being demigods to the state of being saints and Mahatmas then we can become a path for somebody. We can become their way. Not a guide of the path, but the path itself, walking on which someone can take the sinking boat of their life across.

87. Any administration or project is conducted from one central place. Only one person is deputed to do that. Crowds are for violent deeds. Only one person lays the foundation.

88. Many kinds of strange magical enchantments pass through our lives. If on seeing or hearing them you become spellbound or enamoured by them, then you will become separated from yourself. You will no longer remain within yourself. You will end up becoming dependent on someone else; you will become a puppet in the hands of the other, and you will have to keep wagging your tail before the other.

89. A wise and experienced enemy is better than an ignorant friend. A wise enemy knows that things have happened because of the circumstances and someday these can change. But the ignorant friend can set fire to everything.

90. Our actions are so base that we should feel guilty to compare them even to the actions of animals. It is insulting to them to compare thus, for they are more self-controlled than we are. Their actions are more time- and epoch-bound than those of human beings. They live collectively and live with great self-discipline. They do fight, but their fight does not turn into a long-lasting feud. They do not maintain that violent form at all times... But we who are in the human form go so far away from human nature itself!

91. The savagery that is within us, or the savagery that we end up doing — the less time that we let it stay with us, the better we can make use of our time. If we cannot do this, then our whole life will be spent wagging our tails or carrying burdens just to fill our bellies like beasts, and we will not be able to make a history for ourselves.

92. One who is stable, he has peace; he has happiness, he has respite, he has great dignity. In opposition to this, instability

gives eagerness, terror, restlessness, troubles and many kinds of problems, and humans suffocate in them, and they die while thinking about the past. They are unable to fulfil the promise they made to themselves at the time of their birth.

93. You must have seen in your own life that sometimes you become very polite and humble, very kind and very moral, and that at other times you are filled with the exact opposite qualities. This could be an effect of the kind of food and water in which you partake and the environment [and company] in which you live. Sometimes you become very healthy and free from all desires and sometimes you get sick from many afflictions of the world. That is why you should remain very careful about your time and the company you keep, so that you may be able to make a history of your own.

94. Whatever little destiny provides for you, a person living with contentment in that is a great person. He is a saintly person. He is later remembered by people. People who rise on the strength of Godless grandeur are not remembered by anybody. Pigeons excrete on their palaces and castles.

95. A demigod has no sound. You must have seen it yourself. Saints, Mahatmas, seekers and spiritually realized people know this secret. One who knows this mysterious secret keeps all kinds of mysterious spiritual powers within him. His power of making things happen by just wishing becomes very strong; whatever he desires, happens. It is not as if it happens only to world-relinquishing saints. Even householders experience this. Their power to make desired things happen also becomes very strong. If you keep an eye on yourself, if you remain very alert and self-controlled and your search remains right and balanced, then even you can get this power. Whatever you desire will be fulfilled. As soon as you desire something, it will happen, in the same way that the elephant was saved from the crocodile when he said "Go" [the name Govind, a name of Krishna]

and the crocodile was killed. He did not even have to say the whole name of Govind completely. "Vind" was never mentionned. The day you gain this knowledge, that day your search will be over.

96. I pray to that Supreme Soul, to that Mother Goddess and to that God that they give us the strength to spread this peace and happiness to everyone. May we be able to free from bondage those whom we respect and may we become free ourselves.

97. All the people sitting here of the Sarweshwari family are accomplished craftsmen. You people are such craftsmen that you can sculpt whatever forms you want. But your hands remain tied. Your talent and your speech remain stifled. Your mind is under such stress that you cannot do anything. You are not empty. Your mind is not empty; you cannot say anything through your speech and your hands have been tied tightly. You are craftsmen. You have all those instruments in your hands with which you can sculpt many forms in your likeness, and have even sculpted them in the past.

98. There is no home where people have not grown old, where people have never died, and where births have not taken place. Everybody knows this truth. But it is a special trait of ours that we do not even pay attention towards it. We do not give it the benefit even of a glance. It's okay. It's better if you don't look back towards the past. But the situations that prevail in the present are definitely going to pounce upon us. We do not know about our future; it is tomorrow, and tomorrow comes every day. It does not go anywhere, friends. That is why, keeping all these in mind, we believe in the mantra, God and Guru, and try to achieve them in our life. How do we do that? By remaining self-controlled for nine days like an ascetic. Yes — controlling our senses, we look for that concentration which harbours everything, friends. But, if after achieving everything

we remain senseless, then what is it? At that time we need only solitude. Those who remain deprived of this, their life tilts towards old age. They embrace death and, losing their senses, they sleep forever in the earth.

99. We always benefit from approaching saints and seeing them. If we go to them alone, and our desires, wishes, jealousies, envies, attachments and ego do not accompany us, then we achieve an immeasurable wealth. But if we go to them lugging the baggage of our untrue thoughts and feelings then we remain deprived of achieving anything. Because that saint-*mahapurush* thinks, "this person is already staggering under his own loads; if I also weigh him down with something, he might even die. He may lose much." And so they do not give you anything.

100. The light of good behaviour lights up the world too.

101. When you bow your head in front of your demigod, Mother Goddess, great saints or Mahatmas, then this humility of yours takes you towards greatness. If instead you keep standing with your hands gripped behind your back, this means you are hostile, that you want to attack them. When you put both your palms forward it symbolizes that you are very humble, very patient, and you are not carrying any arms. Your folded hands indicate giving up of all worldly arms, and they do not inspire one towards troubles and sorrows. They also inspire others to also bow their head, fold their hands, move towards greatness, and become peaceful like you.

102. When you become very polite and humble with your elders and respected ones, or with those who are lesser than you or neglected, don't you derive satisfaction? It provides great satisfaction. At that time even harsh words said to those dependent on you also provide satisfaction because those words hide the feeling of their welfare. "Love in the heart, and harsh

words in the mouth". You have unfathomable love in your heart; then only must you be using harsh words on your children-grandchildren, workers and dependents. You are under no obligation to say all this to someone you are not concerned about, and you cannot even say it.

103. The use of harsh words or admonishment used by our respected people is an exercise in their love. We should not become afraid by this, nor should we leave our patience. By using such words with us they want to do great justice with us, not to forgive us at that time out of their kindness so that in future we may be beset by even bigger troubles.

104. What will we do by becoming big? What does someone with a big family do, or one with many children and grandchildren, or one with many friends and relatives? It is just like a herd of sheep which is taken to a nice grazing ground for that purpose. It is then made to graze. But that herd of sheep stinks. Donkeys are domestic: they live in villages, amongst human beings, and carry their loads. Their offspring also carry loads. All their lives they carry loads. A tiger lives in the jungle, and will stay without food, but will remain alone. But he is the king of his jungle. He does not carry anyone else's load. He does not carry anybody's weight. He does not wander from door to door. If he finds something, fine; otherwise it's also okay. God will provide for food. One who has a life like this does not have any sorrow in this great wilderness where nobody is really around. Even if he cries, in the forest there's nobody to hear him. But even then, he is the tiger, and within himself he is king.

105. It is said that the company of a foolish person is a house of sorrow.

106. Friends! We who are young should also try to journey on foot at least once. Whenever we walk on foot from here to Banaras,

or here to Mughalsarai, or here to the gate, we should have such careful vision that nobody gets hurt under our feet, which can also lead to our stumbling and falling. If you stumble, that (the one you stumble on) has borne so many kicks by now that it must have turned to stone. Even then we should keep our eyes open, friends. Because of these open eyes and their respective purposes, people find other people with similar temperaments and go amidst them, through the medium of this Sarweshwari Samooh, which is a very small, simple institution. Not even an institution, regard it like a kids-play akin to:

> "The make-believe in play actually happens.
> One who plays the real game is one in a million."

Perhaps a time will return again. All the largest rivers — all have their tiny source, like a little seed.

107. Friends, we are poor. We will also remain poor. We do not want to become enormous, nor do we want to be expunged either. We want to remain in a simple, normal way. We do not want to become too big and then have to listen to our ego. But if we are expunged, then what will remain here? Nothing. That is why purity of the blood is essential, friends. Every species has its characteristics. The species can go bad.

108. Even I know what happens in the offerings of death rituals. Friends, that does not have as much importance as the importance of remembering those people gone by, those people who are no longer here but whom we remember, for we are like them, and this 'Foundation Day' is an occasion to remember them. "The son perpetuates the father." We are in their form. We keep remembering them.

Inspiration

Every human being needs some inspiration to overcome difficult situations that arise in life. Any inspiration that makes an individual work not only towards his or her own benefit but also for the benefit of his or her society, will last forever and will result in a happy society.

1. It is essential for our nation, society, village and city that we show the right path to our youth. We should inspire them towards higher thoughts and sentiments and towards living a life of self-sacrifice. We should inspire them towards good behaviour. Whom? Those youth who are blameless, faultless, dilemma-less, and whose heart is as clean and pure as water.

2. I hope only this from you all, that all of you, our mothers and our sisters and our brothers, that you will understand these sentiments of welfare of the nation and that you will be conscious towards your culture, and that you will have faith in God, and in the soul of God.

3. I have this hope in you and you have this hope in me that Oh God, give us some of that very nice inspiration so that we may be able to do something for the benefit of the nation, the society and for the culture. And, may we be able to inspire human beings towards those divine virtues which make a human being live as he should.

4. That which is in the present with us today: that which is already past, and that which is passing away; I know it will not be of any use any more. The time that we have left from this we should make good use of with good sentiments.

5. It is our duty that we should keep doing something. Whatever valuable time of our life gets offered to God or to the

Divine Mother will act as a great wealth for our future. In the future it will give us happiness, it will give us peace, it will give us glory. The past is gone, and the present is going away.

6. One who does not have any love for living and active beings cannot have any love for the God of stone sitting in a temple, or the formless God of the mosque.

7. When a human learns how to live, he learns what he has to do very naturally. And when he learns what to do, then he knows everything. But if he does not learn how to live, and keeps it all only to the extent of speaking or philosophizing about it, and he does not bring it into action, then that person's mind remains very unstable. It is so unstable that he keeps wandering day and night. He wanders in his sleep, he wanders while awake, he wanders while sitting, and he wanders when he gets up. He wanders while wandering, too. He never becomes stable. Neither does he become stable, nor does that great creative energy, waiting at his door, enter.

8. Haven't you heard, it is due to their words that people are admonished; it is because of their words that people are well-treated, and it is through their words that they are able to please even the divinities.

9. Decorate your bouquet with flowers of many different kinds.

10. What can be pettier in human life than this? That we should be weighed readily (on other's standards) everywhere, that we should be weighed on every scale available! Who, then, can be more petty than us?

11. Manu [one of the ancient law-givers] has directed that, after their monthly period, married women are again pure, and should be fully accepted.

12. Life is short. Do not be eager to burn in the many kinds of fires: of envy, of jealousy, of animosity.

13. If the knowledge that I have is real knowledge, then even you people can make it go a long way.

14. This mind of ours — if it remains bowed at the feet of the Divine Mother, then I have full hope that our faith and devotion will help us, and will dissipate the many faults that we have in our lives and in our society.

15. As long as you stand united, remember to listen to your elders and remain in the service of your old people, you will keep prospering, you will be well, you will be happy. And when you begin to ignore them, when the young people begin to neglect them, they [the youth] will begin to encounter destructive people and we will be forced to live like forest-dwellers again.

16. Break your sword. Pick up the plough and the hoe: the time has come.

17. "I am very clever, I dominate everybody, I fool everyone, I make everybody look down." We should not even glance at such hateful actions, nor should we be forced to do such things.

18. If we have limited needs, then our mind gets absorbed and dissolved in a little happiness, a little prosperity, in a little meditation and a little contemplation. And that soul of ours whom we address as God or the Divine Mother — that too we actually experience, as if a vibration is coming to us from That. But this becomes easy and can be experienced only when you control all the desires of your senses and sit in solitude for ten or fifteen minutes, or half an hour or an hour; when you sit in this way in meditation, in contemplation; when you think about someone, or you look at the world, you see everything there right in front of your eyes.

19. We do not know what crimes we end up committing through our mind or our words or our actions, and it has terrible consequences. To dissipate all this, and for our happiness, and peace, to become close to ourselves, this society (Sri Sarweshwari Samooh) has been established.

20. Friends, if you desire respect and prestige in society, then make sacrifices and undertake difficult actions. That sacrifice, that austere action need only be this: if you do not need to be in the company of undesirable people, then you should not be in such company.

21. One who speaks sweetly, who sees God everywhere, is a gem of mine.

22. The many kinds of wrong actions that we end up doing; those actions, we will have to abandon. Only then can we walk on the right path and reach that goal — on reaching which, all great souls have fulfilled the ultimate goal of their life.

23. Respected brothers, the ultimate goal of life is to enter that point of energy called *hingalaj* created by God, to reach the *samadhi* of that great soul (God), to conduct self-investigation. If we are engaged in self-research, or if we have completed that research, then I have full hope that at its culmination everything will be available within us.

24. Today, humans contemplate Rama, Krishna, Shiva, saints and Mahatmas, but do they ever contemplate themselves? As long as a person doesn't show kindness to himself, as long as he makes no effort to prevent himself from falling into filth, all his meditation and worship are useless.

25. If we save ourselves from the flaws of the eyes, the ears, the speech, and from contentions with each other, this will have a very good effect on us.

26. We should not deceive ourselves with our mind, our words or our actions. We should show some kindness to ourselves.

27. I came into this tradition in my youth, and I used to be a very intoxication-loving person. I ended all that. I have experienced what is the bad effect of that, and to what places it brings human beings.

28. If a human being wants he can become a divinity, he can rise even higher that God. If a human wants, he can also become a beast and can spend his life like a base creature.

29. Friends! If we keep a contentious feeling towards our countrymen, if we keep bickering over little issues with our own people, then we will keep fighting with them, colliding with them. We will bother them and they will bother us. And some third person will keep reaping benefits from this.

30. If we keep getting together, keep meeting together, keep inspiring the youth, and keep respecting women, we will prosper. With that, we will keep up our struggle towards unwanted customs and traditions. If we will have a programme before us, if we will remain occupied within the society, then we will not do anything wrong.

31. We should encourage our youth. We will have to tell the history of our country.

32. People live to fill their bellies; they earn to eat, and all this will continue their whole life. What will our rebirth be like? We will have to make some decision about that. If there is no rebirth, even then we will have to pay for our actions in some way. We will have to decide whether we are making that payment or not. Otherwise, it is possible we may fall into a despicable place.

33. I have only this request to make of you people — if there are people who use such intoxicating substances, then it is right and good to speak harshly to them and admonish them, be they even spiritual seekers or terribly nice people. Because, perhaps then, they will break away from that habit.

34. We may see darkness in our life, but the light is about to arrive.

35. [We have to learn] how to walk, how to sit, how to rise, how much courtesy we have, how polite we are, where to sit, where to stand, how much to talk with whom, how much not to, how to stand in the prayer hall while praying — how to stand in the prayer of the divinity — and how to stand in the prayer to our ancestors, and how to meet with young people, and how to behave with children...

36. Friends! We have to know what will be favourable to us and what will not. If it is a part of the contemplation of the Devi, the Divine Mother, the Bhawani, then we will have to respect that completely as well. We will also have to guard lest we end up doing unrestrained things. Wanton actions, due to which we are getting completely destroyed, and are destroying the traditions of our gurus... Is this why we have been born? Is this what our duty in life is?

37. Some we have lagged behind because of bad company, and some, also, because of our environment.

38. We will have to protect ourselves — then only can we be protected.

39. If a tiny blade of grass or a tiny grain of sand goes into our eyes, then all the panoramic views that we see — all become invisible. We cannot see anything then. The person begins to close his eyes. And when that tiny particle is removed, that great panoramic view becomes visible again.

40. If suddenly God or the Divine Mother comes physically before our eyes — suppose they do — in the form of a human being, then they will not ask you to get away from your duties, sit on a riverbank and just keep meditating on the prayer beads. They will say only this: be of service to the beings on this earth; especially be of service to human beings, serve them, help them, feel pain in their pain.

41. We cannot become Bhagwan Ram [the hero of the epic *Ramayana*], but we can definitely walk on the way told by him; we can definitely serve the servant of Bhagwan Ram. Mira has said: Oh God! Okay, don't make me your servant, but keep me as a server.

42. Friends! We have a great history of Mahatmas, great souls, saints and nice people here, and it is lying here hiding great inspiration. When you see it you will find the activities of these people — in the beginning, in the middle, and the activities that are going on now — these have been remarkable. How can you overlook this wealth of great examples? It is inconceivable.

43. To say, we say many things; to hear, we hear many things; to read, we read many things. But all this is like trying to catch a shadow: the shadow runs right before us, we keep chasing it, it never comes to our grasp, and ultimately it leads us to fall into a ditch. All that our gurus have said is this: we should turn around. Then, this world, like a shadow, will begin to follow us.

44. Within our depths lies a lot of happiness and joy which we forget, for which we do not search. We do not even make any effort to find it. We remain engrossed in many tasks that we have. We do not even try.

45. Your life should not be one of contention. It should be peace-loving. May there be peace everywhere.

46. Our ancestors had to bear with great sorrows, and the reason was that we were divided into castes and *jatis*.

47. God, or the Divine Mother, or whoever may it be in their place — they are not bigger than the human being. If a human wants, he can create thousands like them.

48. There are also Mahatmas who, despite being free, are unable to express things in free speech.

49. Food and water, movement, sleep: these things are available to all living beings. Amongst all these beings we have this good opportunity to be different from them, and it is possible only in this human life. That is why we should try to make the best of begetting this human life. And to make the best of it, worship yourself.

50. Amongst Hindus, on becoming pregnant, women never used to do any wrong act. For nine months they used to be involved in deep thoughts, and very respectable, pious deeds. They used to serve the guests, the Mahatmas, the great souls, their parents-in-law, so that their progeny may be an ideal person. And if there is anything that is negative in that child, it denotes a lack of refinement. And how did that lack of refinement come about? It is a gift from the parents to the child.

51. Whenever a child comes into the womb, when that soul arrives, one should behave very nicely with his wife. He should leave her free to conduct works of charity, pious acts, meritorious acts, for nine months. One should not have physical relations with her for that time or the child can produce distortions later. It can also turn out to be a lineage-destroyer, a destroyer of the whole family. That child then becomes a curse. Its whole life is then a curse for itself and for others too.

52. This is a festival of creative energy; we want creative energy, and with creative energy we also want peace. With peace, we also want to see our children to be well.

53. The more softly and gently you say something to your children or to your spouse, or to your brother or sons, the faster they will be able to understand it. But if you just start yelling at them, then neither will they understand it, nor will you succeed in making them understand it.

54. You must have seen sometimes. If you try to explain something to children in anger, the child will not be able to understand it. And even you may not be able to understand what you actually want to say to them, to explain to them. The same thing said softly and gently, the child understands it immediately.

55. The word *vrat* does not mean fasting. It means that you take the vow that from today you will not do bad deeds, you will not associate with bad company, such-and-such an action is very bad for your health and so you will give it up starting today, or many other kinds of actions which are a hindrance to the search for your ideal and your consciousness — you will not do any of them, you will not do them anywhere. This, then, will be very beneficial.

56. Where we have to give, let us give a bite to eat to someone, and where we have to take, let us take the name of God. Contemplate on the Self, and keep performing everything through our strength. But from within, we should remain steadfast at that one place.

57. You have made a proper determination that, from today, you will speak only auspicious things in life. If during play, or in conversation, or during meals you for whatever reason say something inauspicious, then you will have to be ready for the consequences that follow.

58. The person who gives up harsh words can make anyone, even birds and beasts, his friend. When you have a gentle heart, when you have a soft heart, your voice will become very sweet. It cannot be described through speech.

59. Nobody takes anything away with them [at death]. Not even a needle do they take with them.

60. Just sitting the whole day I indulge in Self-contemplation. I keep thinking and doing something. When my attention moves towards That, I think. I try to keep nice sentiments sitting under the wish-fulfilling tree of the Self.

61. To achieve something, and to give something to someone, the person giving away has to keep what he has achieved with great care, with great attention. Because once you achieve something, if you keep giving it away repeatedly, then you will become deprived of it, and the fear of ignominy and shame will always be present.

62. Don't you see, the more a person uses sweetness and patience at home, the better his family feels, the more fragrant they feel. Everyone remains very gentle. But the one who uses harshness, who takes the support of harsh words and who thinks terrible things, his life remains full of abrasiveness.

63. What will we do with spiritual powers? Do we want to use them to chastise someone, or to do something else with them? What else will we do? Shall we build palaces, shall we build kingdoms, what will we do? No. Achieving those powers, we should be able to help those beings who are in dire need of livelihood, or those who are in complete darkness beset by every kind of sorrow and pain. And to provide that help, too, we need that grace, or we will not even be able to recognize these things [people in need].

64. You would never have enquired this way about your *isht* (personal divinity). Nor would you have enquired about your master, whether he is happy, whether he is fine, is his health alright or not? You couldn't ask the fire about it, but you could have asked the winds about it. At one time people used to make messengers out of clouds and send the letters of their heart through their medium.

65. Many *rishis*, when they made mistakes, they put it in writing. For what reason? The Moon had run away with the wife of Brihaspati [a *rishi*]. He wrote it down. Why? So that one who listens to this story, one who listens to this tale, will become a co-sharer of a sixth of the effect of this incident. So friends, when something happens through you, you hide it. You try to hide it and the result is that it keeps growing. You never think that you should end it. You never think that you should do something whereby everybody criticizes you and you become clean.

66. By keeping a critic close to us they can tell us our weaknesses. Our friends cannot tell us that.

67. If you want to learn something from your divinity, from your guru or from your teacher, then you will have to follow their guidelines. It is not such that you should learn something, get to know something, and then go and do something quite different.

68. That which you think is lost in deep darkness is actually right in front of you.

69. In the same way that a goat grazes on the leaves of a tree growing on the rock, and feels very satisfied on leaving it leafless, the goat in the form of a politi al leader also feels very happy when it sees the tree of the people bare of all their leaves.

70. The acts of human beings at night do not look good during the day, and their bad deeds of the day do not let them sleep dreamless at night.

71. Darshi! We will have to go beyond light, we will have to go beyond capabilities, we will have to transcend even the limits of the limitless. We will have to reach that place from where there are no paths, no roads, not even little trails, Darshi.

72. Only service to yourself can be service to others as well.

73. Good and bad characteristics are like morning and evening. Sometimes our feet are on our head, and sometimes our head is on our feet. An egotistical cloud definitely rains. Making our needs as little as possible, we should keep our life comprehensively covered [by grace].

74. God has given us two hands to respect others and to help others. If we cannot help and respect others with these, then at least we can do so for ourselves. These two hands are not meant to sling mud at others, or to throw stones at them.

75. An independent, joyful life is beautiful. Whatever parochialities produce hindrances, break them. This is where lies the real fulfilment in life.

76. There are only four things in your life, and it is not necessary for you to remember all four of them. If you want to live like a fortunate person, then two things — that is, the good that you may have done to someone, and the bad that someone may have done to you — forget both these things forever. And two things — first, God, and second, death — always remember.

77. Practice to recognize the distinction between the human and the demon.

78. To worship Brahmans because of their caste is a great sin. But to worship one who is a Brahman in deed, even if he be an undertaker by caste, is a great virtue and brings good fruits.

79. If you stop on an auspicious path, the distance gets longer. Do not stop on the auspicious path; keep walking.

80. The ideal behaviour is away from either scholarship or erudition.

81. Without effort and self-confidence, human beings cannot achieve either worldly progress or the other-worldly progress. For worldly progress, education is required, and for other-worldly progress, initiation is. If you have the unshaken faith of knowledge and a foundation of experience, then even the most difficult practice becomes very easy.

82. Whatever has happened through you is not the truth.

83. Only the one who takes away sorrows from others is the one who suffers because of sorrows.

84. [The day of *Akshaya Nawami*] has great importance in itself. It is especially important for the simple-hearted, for those who are guileless and free of wickedness and for those who do not have any kind of artificiality. We sit down on one day every week in a meeting and greet ourselves, and convey our thanks to God, that Unknown who inspires us to live, and also to choose from among the many different experiences of the ways of living, and who also tells us the way to merge our own way into the way of living properly.

85. Have faith towards devotion, and also have faith towards the creative energy. For, without devotion you will not achieve creative energy, and without creative energy you will not be able to have devotion.

86. Instead of criticizing somebody's livelihood you should be inspired to praise it, and with yourself, encourage everyone to praise it. By doing so, your stories will achieve that indestructibility whose sentiment is imbued in today's festival of *Akshaya Nawami*, i.e. that which is indestructible, one that can never be destroyed or harmed.

87. You should not keep yourself empty. Keep yourself full. To keep yourself full, move steadily towards the many good goals that are taking birth before you. By doing so you will leave all the bad ways behind and you will keep finding the good path.

88. Also, keep the company of saints, *mahapurusha*s and good people, but only after testing them well. Even amongst them you can find some very strange people. If you just go by their beautiful clothes, their matted hair or beard and moustache, then you will be caught in illusion.

89. If your posture and style of sitting before your guru, your respected people and your elders is proper then you will understand every word of what they say to you, and they will thereby always remain in your memory.

90. You should not sit wasting time, nor should you speak in vain. You should read those books of yours which are full of great gems.

91. We should do something only after fully considering where we have to go, and where we do not have to go: places where we do things which will make us lose our good character, and where we will lose our self-control.

92. If you do something quietly, then that task has a long life. Its roots go very deep. It is for the welfare and happiness of all. It bears fruit every day, in all countries, and in all periods.

93. Fasting should be done only according to the needs of purification of the body. In worshipping Sarweshwari, in fact, to read anything you like, to fast without purpose, and to go on pilgrimage: all these three are prohibited. All these can give rise to futile efforts and dark thoughts.

94. Speak the truth; it will give you strength.

95. Good action is for the good of everyone; it is for the benefit and happiness of everyone, and it will be for your happiness and benefit too.

96. One should not cheat one's own group, one should not steal from one's friend, and one should not be deceitful with the guru.

97. I hear that nice fruits are found on the tree of contentment.

98. Householders should treat their children over 16 years of age as friends. If they do not do so, then they give birth to terrible difficulties.

99. Even a saint should have a friendly sentiment towards his disciple.

100. Whatever we learn, we should teach it to others too. For those who are lost, who are in the dark, show them the way. If we teach ten people, and of those if even two learn to walk on the path, then it will be very beneficial. This is what is known as real beneficence. If you inspire ten people they can inspire ten more and lead them to progress, who in their turn can lead others to progress. This trait cannot be achieved simply through education. To become educated, to be able to read and write, is an entirely separate thing, and it only carries the sentiments inherent in the book. But these other things are that nectar of life which maintains an everlasting life. This

indestructibility carries on through the tradition, from one to the other. It is completely dependent upon faith and devotion.

101. Everyone wants to be a friend of the house and family that remains united. They do not have any enemies. Nobody even thinks of picking a fight with that family. It is an effect of the power of being united.

102. Friends! Your presence here is indicative of that happiness which will inspire you towards good days in the future. It happens in the life of every being, and it will happen in your life as well. Your desire to enter something new, to find something new, and your desire to make changes in the fundamental rules of this life through your actions: these are very praiseworthy. You used to have many kinds of sorrowful dreams, and their end is coming near. You should eagerly try to follow the good days.

103. For your bright future, you will have to dig out your present from your past.

104. Exaggerations are not the truth. I believe that because of watching your behaviour, your quiet stance, your ability to sit in solitude where there is no solitude, and your ability to listen to things eagerly. That Truth is true, by itself. You all should embrace that truth.

105. You will have to look for peace within yourself.

106. If we save ourselves from deceiving ourselves, then we can save everything. If we stop closing our eyes to the reality, we can see everything.

107. We dream many kinds of dreams in our lives. Somebody is killing someone, somebody is hurting someone, somebody is dying, somebody is living. And it is not that it happens because

of the night, when we dream. In this way we keep waiting for the dawn, when we hope our dreams will end. We will become a human only through perseverance and effort. We will make every kind of effort; we will try and we will create a new world.

108. When we begin to properly use our free time, then the free time hanging on our hands will disappear, and the happiness that exists among us will provide great joy. It will give us so much joy that we cannot even imagine it. It is said that each step taken on the path of the Truth is equal to a hundred thousand *yagyas* (ritual acts).

Culture

Every culture has customs and practices regarded as positive by some and negative by others. Baba always advocated nurturing those practices that benefit the most, even if they go against the grain of prevalent thought in society, such as widow remarriage. In the Indian context, widows have not had a healthy life and have often been subjected to social neglect for no fault of their own. Baba encouraged his devotees to accept widow remarriage, to practice self-control, to be true to one's own self.

1. The end of our traditions denotes the end of our unique character, the end of our unique existence. Such a people do not have good character then.

2. Who is the one leader of injustice amongst us?

3. It is possible to win over people by good behaviour. Gurupad Sambhav, can you become the shining Sun of good behaviour?

4. The Sun gives off great heat. So instead of becoming the morning Sun, or the Sun of the afternoon, become the cool Sun of the evening.

5. Our *rishi*s regarded a second husband as perfectly acceptable for widowed women.

6. A necessary outcome of having a young widow at home is abortion.

7. Journalists are afraid of portraying the world as it really is.

8. The day your house gets transformed by good behaviour, that day you will see even heaven bow before you.

9. One or two hands do not make a country. For that, you need thousands of hands.

10. We need those burning words which will keep alight for centuries.

11. Humans talk about liberating hundreds of people after death, but in their own homes nobody tries to free their mother and father from the yoke to which they are hitched.

12. More than wealth is the value of people. O seekers, gather people, for without people no one can protect wealth. Wealth does not get people; it is the people who get wealth.

13. It is very hard to find saints of good character who can enlighten the entire expanse of the world.

14. The books of every religion are like that burden that people carry on their head. They are not like boats than can take you across the ocean of life. Our own inner experiences, and the scriptures of those inner experiences, are like that boat which can take us across the ocean of life.

15. This is not that, that is not this.

16. Parents should express their love for their children in front of them, instead of spouting forth their latent anger before them.

17. Parents should also get together to think about the welfare of their children.

18. Justice itself is mercy.

19. It is because of all our sins that saints and good people have to bear with troubles.

20. Are not the people of the lower categories in our country fit even to be peons and watchmen tomorrow? Leave aside even the consideration of being I.A.S. (Indian Administrative Service) and P.C.S. (Police Constabulary Service) officers, will not the coming generation be able to use its power of action? This idleness can become a terrible volcano which will burn one's own self and can produce poison in the society and the country. In our country today 20 to 30 per cent people do not have even a sliver of land, and do not have even a thatched hut to take shelter in. All this is not due to the government or the society. It is because of their own idle ways.

21. A man should not go to a pregnant woman, and a pregnant woman should not go to a man, until the time the new baby is born on this earth. They should be told that by doing so a righteous person is born, a person who does not give any pain to its parents, a person who is respectable and full of ideals.

22. Do not use those words that pain others.

23. Not to me, but to yourself
You had made a promise.
Can you remember it?
If not, try to remember it.

24. That woman was saying she will not do anything that will make her children look down with regard to her character. Parents should strive that their sons and daughters never have to look down in society because of the character of their parents.

25. The social organization of the 19th century, or socialism, that the major countries were eager to implement with enthusiasm and effort, will now necessarily have to change at the end of the 20th and the beginning of the 21st century because those people are now demoralized and their progress

has stopped. The destruction of human culture that has happened in the 20th century is unbearable. Human culture cannot be made to change direction by external force; just as if you try to stop a river by damming it, it can also create great destruction. In the same way, if human culture also does not continue under its natural temperament, then it can create major destruction, and then every nation will have to bear these fruits.

26. Today's youth should wait if they want to have children. If they do not want children, even then for their own health, for their peace and longevity, to be stress-free, they should adopt a stress-free style of living. They should become seasonal.

27. The line (of people) that carries a dead body with them walks with great faith and peace. At that time acrimony and jealousy remains away from the hearts of people.

28. Merely the expression on the face of saints begets the knowledge of the scriptures.

29. Except for filling the bellies of a lot of people, a big [political] party does not do much for the people. A small [political] party is better than that because what it does, it does for the people.

30. A big country does nothing except gather together a lot of people and look after them.

31. Europeans say they brought the faith, while the faith of Indians continues from the beginning of the earth. The progenitor of faith is none other than God.

32. It is essential that the pictures of the divinities, owned by a person of good character, should themselves also have good character.

33. Those who have given us respect, and to those whom we have given our word to render service — are we faithful towards them?

34. One should marry that person who has not become separated from the ways of his family, his lineage or his father, so that there are no doubts at the time of paying homage to the ancestors.

35. Over the period when hundreds of thousands of people were destroyed, mixed-category people have appeared as rulers. The rulers, who are of mixed category, and those who are their yes-men, regard it a matter of pride to uphold the mixed-category system.

36. [About being Indian and accepting simplicity:] However spiritual may that person be, if he is hesitant to put on Indian clothes and eat simple food, then he is not fit to be invited to a gathering.

37. It is possible that a person of good character will get wealth, but it is not necessarily so that a wealthy person will get good character.

38. The youth who does not respect his elders is a danger alarm to himself.

39. There are very few connoisseurs of the gurus of good behaviour.

40. Death is a condition. To achieve that supreme truth, this true condition has to be fulfilled many times.

41. Always remember these three things: The best posture is to bring the palms of both your hands together and to join them with your body and mind. We respect others by bowing our head. And, charity spreads peace in society.

42. If our ancestors, our fathers and forefathers have been good, then we should definitely adopt their nature. This is done in the same way that we keep trying to adopt the nature of our great gurus.

43. Peaceful, united humans will never be defeated.

44. Friends, light 'your own' light in the darkness of your heart.

45. The prestige one got in the past will not improve the present or the future.

46. The cross symbolizes crime and death, not religion.

47. I see only that, which you let me see.

48. O Sudharma! The few human beings who can convert into forbearance the unbearable conditions of sorrow, wickedness and pain of the struggle of life, these are the ones who have been declared as the Mahapurush (great human beings) in history, in the Puranas, and in every religious book.

49. Sorrows are what the *rishi*s have called the ocean of the world. Those people who try to go across this ocean without a boat, an oar or a boatman, they are battered about and destroyed by typhoons, hurricanes and stormy weather. Great *rishi*s have called it the demon of ill-fate which does not relinquish even serious, beautiful, sympathetic, bright and virtuous people from its grasp. In the grasp of evil fate, even truth bows down before wickedness.

50. O Sudharma! The common people quail before a self-controlled ascetic saint.

51. The strongest support of the nation and the well-covered home of the society is founded on the pillars of these young

men and women, and will remain so in the future as well. We believe in this. If these pillar-supports who are young men and women are not saved from becoming hollow or damaged by termites, then the house that is the society can rot, break, fall and be destroyed. In that decrepitude, we will have to hear the heartrending agony, the pain, the sorrow, and the pained sighs of the people living beneath the roof of that house, and we will have to watch them act like confused or deranged people, blabbering senseless words and banging their heads.

52. In today's condition it will be a great boon to accept the fact, with a happy heart, that all people of all castes, states and different regional languages are worthy of respect, prestige and love. Erasing the everyday differences, and in organizing together every social category, every caste, sub-caste and family, and to give them a harmonious organization, even religion can be helpful, even if they worship different deities.

53. If, as a representative of that 'Unknown', if as a representative of that God and guru you help the needy people in an unassuming way, and you keep helping them, and your generations to come keep doing so, then there can be no saintliness, no vision of the Truth, and no everlasting existence better than that.

54. O Sudharma! There is no government institution, there is no officer who can provide shelter to the innocent citizens of this highly cultured country, who can liberate them from this all pervasive oppression, to breathe freely. This, which is happening every day in the lives of every sub-category of every social category, is not a gift of that 'Unknown'.

55. In the context of today's conditions, the thoughts and sermons of nearly all religious books, whether they be of the western world, of western Asia, middle Asia or elsewhere, whether

they be the Bible, or the Quran, or Hindu religious books, they all seem inspired by selfishness of political power and politics. This is nothing but crass individualism; this cannot be socialism for social welfare, because despite gaining knowledge and despite entering science, human beings have become distorted and deformed.

56. In the same way that sunlight gets dimmed but does not entirely go away when a cloud comes in front of the Sun, Truth also gets dimmed in front of wickedness. If this is the condition of humans in the world, then it is possible that the necklaces of religions strung together through the holes of wickedness and deceit can break, and the tendencies of destructiveness can also keep rising.

57. It is the ill-effect of the increasingly negative company of lost or beguiled people and incomplete religious books and philosophies which create pollution for one's own self, that the soul also gets trampled upon.

58. Real curiosity has an unbreakable faith.

59. Harmless action and art, and desire free mind and heart, are enough for us, Darshi!

60. In the same way that we try to wheedle and cajole the divinities, we try to cajole Kali and Durga, we try to cajole the gods and goddesses, so also the clever people have cajoled or somehow appropriated — by throwing their net on them — the nice souls, the *rishis*, the saints, the Mahatmas and the sadhus on the slopes of the southern extremities of the Himalayas. By creating a divisive intellect in them they misled these good souls and stole from them the goal, the glory, the aura, the luminescence, the power to think and the virtues of the soul. The result of this has been that we became slaves for thousands of years. All this is happening today as well.

61. Understanding our weaknesses and by trapping us in their net, the people of the west have fished us out in shoals. And like the fish in the western net, we are trapped and listless. Getting into numerous bondages of *jati*, religion, family, friends, relatives, home, city, village, children and grand-children, we have become frustrated and are unable to be free of this net.

62. Our life has become limited to eating to live, and to earn to eat.

63. You live within the confines of parochialities and the mindset of a well-frog. You fear the expanse of the ocean. In the ocean ply huge ships; in the well, only the frog hops around. On the huge ships great nations are carried around and ferried. The frog just jumps around in the well and thinks itself to be great.

64. Have we become so parochial because of our education, or our culture, or the prurient literature in the name of culture, or many other kinds of dilemmas?

65. Friends! You are born on this land of India where many great souls have alighted and have gone leaving their shadow behind, in whose shade you find a lot of happiness, peace and comfort. Remembering that we try to achieve the new force of a new soul, and to achieve security and divine consciousness, we invoke them.

66. When we were praying to these gods and goddesses with folded hands, at that time cuffs were put on our hands.

67. Wherever in the world any people have such an attachment for another's culture, nobody will find it difficult to overpower them and to make them dance to a different tune.

68. The soul of India is misappropriated by other religions.

69. From the eyes of those vulture friends [of mine], tears full of slime were dripping. They were saying that even now in the rivers of the northern slopes of the Himalayas, so many bloody knives were still being washed. These vultures had hoped to take care of that environmental pollution, [of the effects of] that cruelty and that heartlessness, but when they saw the turmoil in the sky there, they came flying straight to this palm tree and sat on it. Watching the smoke of the cremation grounds of the north, they were somewhat angry that their food-stuffs were being quietly disposed of, food they could have used to fill their bellies, and they could have removed the pollution of the environment which had been wilfully spread. I cannot say what mystery lay in their conversations, and in these thoughts of theirs.

70. The tendency of ours to destroy the temples built by God [the human body] and to protect the divine places made of concrete and cement is like cutting our own limbs with our hands and then asking for forgiveness. For this, our own Self will not forgive us.

71. Our entire country and every house here is that ashram, that divine place, that *dargah* where people continuously spend their spare time left from their livelihood in the discussions of that Unknown. Will all this of ours be snatched away from us?

72. In our India, all the villages and dwellings are like the huts of the sadhus. But those who live in big houses, those who live in palaces, are never ready to even light a candle in these huts, nor does their heart ever prompt them to do so. The day our inclination becomes so [like the inclination of a saint], on that day candles will be lit in huts even before they are lit in palaces. Many of our Gods live in huts only. Then we will worship them first, and only after that will we worship ourselves; such would be our inclination.

73. There is enough to learn and to teach even within the boundaries of the ashram itself.

74. Friends! This ashram is very different from the *varnashram* (a fourfold division of society into Brahmin, Kshatriya, Vaishya and Shudra, according to the ancient texts, plus the successive age-based stages of *brahmacharya*, *grihastha*, *vanaprastha* and *sannyas*). All the Vedas and Puranas were only written in ashrams, not in temples, mosques or churches. These were written since the time of the inception of incarnation-ism. This is an ashram of an Aughar. Here you will not find *varnashram*. Only the ashram exists here.

75. When the country was overrun, from the north until the Karnataka region, by bestial people and the men-folk were helpless in facing them, at that time a princess living in a fortress destroyed those people with beastly mentalities (*mahishasur*). Because she lived in a fortress (*durg*), she is known as Durga. She was not an idol of stone or iron. For weapons she had the trident, the mortar and the leg of a cot. At that time, swords and bows and arrows did not exist. At that time, she gave a backbreaking reply to those people with beastly tendencies.

76. There is a Supreme-ism away from all dilemmas, separate from our incarnation-ism, our idol worship, and our God-ism. And that is you and I and all of us. But if you and I and all of us accept the subjugation of someone else then we have a very bad fate in store.

77. What is the importance of the imaginations of the gods and goddesses and the divinities living in the sky and in heaven for us human beings who live on the earth? I can't understand it. This is simply a pointless lie, a harness that we tow because this is the livelihood of some people, due to which we are made frightened, and we are made suspicious, and we are made blunt.

78. Many matters of the scriptures have turned merely into puzzles, and you have lose your whole life trying to solve those puzzles.

79. Today's legal rules are also like a certain kind of religion which was born only 125 or 130 years ago. The pundits of the constitution, living in legal offices, adopt a process of distorting the facts and creating delays to bother the people in the villages and to exploit them, in the same way that many kinds of fabrications were made in our scriptures for exploiting people, and due to the bother and troubles created by them, people of all religions are fed up. We are so fed up that we are now bored with religion and we have no faith in it. How long will we keep reading these puzzles that are so misleading? How long will these puzzles continue in our lives? If we don't forget them, then our prayers and worship will have no meaning.

80. If you think that you are very pure and clean, that nice clean clothes will keep you in the category of 'nice people', and that you will always escape unscathed, then it is just a futile dream. In fact, better than you is that person with only a loincloth, who bears no risk of ever falling. He will jump over and escape from any quarrel. This country has even been liberated by these people wearing loincloths. And other religious institutions have been made in this country, in their name and memory.

81. [About Kinaram Sthal]: People have many misconceptions about the tradition and age of this place. They easily say that this place is three or four hundred years old when, in fact, this place and this tradition, both are ancient. Even before Maharaj Shri Kinaram, whose festival we are celebrating today, there have been many saints and *mahapurush* in this tradition, and this place had existed even before them, it exists today, and it will exist tomorrow, too. Behind this house is a remnant of an old monastery. Even today you can see some *lakhauriya*

bricks (a special kind of thin bricks) by studying which you can easily gauge the ancient age of this place.

82. If you read history you will find that in the Prabhas region of Somnath, where exists Aghorwan which is also called Somnath-Pattan, and where the Sultan of Ghazani had met Aghor Rudrabhadra, in the same series this [Aghor] tradition has continued since ancient times. Friends! The tradition, whose great *samadhis* you see here neglected, have been through a lot of times and troubles. Many blows have tried to erase them. It is by the grace of that 'Unknown' that they are to be found in this form today. It is the blessing of that great soul that even today these are present to provide good inspiration.

83. [Aghor tradition]: Be it Hindu or Christian, or any of the other eighteen or twenty religious traditions, each one of those has many schools of thought and differences among those schools of thought. In a single thought-flow of theirs, in time, there appeared many different streams, that is, different though-flows. But this [Aghor] tradition is the only such thought stream which remains the same from its source till its union with the ocean. On its way, in many towns and cities, many drains and rivers [other thought-streams] have joined it and so it has become a huge divine river, like Ganga. This is what we call Aughar. We call it Aghor.

84. Regarding alcohol and prohibitions, the opinion that people have is that all this has come from Mount Kailash (in western Tibet). This is not so. The people of Kailash never even used them. They had a different joy, and they used to be absorbed in that joy.

85. I do not have any hatred for politicians. But I do hate the present form of politics. Today, because of the thoughts and behaviours of politicians, terrible hatred is being produced towards them in the psyche of the common people.

86. Before independence, Hindu, Muslims, Sikhs and Christians in this country all used to work together. They had sentiments of love and friendship for each other. They used to have sentiments of faith and belief for each other, and for the benefit of the nation and society they used to be eager to make collective sacrifices. But merely in the span of 43 years all these sentiments have disappeared. The place of divine feelings for each other has been taken over by feelings of hatred, jealousy, envy and animosity. Everywhere you find riots, fights, violence and lawlessness. Who is responsible for this? Will the new generation think about it?

87. This country is very old. It is a country of old people, and it is very mature. The people here have a lot of wisdom. But they rise [to action] only after some time. They stretch themselves only after a long time.

88. These ashrams are to provide support to human beings burnt by the flames [of life]. This organization of yours also has a distinct symbol, and has a distinct character. If the virtues of humility, saintliness and innocence are found in you, then you become worthy of respect and prestige.

89. In these ashrams of ours, many people of the world who desire prestige, people who are very good people, they are eager to be ridiculed by these sadhus, fakirs and alms-seekers. They know that an insult from these people will only add to their value.

90. Friends! Our picture was not like what we are portrayed as today. Our Goddess did not have such a distorted character that people have slyly tried to portray her with swords, arrows, knives and maces. She is the Goddess of forgiveness. Such pictures are a product of the Islamic period, and it is the people of these higher castes who have produced such cartoons to show us. Is the gaze of the Goddess with a sword and a begging bowl even more cruel than that of our worldly mothers?

Absolutely not. Her gaze is very nice. But the way our divinities are portrayed in stories and legends, we feel ashamed of telling them to anyone. Wherever the question of character, arises we cannot narrate them. That is why we have no special interest in that.

91. Do not inspire self-controlled fellow countrymen to become uncontrolled. They will break and disintegrate.

92. The young seekers see many fires [of desires] pass before them every day, but they remain very careful. They know even if they are a little uncontrolled, they will be promptly ousted. But you householders cannot test your children this way because you have not made friends of them. If you so much as think like this towards them, you may have to face terrible opposition.

93. Our condition today is such that we are unable even to safeguard the wealth inherited from our ancestors. We are fighting even over a broken hut, and are not able even to save the hut from destruction.

94. Despite worshipping the Goddess of strength we remained enslaved for thousands of years due to a lack of people-power and the strength of unity. We have become free of those chains of slavery only when we added the power of the people to the power of the Goddess, and respected it.

95. Our country is ancient compared to the nations considered to be wealthy today; before the British rule, it was the wealthiest nation of the world. Everyone had their eyes on this country. Is all that not there anymore? It is all there, friends. Hell has not arrived from heaven. It is we who have created a hell here. It is not that hell was abolished after the creation of heaven. It just does not exist in heaven. The dawn will definitely come. You should not give up your desire to see the dawn.

96. Now our time should come when becoming united, strand by strand, we become so strong a knot that we cannot be destroyed by anyone. This is what we need most of all now. In the coming times it is necessary that all of you join with your good souls, and considering their thoughts, cultivate the abilities within you to act on them.

97. We gather together regularly with our well-wishers to think about and understand the path of life, and to evaluate our ways of doing things, to meet with each other, to renew our resolves, and to remember things that we have forgotten within ourselves by seeing a few faces.

98. [Regarding the idols and pictures of Gods and Goddesses]: Those we worship are portrayed as having violent temperaments, carrying weapons and fighting. But that is not eternal. That was limited only to the battlegrounds. After that, each one evaluated themselves according to human inclinations and human values. Seeing weapons in the hands of our gods and goddesses, in our innocence we consider that as ideal behaviour; it indicates a violent temperament and instead of making us fearless, it inspires us to be violent.

99. We have considered the Gods and Goddesses to be something else for generating interest in stories and legends, but like wheat and rice and other things that we produce, they too are Gods and Goddesses produced by us. They can only fill our bellies, these bellies because of which we are related to each other.

100. Initially, humans were made in the ashrams of *rishis*, in the ashrams of *mahapurushas*. Then religious books were written, and Vedas, *shastras*, Puranas, and many gods and goddesses were produced. All these are derived from the ashrams of the *rishis*.

101. We spend our life like a prisoner in the soil where we have grown up, whose weather and the wind has touched us, and touches us still. We cannot stroll freely on the road, nor can we freely exchange ideas with each other, nor can we talk with all our fellow countrymen about our friendship and kindness. Even the British weren't able to foster so much animosity between us.

102. You have become so soft before your mother, before your father, before your guru, that the practice that you have, you cannot even practice that practice. You are not gaining stability; your faith is not becoming firm. The reason behind this is the present environment. Our environment today is that of newspapers, radios and televisions.

103. May God save that country where you find too many divine speakers, nationalists, socialists, opportunists and leaders.

104. At Parao in Kashi, millions upon millions of mantras have been recited, uncounted sacrifices have been made and many good thoughts have been meditated upon. At such a place if you are sharpening your sword of the Guru-mantra, then you will be able to know completely the knowledge of the five elements (earth, water, fire, wind and ether) and their 25 subcategories (five for each element). On learning this, at the time of knowledge-absorbed consciousness, all that was hidden or revealed will become apparent separately.

105. In this culture of ours, the process of worship is very great and full of deep substances. It is scientific as well as heart-touching. It is also difficult to understand. If you merely try to understand it then it will take a very long time, and your understanding will also remain incomplete.

106. I see that you greet someone by standing up, then sitting down, and in the same way you greet gods and goddesses too.

On this pious occasion, this greeting of yours, your prayers, denote for you greatness. By doing so you do not greet any God or Goddess, nor do you greet any saint or Mahatma or guru, but in fact you give an indication of your politeness, humility and patience. You may not be able to understand why you do this or why this happens. Perhaps you've never paid attention to it.

107. The thoughts of the West are putting great pressures on us today, and there are many things [that pressure us]. Two generations of ours have been lost in these ponderings. Perhaps, after the end of the 20th century, our new generation will once again become conscious about its culture in temples, and will again search for it with vigour.

108. The person to whose name the word 'Ram' is attached, they are better than us, even if they are fallen people, neglected people, downtrodden people, scheduled caste or people of any other caste. It is believed that Shudras (the lowest caste) had arisen from the feet [of God], but this fact is very important. Whenever we pay respect to our gurus, elders or saints and Mahatmas, we say "Baba, I touch your feet! I bow at your feet!" We never say, "I touch your head" or "I touch your forehead".

Attachment

If the goal of life is to be free, why do human beings bind themselves with so many attachments? These attachments can be towards possessions, or prestige, or loved ones. Baba did not say that everyone should become as detached as the ascetic who has no concerns in life, but he did say, lessen your attachments, they are what weigh you down.

1. The more attachment people have, the more infatuation they have, be it towards gold and silver, house and home, position and prestige, or respect and praise, with double strength does the fire of sorrow burn them.

2. If we can catch and let go of something, how can it become a bondage to us?

3. As for two-faced people, even the desire for a blade of grass is the mother of great pain and sorrow. One who gives up even this is known as a sadhu, and only he can live a simple and unostentatious life.

4. The genitals and the tongue — excessive involvement in these two soon enslaves humans, and makes them fall, inciting them towards a wrong way — in fact, it forces them to do wrong things. This is like expectorable phlegm.

5. Friends, how deep we are in attachments. We know none of them is going to be with us. Yet, we remain with them. And we stay with them to such an extent that we begin to think they are ours and we are theirs. But if I pinch your body, it is not going to hurt anyone else's body. It will hurt only you. If both your and another person's hair catches on fire you both run to douse your own head first. They do not put out someone else's fire first, and remain deep in attachment.

6. This is an illusion of the Mahamaya, friends. We are all deeply covered in attachments. Because of these desires we lose this world as well as the other world. And in this world too we become involved in insulting others.

7. The dilemmas of a wayward heart also produce anger. Covered with the slime of dirty thoughts, a wayward heart, keeping the company of troubles, inspires one towards low actions. It forces us to do wrong things.

8. One who creates discord and animosity for himself is a person who betrays his own Self.

9. If the person is not balanced, then his pilgrimage and prayers and worship are all useless.

10. Those who merely indulge their senses, especially those who indulge excessively in pleasures of the reproductive organs and those of the tongue and taste, and inspire others towards such standards, become absent minded and very dry-hearted.

11. We have amassed material things for a hundred days while our life lasts only two days. We can't even get up from the bed, and yet leave the world and go away.

12. The natural temperament of any person does not change by prayer and worship. Desire, anger, attachment, greed, sorrow, hate, jealousy, envy: all these remain and, as soon as they get a chance, they begin to reign supreme. They then make that person do whatever they want him to do.

13. Even those seekers who leave their place and roam about from door to door are valued very lightly, like potatoes, tomatoes and eggplants are in the marketplace. Even diamond has its value in its own place.

14. Because of a lack of the right vision within you or because of a vision of duality, because of mutual non-cooperation, and because of living with sentiments of discrimination, we see everything opposite of what it is, and hence we have obstacles.

15. We want to do something while what happens is something else. The energy which should be utilized well is being misused. It is a strange situation.

16. In the same way that after relieving yourself you do not even look towards it, so also the thoughts with which you have lived and grown up and which have produced so many sorrows, so many pollutants that have contaminated your thoughts, they are to be given up like that excrement. In the same way that after relieving yourself you feel good and the heaviness of your head goes away, so also after giving up dirty thoughts, feelings and sentiments: you will achieve great happiness and peace.

17. What a crime we are committing to ourselves. Even if God forgives us, how will we be able to forgive ourselves?

18. It is because of this baggage of ours that we have come to this situation. We have made a heavy load from many kinds of frustration and because of its weight, we have become dull-headed. Where we have to say something we do not say anything, and where we should not say anything we keep on speaking. Where we should listen, we do not, and where we should not, we listen very carefully. In the same way, because of our obtuseness with regard to seeing things, going to different places, and doing different things, everything that we do has an opposite effect to that which is desired.

19. Not feeling good feelings for anyone has bad effects.

20. If things in this world get spoiled, then how will the other world be better? The other world will merely be a thirst before us, then.

21. If you are sitting at your place of worship and are thinking all sorts of negative things, if many kinds of dirty thoughts arise within you there, then it is better not to go to that place. Then you should sit in a dirty place and await the arrival of nice thoughts.

22. A matchstick stays within the matchbox and, on shaking it, make a rattling sound, too; but it does not burn until a third person produces friction between the phosphorous on the matchhead with the phosphorous on the matchbox. This is known as the ill of bad company. Wise people use it to light lamps to derive light, and perform *hawan* (fire oblations) etc.; wise women prepare meals on it. Uncontrolled and ill-understanding people turn it into a poison which can burn everything, unacceptable everywhere in the absence of Aghor.

23. Because of our wrong understanding, we have become enemies of worship.

24. Lazy people are family destroyers, ancestor destroyers and traitors to the nation. It is useless to expect anything auspicious from them. Because of laziness today's young people are rabidly becoming afflicted by deadly diseases. They never can repay back their debt to the nation for the food and water that they consume. Their life becomes deadweight. After death they get born in the form of animals and other lower forms and keep wandering lost.

25. It is necessary even to have criticism and censure. And it is even better if it happens in the presence of the person. At that time our lack of control, anger, or any other excitability can push us very far back.

26. Regarding duty, action, policy, justice, daily activities and daily behaviour, we all know that if we keep getting only praise then we can take a very wrong path like this also, and then we will not be able to stop ourselves from wrong actions.

27. If different kinds of situations come before us, then we should not hesitate to perform whatever big or small actions they demand.

28. Excess praise can make us become participants in miseries, like hell.

29. One who listens to the sins of others becomes a co-sharer in one sixth of that sin, and the one who narrates it keeps five sixths of it.

30. I see that your heart becomes very eager on seeing small things to eat, intoxicants, and other useless worldly attractions. The result of this instability is the same as the dance that young men and women of today perform. We will acquire those same vibrations. When we acquire those vibrations, our condition will be such that we will end up dancing all our lives to different tunes. We will end our life dancing like this, and would not have gained anything.

31. That divinity in heaven, in whose name we are intimidated regarding various sorrows and troubles — we will have to become fearless of that. Then only will we be a true worshipper in a real way.

32. Everybody knows that every single person is born with their own fate, and with their own conveniences. What we do will not have any effect on that, nor can we do anything.

33. We are in the bondage of the chains of desire. We are a self-emergent divinity but have turned into this chained person

— and this chain never breaks. We have lit many fires and done much meditation to break it. We have taken refuge in the waters to break it. But even the water of Ganga couldn't break it. We have tried to break it with blows of words and sentences, but even then we haven't been able to break it.

34. One who speaks many nice ideas but doesn't practice them is like that bank official who counts millions of dollars every day and distributes them, but when he returns home in the evening, he hasn't even a cent in his pocket.

35. A narrow-intellect produces fear. Stop the mind from going in the opposite direction. A wise person should keep his intellect straight, as a fletcher keeps his arrows absolutely straight. Listen and follow, O seeker.

36. Whose mind is unstable, who does not know the path to the truth, whose faith and devotion keep getting shaken, he can never achieve absolute wholeness and knowledge, O seeker.

37. One enemy can hurt another enemy. One who harbours hatred can harm someone else. But if a person's own mind goes in the wrong direction then it can harm him more than anything else, O seeker.

38. Who will win the world over? The enemies in the form of our poisonous thoughts rise in us and poison us. Divinities, the God of death, death itself, and pain: these all poison us. They aren't really there, but it seems as if they are, O seeker.

39. O my wise, virtuous, well behaved disciple! Acquire a comprehensive vision. Only then will you be able to win against the intake of poison in this toxified world which you have been living in. For, those who have accepted the slavery of the senses are like the little insects of hell. So, do not get tied up in the weaknesses of the senses, in their attractions, or by that

arrow of Kama — bedecked with flowers, so attractive with its beautiful words: like this, on hearing the music from a *veena*, a deer will become lost in it, and thereby loses its life. Do not lose your life like that. Be victorious. Be victorious, O seeker.

40. The person who considers it a matter of pride to ridicule pure and high souls is an extremely weak person.

41. Because of fear people go into temples, into sacred places, under sacred trees, and to the rivers. They even build nice fortresses because of it. Even then they have sorrow. They are incapable of being free from sorrow.

42. Any kind of victory produces hatred. Hatred gives rise to every kind of blackness. Those clouds of ignorance may appear very beautiful, but they also produce fear. Every wise person knows this.

43. O seeker! Through the mouth of Rama, Tulsi made it be spoken: divinity, divinity. He had the right thing be said. Neglecting your own efforts, mere God-ism also produces sorrow.

44. There must be some negative entity amongst us who does not take care of its habits. Your mercantile and indulgent intellect is not able to catch it. And this is the reason why you get cheated every time. And it also puts many kinds of negative effects on your mind.

45. Whether the amount of excrement be less or more, it is bound to smell.

46. As everyone knows, the intellect of one who indulges in the wealth of negative people becomes negative. One who imbibes alcohol and *ganja* is bound to get intoxicated. His mouth is bound to smell.

47. To use a plough, to do manual labour, to do hard physical work, to keep your hand overhead or to spend your life standing up — these do not count as austere practices. These are not known as austere practices. They merely denote: "different ways to fill the belly".

48. The praise of a few minutes is just another form of negativity.

49. Forgetting your unbreakable faith within you, which is your own, you are searching for something which just is not there.

50. Despite all kinds of situations you are still hopeful someday that entity will catch us by the arm and pull us out of it [the ocean of illusions]. It will pull us out. But that is possible only when you are drowning. You are not drowning; you are floating. And regarding the body that is afloat: as everyone knows, it's a corpse. You get liberated, you die.

51. Everybody is himself free, although freedom of this kind sometimes also can act as a poison in life. This poison can take your life, and can take you on a wrong path, as well.

52. The good thoughts that are given to you in the beginning that for now do only this much, for now you do not need to know any more than this, if instead of doing this the person begins to feel restless and jumps around and looks in this too, and thinks about that too, and looks into this and that book, then his thinking will definitely get contaminated.

53. Excessive cleverness produces great sorrow. It is excessive cleverness which brings poverty, mental stress, hatred, jealousy, and envy home. We people have become so clever that even we act cleverly with our divinity, our respected people, and our elders. We think that nobody else is watching, or understanding, or knows what we are doing. The result of this is

that, although we already were in darkness, we fall into it even deeper. Excessive cleverness indicates stupidity. Cleverness does not provide the desired stable success to anyone in the world. Like lightning in the sky, it may provide light or success for a little while, but it does not remain stable. If this cleverness goes away from us then we can become a good human being. It is because of our excessive cleverness that we achieve failure. Failure produces anger, and our heart begins to move towards destruction. Destruction then generates attachment, and that produces sorrow. In this way many kinds of enemies begin to attack us.

54. Those who are imprudent people do not even realize what they received from a particular moment of time. Such people themselves lose their time.

55. If you know something and you insult it, then you will not achieve success. That light will not light your way. But if you do something unknowingly then it is forgiven. The same is the condition of your life. If knowingly you are insulting a nice person and are respecting cruel people because of greed, then this will not be forgiven.

56. It is because of this unstable mind that we have met this bad fate. It is the mind that shows us all the good and bad dreams, and keeps making and breaking, joining and destroying every relation. It is this that has made us mad in this world. It is this mind that is the cause of every adverse effect. It is this mind that is kept under control by saints and yogis.

57. Because of our weaknesses, our mentality doesn't stay right. Due to this distorted mentality, we can't worship the peace and stability that we want to worship; we can't be satiated by eating only a little, as we want to do. Despite eating a good meal, lugging our baggage around, despite having everything, we are not able to sleep well.

58. We people are lost in ourselves. Our sickness is one thing; the medicine that those pundits are giving us is something else.

59. By going to the shelter of saintly people, what we receive — if it does not seem palatable to us, this means we're suffering from an illness, or that we are so destroyed by our own mentality that we are no longer fit to receive it.

60. If you speak lies then you will remain fearful, your heart will tremble and your mind will remain tainted. Then troubles will surround you and you will grow very frustrated.

61. Today, because of their selfishness, narrow-minded people are overlooking the laws and inspiring others towards hatred, but one day, at the appropriate time and period, hatred will arise against them too. The day your children are deprived of their comforts and conveniences, they day they are forced to drink all kinds of poisons, that day they will become mad, and act accordingly.

62. Let us not cooperate in the negative deeds of our dear ones, our family and friends, nor should we try unsuccessfully to hide them, for those actions cannot be hidden.

63. Try to explain this again and again to your mind: O mind, whatever you think, all that is nothing. And what is not, is actually what it is. This you should understand. This is the truth. For the rest, all that you understand is futile and untrue. Nobody ever derived happiness from it. Nobody ever derived peace from it.

64. In the search for peace and happiness we get beguiled by desires and end up spending all our life in futile efforts, ultimately gaining nothing but hopelessness. We think after getting married we will have our wife's cooperation and together we will pull the chariot of life very well. But everything seems to

happen the opposite way in the lives of ninety-nine percent of people. Leave aside the talk about pulling together the chariot of life; because of their small, narrow selfishness, so much bitterness arises between the two that all happiness and peace disappears and life becomes full of acrimony. Life feels like deadweight. Then between the two a third arrives in the form of a baby. For its suitable upbringing, in getting together all the comforts and conveniences and all sorts of essential things, the struggle taints the quality of our life and actions becomes very low and our social ties become strained. We get forced to live a life full of neglect, enduring everything. Even our parents and relatives, who have great expectations from us, neglect us.

65. As soon as you become four-armed (the family with husband and wife), you become an object of neglect from your parents and your friends and relatives. When you become two from one, enemies begin to rise against that Vishnu in your heart. All four-armed people generate enemies. When you were alone you used to receive love and affection from everyone, but soon as you become four-armed you become the object of their anger. When the third arrives and you become six-armed, then what can be said! Now a war begins to be waged, be it internally or externally.

66. Because we are overpowered by desire, we wander around temples and divine places in search of happiness, joy and stability; we try to follow the life-ways of saints and Mahatmas, nice people, and religion; when all that appears futile, then lack of faith arises in us and we achieve nothing but frustration.

67. We should take the support of stability in our life. Gaining concentration in solitude, in that concentration we should try to root out all our stresses, all our sorrows, and to limit our desires. Because the more your desires keep growing the more you will have stresses and problems in life, the more you will have sorrows, and your life will be spent in disorder.

68. You should definitely stay in this world but if you do not save yourself from its muck then you will be met with ignominy.

69. You will have to stay thousands of miles away from all kinds of hatred, jealousy, and envy. It is not that you will have to walk away from it all, but that you stay in the midst of them and they should keep happening around you. It is not as if you will profit anything by relinquishing these. These should keep happening, but even amidst this fire and storm you should remain unmoved like a mountain.

70. [People who are like] animals without tails deserve kindness because they are not able to exercise control over their thoughts and conduct, their behaviour and their senses, and as a result end up grazing their whole verdant life. Due to fear, or to fill their bellies, or to achieve praise or authority, they indulge in all kinds of negative deeds and keep wagging their tails. To think of overlooking them or punishing them is not right, because they themselves are overlooked and punished. Saints should think in this way. They have many desires and emotions. Keeping that in mind do at least this much, give this boon to them, that at least they may be able to understand the symbolic language.

71. We never get tired of criticizing others, finding faults in others and we spend a very large part of our time in futile thoughts, because of which our free time becomes a curse for us and our life. Despite sitting in the company of saints and great souls, we remain deprived of the effects of the vibrations of power and light that emanate from their bodies. We remain deprived of the inspirations that we could have had. Keeping our eyes closed towards them, we keep ourselves in darkness and then become forced to do that which should not be done. We waste free time, when in fact it is this 'free' or 'empty' that receives that voice and brings it to us.

72. We should decide after due thought about all the places to which desire makes us wander. You are standing at a shore where, with the boat of His grace, you can go across the ocean of life.

73. New inspirations come in our lives every day, again and again, in every way, but they go away. Good days also arrive, but they go away. So, our lives remain dissatisfied. We are never satisfied because of these mental aggravations.

74. We have never learnt to praise anybody with a pure heart. The result of praising the deplorable and deploring the praiseworthy is that we begin to suffer from insomnia and loquaciousness. We perceive all kinds of discriminations and category distinctions and many kinds of tainted thoughts and sentiments arise and put us on the way to destruction.

75. Praise, in fact, gives rise to great weakness and makes us very egotistical. Thus it keeps us away from a face-to-face meeting with that Unknown because that God does not like egotism, wickedness or deceit.

76. Even wandering lost has its own importance. Because if we did not have these lost wanderings, if we had not been sinful today, if we had remained absolutely pure and righteous, then why would we have imprecated each other? Even our tendency to imprecate has a character of its own. Even that has a mystery. Sometimes God chastises us to make us worthy of praise. Until such a time as we are put into the fire like gold, we cannot acquire that lustre. Until we experience friction like sandalwood, we cannot have the same fragrance.

77. Worshipping Lakshmi (the Goddess of wealth) and Ganesha (the God of prudence) together does not make sense. We all know that Lakshmi is a descendant of the ocean and Ganesha is a descendant of Rudra. But tradition prescribes worshipping

the two together. For, without intellect, even Lakshmi can burn a person. She gives great strife. She also gives great pain, and with her the humanity of a human being can also go.

78. From ants to elephants, every living being is running to fill their belly in the exact same way. Despite the difference in the amount of their needs, they both have the same troubles.

79. With your wrong behaviour and conduct, your covetousness and unwanted deeds, you cause your children to be deprived of any good cultural upbringing, and then you yourself suffer all your life long and pave the way for their suffering, as well. I see this in thousands of homes today. Because of this, today, our children have no value.

80. Whenever we have been cheated, it has been due to an ignorant friend.

81. The fear is not that the old woman might die, the fear is that Yamraj (the God of death) might become used to this idea.

82. This attachment does not go away from our hearts. If this attachment goes away then we can definitely live a good, long and peaceful life. But we are tied by the bonds of attachment making us suffer at home from our families, we listen to all kinds of things, and yet we remain forced to spend our lives like animals tied to a hitching post. Despite living in this world, those who remain away from the bonds of attachment — like the stage manager for a play — spend their life in happiness and peace. A human being does not progress on the path of liberation as long as time his attachments remain unbroken. The path of his numerous desires is so intoxicating that, despite its being unbearable, he hankers for the same intoxication. To leave all this and be separate from it all, we will have to give up attachments. We will have to give up our feelings of jealousy, animosity and revenge.

83. The way we look at ourselves — that we are this — we are actually not that. It just seems that way to us, in the same way that something hanging above some water might show us its reflection. It is not true that we will understand the truth just by looking at the reflection. The truth of that reflection lies somewhere else.

84. We think we are awake and that we are sitting here. Even this is a dream, friends. That we are moving and walking is also a dream. And this dream will end only when we understand that essence, that truth. That is why, at the beginning of any worship, meditation, contemplation, thought or prayer we say "*Om tatsat*" [literally, "Om, that which is true"]. By saying this much or by remembering the guru we expiate the sins of internalising unworthy things and going to unworthy places; because of these sins we experience guilt, we consider ourselves to be cruel; we deceive ourselves, and by closing our eyes we try to escape reality.

85. Even while awake we remain asleep, and even while asleep humans remain awake. One who remains awake remains away from sorrow. One who remains asleep dreams of all kinds of sorrows.

86. Friends! The free time that we have can inspire us to many negative deeds. It makes our young men and women lazy. They keep sleeping, and they do not understand all that they lose because of that sleep. Their health deteriorates and their intellect gets distorted. Many futile thoughts arise in their minds. They do not understand the import of the saying, "Sleep, a yawn and laziness: these three are brothers of death".

87. This life is like a mirage, yet we constantly remain involved in it, and this troublesome mind of ours keeps letting us experience many kinds of illusions. Because of this mind we forget the promise we had made at birth in crying "where, where".

Our guilt and attachment and —even more so — this ill-perceiving mind of ours trouble us constantly to make us suffer more. It takes us to so many distant places! It makes us wander even in places where we should not. Our life remains so ghost-like. This mind forces us to move when it is not the time to do so — under the strong sun, in terrible heat, through pouring rain, in harsh cold, and in bad times. This mind forces us to act like a disease-ridden dog, despite our not having the courage or strength to do so from within. It is only this mind which generates all kinds of weaknesses in us. But if the person makes a resolve then he can be free of the curse of the mind.

88. Who doesn't know that you can't catch your shadow? The more you chase it, the farther it runs. But if you turn around, it begins to follow you. What does this 'turning around' constitute in life? To slowly end the contaminants of the mind, its superficiality, its desires. If we do not do anything prompted by base mental desires, and if the base mind does not do anything for us, then this will be called 'turning around'.

89. Because of the mind, the pleasures of indulgence are unstable. They are momentary, and momentary pleasure is nothing but sorrow. Let us remain within bounds. Let us look for our happiness in every kind of situation. It is difficult to be free from the bondage of the slavery of the mind. We can be free from every bondage, but the person enslaved by the bondage of the mind suffers everywhere.

90. The tendency to amass wealth by wrong means and to give it to our children due to attachments gives rise to future inaction and laziness [in them]. Because of such attachments, our coming generation indulges in futile acts, becomes impotent, and becomes forced to suffer sorrows in inaction.

91. You should not leave yourself and you should not overlook the pure words of your guru, his pure ideal and the very good

thoughts that arise in you. If your wife, children, sons and daughters say something with a pure heart, then welcome it; if they say something out of jealousy, acrimony, greed or illusion, then don't be eager to follow.

92. It is a paradox: when we go to our gurus, saints and Mahatmas, we pray so that our baggage will feel light and relaxing; we do not pray that it be removed from our heads. The things that cause all our troubles, these very same things we beg from our guru and our divinity. And if he thinks about your welfare and doesn't give it to you, then you begin to think and say inappropriate things.

93. It is because of your egotism that you people fall behind in our search. You remain deprived of knowing that divinity who creates the vibrations in your veins, arteries, blood, flesh, marrow and intellect, those vibrations which make you think and do nice things.

94. Even a moment of ours spent with saints or great souls or nice people destroys our darkness of illusions and attachments.

GURU

In the Indian context, perhaps the most important figure in a person's spiritual life is his or her guru. A guru is the teacher par excellence, an instructor who has himself tried and tested and succeeded in whatever he is imparting to his disciples. A truly enlightened guru, therefore, is a rarity. That is why a guru is like God in human form. If a disciple finds a truly enlightened guru in his or her life, then their spiritual success is only dependant on the firmness of their faith in their guru. Baba understood this fact very well. What is presented in the following pages is what he said about it.

1. [Guru]... He is the life-force (*pran*), and as long as you are **alive** with your life-force, he will remain present within you.

2. I embrace you from my heart, all of you who are present here in the many forms of my own soul. May your heart and mind feel as good as mine does, as when the clarity of divine vision awakens within a person.

3. The company of your guru in the form of *pran* is the only refuge which can see you through all the strife and strains of life with ease and happiness.

4. O devotee! Above everything else, you will need faith in the careful words of your guru. You have to believe in and see your guru at a place much higher than the gods of the trinity. This will be an expression of prudence.

5. Whichever work you want to be successful in, think of your guru's expression, appearance and state while performing those actions in different times and situations. Pay attention to it, remember him, and bow to him with your life-force.

6. Scriptures bind us within limits and confuse us. They do not allow our thinking to roam freely in the realm of thoughts. They make our thought very limited. But the words of your guru, even if they are not derived from the scriptures, are in keeping with necessities of the time, place and nation of your existence. Chopping away all your limiting ties, he will make you reach salvation.

7. Guru's words reveal a whole host of mysteries and show you the right path for your bright future.

8. Guru is not this body made of flesh and bones. Guru is that firm support whose expressed words will ripen you to maturity. If you follow those words they will enable you in every way to realize guru-hood. Guru is the maturity of your thoughts, the firmness of your faith, the strength of your beliefs.

9. Nobody crosses the ocean of life to salvation without a guru.

10. There is not a single person who is not sick. Eating and drinking, moving and walking, every behaviour is a disease. Great souls, gurus, do not speak only about medicine to cure such diseases; they also show you the post-medication practice.

11. There are no troubles in the refuge of Mother-Guru (Ma-Guru).

12. Worshippers of Ma-Guru! Nobody teaches the tiger to hunt or the fish to swim. Worshippers of *guru-mantra*! Understand it. Know it.

13. Praying to Ma-Guru bestows immortality to a person.

14. Whoever your guru or teacher may be, have unwavering faith in that person. Then only will you be able to acquire their virtues and experience peace within yourself. Away from faith and devotion, even the greatest ascetic aspirant cannot achieve

God's grace and peace, however learned a scholar may he be. Only with a pure and guileless heart can you achieve absolute peace and God's grace.

15. Guru sculpts a guru, not a disciple.

16. A guru's mere company teaches the disciple by itself.

17. A real guru is one who turns the disciple into a guru like himself, and imparts him the ability to sculpt great gurus.

18. The only difference between a guru and a disciple is that the guru gets to know a little earlier and the disciple, a little later.

19. A disciple does not get to be bigger than his guru. But a self-realized disciple merits the same position as his guru — and never a position higher than his guru.

20. When the disciple has belief, approaches [the guru], serves him, asks him questions, listens intently, accepts the knowledge he hears and ponders over the meaning of knowledge he has accepted, only then do the thoughts and blessings of the Aghoreshwar get propounded.

21. The disciple who really believes in me is a recipient of the blessings and grace of Mahakapalik Aghoreshwar. He is amongst the gems of Aughar ascetics; he is an invaluable asset to the Aghoreshwar.

22. The guru has the responsibility of imparting knowledge. But the responsibility of acting on that knowledge is that of the disciple.

23. Friends! Up until now we have dealt with the dead. We hunt dead flesh, we keep it, we are happy that we have meat to eat. But we never understood that we deal only with dead flesh. Real

gurus, great souls, deal with live people, associate with human beings who are alive. And that person acquires such a beautiful persona, blossoms in such a manner, that he understands many things in his life, does many things, and achieves many things. And that Divine Mother also keeps her grace on him.

24. Look: I will make you meet with our Divine Friend. Do not be afraid; be patient. Put on your clothes. Wash your body with clean water. Get cleaned of this dirt and impurity. Become pure.

25. Friends! The real son of a father or mother carries their influence, their features and colour, their ways of acting and behaving, even the ways of dressing of his mother or father. Similarly, the disciples of a guru become very much like him. They sit, stand, speak, explain, analyze, elaborate, understand, teach, become humble, become patient like him. They do not have any bitterness in them.

26. [On the subject of guru:] This subject is harder than the hardest, and simpler than the simplest. It is peaceful, and is a narrow trail of supreme virtues which, when trod upon, gives to an aspirant his guru's forgiveness for all his actions, non-actions and mis-actions, done knowingly or unknowingly — which even God, the Supreme Being, does not forgive easily.

27. Regarding guru, the first thing is to believe in him. And that faith is difficult to achieve. This is because the guru is not a dummy made of skin and bones and flesh. Gurus are in all castes, categories, periods and places. When our circumstances favour us and the Divine Mother has her grace on us, we find them easily. Otherwise, a person can keep trying and crying his whole life but he still might not find his guru.

28. A person seeks a guru from pillar to post, from place to place. It is not certain in what conditions, where, and how that great

soul will come to you. But on finding him, how will you believe in him?

29. Until one has full faith and belief in his guru, he cannot be successful in the knowledge imparted to him. This is very difficult to achieve in life. You can lose your faith due to many kinds of treatment the guru metes out to you, or many kinds of humour to which he subjects you. When you experience even the slightest disdain for your mantra, for your guru, for the divine being you worship, then that knowledge takes a very long time to be achieved. It becomes very difficult to find success. Then you cannot achieve it. It goes away.

30. Making one disciple, the guru accrues the sins equal to killing a thousand cows. The guru has to bear all responsibility for the disciple. If the disciple turns out to be wicked and immoral, a sinner and a criminal, and does nothing but useless things day in and day out, then who is going to digest his sins, and how?

31. Great is the importance of both the guru and his disciple. If the disciple wants, he can lead to the guru's deliverance, too. There have been many disciples who have raised their fallen gurus.

32. Sometimes you can see more power in the disciple than in the guru. He can then lead to his guru's redemption on the strength of his faith and belief. Then, he has the power and authority to buy even heaven, if he wants.

33. Many gurus, over time, have strayed from their paths. Many disciples have strayed too.

34. Is the guru like Brahma, Vishnu or Mahesh?! No. In fact, he provides light to all three of them. He is greater than the three of them. Because he is the one who takes you to them, he

makes you meet them, and he gives you a position equal to or higher than theirs.

35. A Sadguru (self-realized guru) is not one with special characteristics, or with a beard and a moustache, or in red or yellow or black clothes. A guru, by nature, is very simple, and is just like you or me, amongst us. He speaks and acts like us. He plays and works like us. But that one word of his — one sentence holds the truth, it is real, it has the endorsement of age-old knowledge. He never tries to keep you in the dark.

36. You are working very hard, my friend. But if you do not save and accumulate, these same people will ignore you. Your guru will never ask you to be extravagant, to waste everything you have so that society may laugh at you later on.

37. A guru should not be conceited. He should not neglect his disciple.

38. Brahma, Vishnu and Shiva are not gurus. To count them as one with your guru is a mistake. The fruits and flowers that you offer your guru are nothing but so much deadwood to him. The right offering for him is not flowers, but faith. And that faith is the flower of your heart. There, you do not need to spend either money or time. If you keep offering that, you will never find yourself lacking. You will never want for anything. You will be inexhaustible in wealth, inexhaustible in strength, inexhaustible in intellect and inexhaustible in esteem. It will never perish. Wherever you go, my friend, you will find what you seek. A circle will grow within you.

39. I say to myself that I make a resolution not to break this word to myself. This is what is known as guru-initiation or guru-mantra. This mantra then grows and blooms; blossoming, it yields the sweetest fruits.

40. On seeing a real guru, pure thoughts and emotions rise in you, new ideas emerge in your heart, and self-purification is easily realized.

41. Whom you find peace in your soul on meeting, he is a guru.

42. Some people say the *sadguru* is a *paras* (Philosopher's stone). *Paras* can turn iron into gold, but that gold does not have the ability to turn another piece of iron into gold. But a real *sadguru* is one who makes his disciples like himself, and enables them to make *sadgurus* like him.

43. The sun [the *sadguru*] carries light [disciples]. But even light should lead to an experience of the Sun. Only then will the oneness of the sun and light be for the benefit of the world.

44. The rain of guru's blessings and sermons does not only fall on high mountains. It goes to the deepest realms and ends in the ocean. It's unfathomable, that's why.

45. Guru is electricity. If all of your ten rooms are well connected, they will all conduct electricity naturally.

46. Even the rays from a guru's toenails provide the power to see through things.

47. You will have to come out of darkness for yourself. Your guru's coming out for you will not help.

48. By practicing the mantra given by the guru, the lines of fate get expunged. Your ill-fate wanes away.

49. Guru unlocks the insightful speech of the disciple who has faith in him, and that disciple begins to speak, word by word, of things that are ten years hence. This is indicative of a state of godliness.

50. I will not be able to satisfy a sceptic's doubts. However, I will certainly satisfy genuine curiosity and inquisitiveness.

51. You are all happy because of the happiness of my spiritual being.

52. By the flash of a spark of spiritual energy Sarveshwari I was born the first time, and after my birth was born the creation.

53. Friends! I am an ascetic. I should not have any attachment towards you. I should have no affection for you. I should remain far away from your actions and activities because neither have I added to the population growth, nor increased the impurities of the environment anywhere. Even then, since I accept food and water from you, I do not wish to let you remain as a well-frog. Having acquired the beautiful flower of your heart and mind, I try for your happiness so that your heart and mind don't get alienated, that they remain within themselves, so that you may live in a wholesome way and learn an ideal way of living.

54. If our guru is angry with us, is being indifferent to us, or is using harsh words towards us, then we should become attentive towards the causes for it. Behind his behaviour lies only your welfare. He must be striving to protect you from possible troubles by chasing away your laziness, cowardice, worries and obstacles.

55. If your guru has asked us to look straight, towards your nose, like the way people explain about meditation, that you should meditate straight; this does not mean you should sit down and keep looking only at your nose and ears. It is not limited to this. Its limits are extensive, and that is that, in every situation, our vision should be such that we look at ourselves, that we are aware of ourselves. We must look straight at ourselves. If we keep looking left and right, we can meet with an accident or get hurt.

56. You may become a great person, a saint or whatever — but without your guru, the success of the mantra is impossible, the ultimate success of your life is impossible.

57. The sacrament of initiation should certainly be performed. How far to sit from his seat after approaching him, in which direction to approach, how to sit, how much to talk to him, when and how to present your curiosity and questions to him — all these things should be learnt.

58. If you have some question in your mind, then it should be expressed only after judging the mood and mental state of your guru.

59. After a time, by looking at guru's dress, by hearing the fall of his footsteps while strolling, or by looking at his expressions, we can understand his mental state. These are very small and simple teachings, and these should be learned.

60. The *kalash* (the pitcher used in rituals), in a way, is like the hen which incubates her egg, gives it warmth, and slowly a being just like her emerges from it. Similarly, the disciple also becomes like the guru. His behaviour, dress, and attire become like that of his guru. If you are a worshipper of the Divine Mother and are initiated by your guru, between twenty-one days to twenty-one months later, your nature and temperament should change to be like your guru's.

61. Today, in western countries you will find every kind of religious teacher. They speak about very nice things, they do things like drawing maps and describing things. The path that they show and sermonize about, however — have they trod upon it? The right of showing the way should only be given to that person who has walked it, because he knows the ups and downs, the good and the bad, the turns and pitfalls of the path. By walking the path shown by such a person, anyone can achieve success.

62. A completely stable disciple is known as *akshobhya* (imperturbable); he does not get perturbed by anything. One who is not like this is neither an animal nor a human being.

63. Unless we seek guidance from our guru in the worship and prayer that we keep doing, and until the guru teaches us about it, it is impossible to be successful in it.

64. The mind that meditates on the words of the guru is introspective; it achieves a comprehensive vision. His mind and heart remain within themselves. He does not experience internal alienation, seekers!

65. I am speaking only of that which is in my memory. These matters from memory may be different [from your actions and expectations], and therefore, they may not be understandable to you. It is also possible that they may be appropriate, and will even be seen to be so after your eyes are opened.

66. I am very afraid I should not become a part of that category of teachers whose whole life is spent telling about things within a limited boundary, within the same college. Even then I speak to tell you of what I know, and to have you practice them. If this practice is relinquished then many problems will arise for us and for those who come near us.

67. Deceiving your guru results in the failure of the knowledge he is imparting. It will bear no fruit. You may learn any particular knowledge by deception, but it will not be fruitful.

68. You people fall in the category of those students who, if you understand what I say and practice it, you will surpass me. You will go far ahead of me like that student who leaves his teacher behind.

69. Persevere in one thing only. Do not be ensnared by myriad things. If you are, then neither this nor that will be accomplished. Both will go away. This is known as the deception of your guru.

70. Those who are careful with moneylenders, friends and gurus, who are attentive towards them, who are not enslaved by their minds, they will not run after whatever their mind wants.

71. You become suspicious when you see your children as very different from you. So, when I cannot recognize any sign of our tradition in my disciples and sadhus, I am forced to become indifferent to them.

72. I embrace all of you with my heart and pray to that unknown, in whose lap and refuge I have grown, that new inspirations come to you in the new dawn. The unfinished and faulty task that you have, may you be successful in finishing it.

73. I may have left my home, but I have not been able to leave society. Somewhere, somehow, a society gathers around me and a few people become my friends and companions, and I look at their faces, wondering, what it is that they want to say and what it is that they end up saying? What do they want to hear from me? Is what I am telling them to their liking or not? Seeing this condition of theirs, I begin to see myself in the form of their ghost. Instead of looking at myself in the form of supreme-nature, I see myself in the form of their ghost and become agitated.

74. An ascetic teaches his disciples an ideal way of behaving and conducting themselves in daily activities. Those who transgress that training and discipline do not fall in the category of disciples of that ascetic. It is not at all expected that a disciple have a wicked virtue and bad behaviour and give rise to falsities. Rituals, meditations, concentration, all should be understood only in this sense.

75. Having given wickedness and deception to the guru, expect no success. These grant only lifelong sadness and heartache. After death, and especially on one's deathbed, one has to undergo great agony.

76. Being favourable to our guru's mental state and remembering his expressions and state while performing various tasks profits us immensely in our own activities. In this exercise, there is no such thing as loss.

77. It is possible that, if you have not met your Divine Power yet, you may meet him through your disciple whom you have taught.

78. In guru's name, the impossible becomes possible. From then on one knows intimately that particular knowledge and becomes a wise person.

79. That guru of ours, that ascetic, that Divine Being, is very tranquil and 'stable'. Every level of his is linked to this earth.

80. With our intellect, heart and mind, with our deeds and words and our steadfast determination we should salute that boatman who has come to the bank to take us across the ocean of life, whether that be the last boat of our life, or a boat in the middle of our lives.

81. You should be attentive and stable. Otherwise, by your restlessness and perturbation, you might be uprooted and thrown away in the storms of life-circumstances. To get above those sad situations, pay attention to the signs in your guru. Those who depend upon their guru and who walk the path he shows are affected less by these trying circumstances. But if we keep ignoring him, if we have no faith or belief in him, if we have no interest in his instructions or directions, then to visit him is useless. We, then, exemplify the saying "A pig only likes slime, and *ketaki* wallows only in mud".

82. Brothers! Do not take whatever I am tell you the wrong way. It is not that I am trying to lead you on a wrong path, or to make you remember those painful blows to your emotions. I vow by my heartfelt best wishes, by the name of that Divine Mother and by her feet, that I say nothing false to you. Whatever I am saying is for your own good, for your welfare, and if you think this is right, you will pay attention. You will contemplate what I said to you, and what kind of a sculptor I am.

83. The doctors and healers of time and situation are the guru and the ruler. When they perform [as healers], they are very life-fulfilling.

God

Where is God? And how do you worship God? Baba's message is clear. God is everywhere and the best place to find God is within your own self. You yourself are nothing other than a reflection of God.

1. You should keep faith in God. God will also keep faith in you within himself.

2. One who sees Him everywhere keeps his behaviour and conduct self-controlled for fear of punishment or admonishment from Him. If we are even a little conscious towards that guru, or that Supreme Soul, or that Supreme Essence, then our actions can take good shape.

3. The moment just past, in which we meditated on the Self, is a Godly moment. The path that this thought of ours has shown us is a Godly path.

4. If we represent [in our characters] that entity of ours to whom we belong, it is completely within our rights to do so. Nobody can deprive us of that right. If we love God, if we love the Goddess, if we are worthy of their affection, then we will definitely have this character. Most definitely, yes.

5. It is not that I have known God only by experience, or seen Him or have understood Him. I have also talked with Him, I have heard His humming, and I have also received His inspirations.

6. It is the 'Unknown' who is the One that is everything, but seems like it is not. This is reality, Sudharma!

7. This instrument [of ours] within [our body] does not remain ignorant of that 'Unknown' deep within us whom we also

address as the 'Pure Essence' and the 'Tripura Bhairavi'. It is the destroyer of black thoughts on the path, and inspires s towards fearlessness, enthusiasm and affection.

8. In your own absence, your God does not even exist. First you are born, and then your God. First your understanding, and then the understanding of your God.

9. The supremely conscious mind has been addressed as 'God' here and there in these words.

10. Nothing ever happens within God. Human beings make God and then pray for all kinds of traits and virtues.

11. O human, frightened of the world! O saintly person who has come to the refuge of God! O traveller of the path shown by the soul! O [people who are] unmindful of the distractions of the mind! O people trapped in the mire of truth and untruth! Light the way to find the one who is beyond all this who is present within us. This organization is made up of people who do so. That is why it is known as Sarweshwari Samooh.

12. It may be that we regard that 'Pure Essence' as favourable to us and the Truth, but, actually, nothing happens within it.

13. O lost being! Do not lose your path while looking for God. If your heart is pure, God is with you. Don't you know that you are a temple of God, and that God resides within you?

14. No one person has a right on God. Also, God derives not pleasure from just one specific person, nor is any specific person a special devotee of God. Everybody has a right to Him. He is pleased with everyone. Everybody is His devotee. But to build a relationship with God, it is necessary for everyone to keep their soul clean. Only the one with a pure soul is worthy of achieving the Supreme Soul.

15. One whose mind is lost only in food and drinks and clothing and jewellery, his condition is worse than that of an animal. Only by becoming dependent on God can one be free of this slavery.

16. That who is 'Unknown', whom we do not see, nor know, nor understand, but who sees all our deeds and provides us with inspirations like a background shadow, I even feel affection, love and respect for that 'Unknown'.

17. You will not find any God or Goddess in any temple, religious place, in any idol or in heaven. It is necessary that they live in the company of saints, and the person who lives in the company of saints achieves Them. But the person whose temperament is exactly the opposite — incurable, who has no remedies within him, for him it is difficult to find Him.

18. We are searching for God. We look for Him in singing hymns and devotional songs, in monasteries and temples, and all the while, perhaps, he remains in the company of a sad woman in her sorrow, keeps standing with her at her little hut... He must be flowing in the tears of a helpless woman.

19. [This] is not a divinity which can be described [in a befitting manner] by any name or form. That is beyond name and form. My head is bowed to that 'Unknown' beyond all name and form. And if the hand of grace of that 'Unknown' is on us, then slowly everything in our life will pass away. Even difficult times will pass away; they will go away, there will be no obstacles.

20. If we pray to That, or think about That, or contemplate about That, for even a moment or half a moment in 24 hours, then that is sufficient for us.

21. God's traits and virtues arise in us every day — when we pray or contemplate on Him.

22. The one we call the Supreme Soul, the Great Soul, the one that is the Heavenly Soul, let us be completely covered by the lustre, the luminescence, the rays and the vibrations that arise from His body when we meet Him. So, we need to wake Him up. To wake Him, we sit in *asana*. We become triangular, like an instrument.

23. The Supreme Essence that we make all kinds of efforts to find is imbued in everything around us.

24. God, the wish-fulfilling tree of our own soul, should have nice desires about us. And those nice desires should be such that they make us think nice thoughts all the time. Think nicely about yourself, and think well about all those who are in your shelter, those who are dependent upon you. The day you begin to think in this way, and do not utter any inauspicious words towards them, then nothing inauspicious will happen.

25. God has already made all arrangements for every individual to know instantly all that happens from one end of the solar system to the other. He has not done this collectively. But your science has described it collectively and has demonstrated it before you.

26. He is not only kind; He is just too.

27. Friends, the one who is God will forgive everything of ours. But forgiveness does not mean He will let us leave with our ill-conceptions. He chastises us as well. That is why someone once said: "O formless God! How can one serve you?"

28. O formless, O Unknown. We want to serve you. But you are not an idol. You are not a picture. You are not a work of art created by an artist. You are incomparable. We cannot say you are only so long and this wide, or round or of such-and-such

a shape or form. That is why we touch you; we understand everything.

29. How can you designate something in one word as *alakh* (imperceptible, unknowable), when that entity is beyond the limits of words? How can you describe it in one word as *niranjan* (faultless, unblemished), as is popular in the language of the laity? This is not at all possible.

30. You should perform good deeds with your hands so that your hands may be effective in accomplishing their potential, for they are a symbol of great action. O Darshi! God is nothing different from this. Untiring effort is also known as God. The effort of the hands to seek *pran* is itself an untiring effort.

31. God's existence is in every particle of the world. A saintly person considers every particle to be a part of God.

32. O creature! To establish a close relationship with God, it is essential that you respect the existence and designated ethical conduct of every particle.

33. God is not achieved by leaving the home or through austere practices, difficult discipline in solitude, fasting, yoga or any other such path. In fact, he can even be found within a householder-life, without austere practices. And the only way to achieve God is the purity of the soul.

34. One who knows the reality of atheism cannot forget the reality of God.

35. One who gets to know the mystery of life both inside and out, and every way around, he gets to know both God and Godliness.

36. Where there is a lack of desire for luxury, in that heart God resides. It is very difficult for those who desire luxury and fame to achieve God.

37. Only after freeing yourself from all bondage can you become worthy of the company of God.

38. The point where our intellect gets tired and gives up — there, after that, it becomes easy to find God.

39. One who reflects well the beauty lying within, it is like that person has accomplished in a physical way the form of God right before him.

40. Brahman has neither form nor colour. It has no length, breadth, height, depth or dimensions. It is neither visible nor invisible. If you really want to look for Brahman then you should free yourself from all conceptions of form and colour, depth and dimension, visible and invisible, and worship your own Self truly. You will definitely experience Brahman; you will yourself will become Brahm-like.

41. It is not as if it rains but a little for a sinner and it rains more for a virtuous person, that the sun and the moon do not exist for the sinner and that the sky does not ever light up for the sinner while all these things do happen for the virtuous person. At the root of all these aggravations, all such divisive thinking lies our own ignorance and faulty understanding. The actual direction of that Supreme Essence is 'beyond all prescriptions and prohibitions'. We are the ones who give birth to 'yes' and 'no', not that Supreme Essence. We are the ones who give rise to good and bad and big and small, not that Supreme Essence. We are the ones who have created Brahmans, Kshatriyas, Vaishyas and Shudras, not that Supreme Essence. That Supreme Essence lies beyond all this, beyond time, beyond actions and deeds, and remains situated in that unfathomable state.

42. The bigger a vessel you become, the more can be filled into you. That 'Unknown' measures all on the same scale of worth and doles out to all with the same ladle, from humans to every other moving and non-moving being of the world, despite their roots differing according to their actions and backgrounds, form and colour. It is possible that, in the absence of appropriate worth, his distribution might appear to favour some more and others less, but that Supreme Essence as guru, as Truth, carefully measures and evaluates everyone on their worthiness and according to that, gives to them.

43. Despite being insulted by someone, or upon receiving invectives from them, you do not have the right to judge them. Justice will be done by God. You have the right to act — if you listen to the negative acts of others, then you become a co-sharer in that act.

44. Embracing each other makes us four-armed. This is a form of Vishnu. The God Vishnu has been addressed as ecstatic joy — he is known as a repository of unfathomable happiness and peace — an ocean of all graces: that is Vishnu, with his four arms. Like two lovers. This is what the wise have said in their colloquial language.

45. You turn back towards me. I will turn back towards you.

46. *Bhag* (vulva), *Bhagwan* (God), *Bhagawati* (Goddess), *bhagati* (*devotion*) — these are four names of just one entity. Not *Bhagwan*, but *bhag-yan* (the creative vehicle of the vulva). *Bhag* is a form of Vishnu, and is a source and centre of attraction for the world.

47. Sometimes, become stable within and contemplate the sky in whose emptiness you can see the good souls from far-off places whom you call God or saints. They don't really exist some-

where distant. If you can harmonize with them, this life of yours will become very accomplished.

48. The point beyond which we are not able to reach, there definitely exists a power beyond that which is acceptable to all. People of all nations and cultures, of every religion and community recognize that power. People with clear thoughts who are wise are always respectful towards that power.

49. We should definitely pray to God and to our guru like so: O God! Let me never insult or overlook saints and nice souls. I am very ignorant, I have never become wise, and it is unlikely I will become wise in this life. It must be the good deeds of many of my past lives that I have got this life, and with it the opportunity to contemplate on you and the company of my guru. Despite receiving all this I am still not able to do anything; I am dying, I drown in this ocean of life.

50. We pray to that Unknown: O God! O Mother! Please let me feel love and affection towards all. Let nobody be neglected by me, because this life is very short. It has very few days in it.

51. What we have been told of 'That' has all been proved wrong.

52. Gods and goddesses are not like what you see in cartoons. They do not carry swords and arrows and other weapons in their hands, but in fact are like you and I, and they also live amongst us. They are the Gods of the earth.

53. The talk about a God in the sky or in heaven is pure imagination. You will keep thinking about that all your life, and you will achieve nothing.

54. The worship performed with gold and silver can be ostentation. It can be counted in the category of egotism and

wickedness or deceit. Wickedness or deceit is not liked by God. God is never pleased by it.

55. If we really want to do something then let us get away from the worship of the God in heaven. God in heaven does not provide us the necessary materials of our life like flour, rice, water, salt and vegetables. If we are told about worshipping the God in heaven by an ascetic, or by a priest, or by a teacher or by a person weighed down by ephemeral ideas, then we should take any decision only after thinking about it thoroughly. Only then is it of value for you to come to this place of Aghor. After getting familiar with these [Aghor] ideas you will have to decide how big a war you will have to fight against the name and the form to which you are tied. You can be victorious by sacrificing it in the same way that you sacrifice anger. Every quarrel is only about this name and form... If you remain trapped in the ideas of the gods of the heaven, then you will remain neither of the earth nor of the heaven. We are forcing ourselves to go into a hell even more fearsome than hell itself.

56. Living a good life is like walking along the signs of God. To be able to do everything well, to walk on a straight path instead of a crooked path, is like walking where God tells us to.

57. Whatever we have received as God's grace from Him, let us live our life within that like a good human being.

58. When you gain true knowledge about that reality, then the boat of your life will go across the ocean of life even without oars, sail or a boatman. Otherwise, there are storms all around.

59. It is said God can be achieved within twenty-four hours. God can be found within twelve hours. God may also not be found even after trying for 24,000 years. Say what? You should sit with a concentrated mind. Let no form arise in your mind.

Let no word arise in your heart. When your mind will be cool, within it shall be born your dear divine's form. You will hear his voice in there. But as long as other voices are echoing in there, you will never hear his voice. At that time many kinds of assaults will also be made upon you [to distract you]. Bad thoughts will begin to arise in you. Some very beautiful women may walk right before of you. Naked women may walk right in front of you. Many beautiful people may walk right in front of you. If you feel attracted even a little bit to these, if your eyes open and you feel like glancing back to look at them, then you are lost. You have been defeated. The thing you seek will not come into your hands. So, first, make sure whether in the course of 24 hours you can keep your mind calm like this! If you can, then it will not take you even twelve hours.

60. O friend! The thing that you want to conquer with cleverness, the same cleverness has produced the being that conquers you. You should not forget that death has been following you since the day you were born. The day you started being clever, you produced a being 100 times more clever than you, a being who will destroy you. The place where you will realize your ambitions, from that same very high place he will push you down so that you will fall on the rocks below; you will splatter into smithereens. However big a person may you be in this universe, you will not be excused. Nobody is excused. Even Krishna was not excused.

61. The person who goes close to God takes his society with him.

62. Your own faith should be in yourself. You deserve your own worship. You are, wherever you are. If you had not been here then I would not have been either. Because you have come, so have I. In the same way, your own presence is also the presence of that God. Your own birth also gives birth to that entity we call God. Your being, itself, is also his being. Your life itself is also his life. Without you, he is nothing. The day you recognize

your own glory, your source, that day you will be counted in the category of the very great. You are no less than God. You yourself are God.

63. We cannot say taking what forms and in which places and in what ways He comes amongst us. The tendencies of animosity that arise amongst your parents, and your friends and relatives, this is no gift of His. It is a gift of ours.

64. God always lives with his devotees who are ego-free, deceit-free, and wickedness-free.

65. You can only look at an idol; it shan't touch you. That idol will not ask you to sit next to it. You will be only asked to sit by those two-armed gods, Shiva and Vishnu, who move and walk like you. They are not four-armed because the four-armed entity remains absolutely absorbed in itself.

66. You won't find the God you are looking for until you find yourself.

67. When you are able to establish harmony with divine souls, then as soon as you start reciting your mantra everything begins to happen according to your desire. You will begin to understand the indications of your dear divinity and you will experience joy in solitude. The happiness and joy that you experience in solitude is only a gift of this; otherwise, who wants to be alone?

68. It is you who becomes God. It is you who becomes the divinity. When your conduct and behaviour, thoughts and action become good, when your desires and determinations will become good, then you will become great. That Unknown will be aware of your greatness. Many souls, who even divinities meet only with difficulty, will arrive in their bodies to converse with you, and you will talk with them, move with

them, walk with them. In every kind of happiness and sorrow, those souls will help you. It is not that you will just catch a glimpse of them.

69. I speak neither about the formless [form of God] nor the with-form [form of God]. I speak about what lies in between the two — and in today's times, this middle ground will be best for us.

70. The day our intellect becomes right we will not perceive the difference between the formless and the with-form. If you have a properly discriminating intellect, and if you are able to use it, then your God, your Goddess, your divinity will appear even in stones, trees or leaves. That divinity will appear through your love. Whether or not it be God, they will take the form of our love and become God. This is what is known as worship with form; that which is formless is formless itself. That is omnipresent. That appears only through love. Where there is love there are no rules, no regulations, no formality. Yes: an intellect which makes right determinations is important.

71. Regarding that God, your own presence, you purity, your faith, your affection, and your interest in auspicious actions is more important.

72. The humans who are conscious of that Truth, and the essence of that Truth, and those who have faith in it, all their tasks are successful.

73. O Supreme Soul! Make me as you want me to become. What I want to become might just be a flight of my fancy. It is possible this might leave my life incomplete. And I may lose the justification for begetting this human life. Then I will remain stuck in this same muck, and remain afflicted by attachment to others, like a bull tied to a stake. Then I will remain afflicted by illusions that will never go away.

74. If we properly understand the divinity of our worship then we can understand the Supreme Being who has been spoken about in all religious books and who has been sought by every saint and *mahatma*. That is a very small spark which ignites the whole haystack of sorrow; the sorrows burn up and turn to ash.

75. When you slowly begin to experience that Supreme Essence in your life, then, rising above the attachments and desires in this life, you will be successful in everything.

76. One who has found has not found it.
One who has understood has not known it.
One who did not see, is the one who has seen it.
One who did not find, is the one who found it.
One who did not understand, is the one who understood it.
One who says he understands 'That' is himself in a bad state. He is giving rise to all kinds of troubles. One who says that he has not seen 'It' — he's fine: he's stable and calm. He is free from the slavery of his mind.

77. O Supreme Soul! O Truth! O Unknown! All that I have said or done has been because of this mind. So please do not listen to it. For, our mind does not move with our body. Our body is running to one place. Our mind is running someplace else. When our mind, body and our action, when all three are running in different directions, how can we say we are present and devoted before you with everything we have?

78. We can see our gods and goddesses in every bird, all vegetation, every vine, every tree, and every animal. The vehicles [of the gods] have been described [in the sacred texts]; when we begin to recognize the signs of the gods by seeing their vehicles, then we will be fully capable to have their knowledge. And this is what is known as true knowledge.

79. 'That' is moving very fast, 'That' is never there. 'That' is not like what we say is its nature and character, its name and form, and imagine it and pray to it as that. 'That' is not like that at all. We just feel it to be so, like a dream. Whatever is happening within us, 'That' is like that, and similar things happen within 'That' as well. To understand differently than this is to keep ourselves in darkness, the ultimate consequence of which is that, instead of fighting our beastly tendencies, we run away from them.

80. To think that we can do everything or that we are indispensable for a certain task is wrong thinking. We cannot say how, when, and in what form His grace alights upon us, sitting in whose cool shade we remove the burning gasp from our breath, we give up the desires and stresses and worries burning us, and become stable. After becoming stable we become enlightened, and become such heroes that we prove ourselves worthy of destroying the bestial tendencies that exist within us, within society, and within the nation.

81. When that divinity of ours, our own Self, becomes favourable to us, then all our senses —which are doorways for lesser divinities to feed on us — will become quiet. We will achieve that great *samadhi* (ecstatic consciousness).

82. Without uttering a single word, if you say something silently, from anywhere [in the world], He will hear you immediately. If we utter what we must say, our voice might break, our words could get dispersed or be misdirected. Those words can then get transformed into something else, and He can impute some other meaning from it. And the entity who understands it, if He does not have His mind with Himself, then he can end up doing all sorts of things. Then how will He provide liberation to us? How will we become liberated?

83. An idol of the divinity does not produce any sound. Its closed speech and unsaid words produce a certain kind of reaction in your body, by which a strange chemical is produced in your blood, flesh and marrow which makes you feel that your dear divinity, your guru, your God, has given you much. It is immensely satisfying.

84. All our divinities have good character, and we worship divinities with good characters. Our divinities are not given to anger, or to greed, or to attachments, nor have they ever indulged in these tendencies.

85. People of questionable blood or birth are not our leaders. Our leaders are our God, our Goddess, our Unknown, whom we cannot see, to whom we pray. We think He cannot hear it. He hears everything. He does what's favourable for us, and doesn't do what isn't favourable for us. He knows by doing unfavourable things, bad traits will rise in us.

86. May that God, may that Goddess give all of you the inspiration from my side, that you should not lose your path even in the most difficult circumstances.

87. O Mother! I am seeking shelter in you. Give me the grace of being fearless. If her hand is upraised then it is known as the grace of fearlessness; if her hand points downward then it is known as the grace of boons granted. We do not need a boon right now. We do need fearlessness.

88. The divinity hidden within us rings a bell before each good or bad deed. He makes us aware of each of the good or bad action of ours.

89. If your life is self-controlled, you will get to know the essence of the mantra *tatsat*. After knowing all this you will see right before you the idol that you want to see. You will talk with it.

You will sit and move with it. You will be able to tell your sorrows to it. It will be ready to listen, because that entity also lives in great sorrows and troubles. Because He has given His word: "I do not live in the heaven, nor do I live in the heart of the yogis. I live with those who sing about me, who remember me."

90. He is completely imbued everywhere, in every particle. Now how much worthiness do you have, how big is your vessel? Depending upon that, He will alight to that extent in you.

91. When you begin to follow your real livelihood with enthusiasm and if you have the eagerness to get to know the Goddess, the God, or the Supreme Nature, then they will rise within you, and you will be able to know them. They are nothing different from you, friends! Whatever gods and goddesses and divinities that you see around, all of them have been determined by you. When you get to properly know that Truth you will think that, if your behaviour, conduct and ideals remain pure, then everything will remain pure. Every god, goddess, divinity, tantra and mantra will be within your hands. That entity will remain within your hands like a fruit in your palm, the one whom many devotees address as the Mother.

92. He has a very bad name in this world. God has to hear invectives not a hundred thousand but a million times every day. That much he has to suffer, those words — not only in this country, but in every country. How do I know! How did the same happen to me, I don't know, friends. And then there is the word Aughar attached to it. Even this is a strange word [to most people]. I cannot say whether because they understand it, or whether because they do not understand it. But it is a name that is constantly ridiculed because when you are good even then you are called bad, and when you are in a bad condition even then people say, "O, beat him up, he didn't do things that I wanted him to do for me". In these conditions,

in this hut lives the being who has this name [God]. And I am with that being. Now you will understand that if somebody lives with a person who is notorious, then the person living with him will also get a bad reputation. As it is, I have a bad name anyway...

93. Let us remember that Supreme Soul whom we have never seen; we do not see it, yet its grace remains on us. You have seen how by twelve noon, your shadow comes very close to you. When darkness arrives, your shadow will begin to run farther and farther away. Who gives us this knowledge? That Supreme Consciousness, the Super Nature that is within us gives us this knowledge, saying "Listen and beware, for bad days are going to come upon you". Or, "Good days are going to come to you now". This is where we have to keep our feet steady, friends.

94. If we do not provide indulgence to our senses then how will the lesser divinities [who are the masters of these senses] eke out their livelihood? All those beings we call divinities will die away.

95. This is the supreme knowledge. We will have to give up the [prevalent conception of the] Truth as well, which we know as such-and-such a person being so-and-so, that this is the good, that this is the divinity, that they have these traits, that they have these characters, and that they have such and such things.

The Living Being

In Hindu philosophy the living being has two integral aspects, the jiva or the living organism, and the atma, the soul, which animates it. But is the jiva just a body made of flesh and bones? Not at all. In this jiva, the body that is animated by the God-particle atma, resides God himself, and the combination of these two, Jivatma, should be treated as such.

1. *Jiva* (the subtle living being) has no form. It is experienced like the air, like a fragrance, like the rays of the Sun. Its form and figure, its life-breath is to be experienced in every living being — but it is not seen. Aughars, you should know to be so.

2. *Atma* (the soul) is imbued in everything, like the sky. The soul can be known by the instrument of memory through the power of the intellect.

3. Our mind and heart are reflections of the soul, and knowing these lets us experience the soul.

4. There is as much difference between the mind and the soul as is between the sight and the scene. The sight itself is the scene.

5. You should know that you are a temple of God. That is because God lives in you.

6. In the arsenal of the soul, speech is the best weapon. To use it appropriately makes your life successful.

7. To recognize the voice of the soul according to the changing times is a supreme duty of human beings. Properly understanding what the soul says, make auspicious and divine resolutions.

8. Through the with-form (*Sagun*: God with qualities) itself, you can get to know the formless (*Nirgun*: God beyond qualities).

9. Brahm cannot be achieved through physical strife or yogic practices. A true householder should adopt a more appropriate path of achieving the Brahm. If you want your life to be imbued with Brahm, adopt its virtues.

10. Listen to the voice of the soul. Do not act on the voice of the mind.

11. We do not even know how extensively the ghost, the bad soul hiding within us, pushes us into difficult situations and takes us towards wrong actions. The reason for this is that we do not believe the words of the guru, the saints, or good people. If we believe in their words, if we walk on the path indicated by them, very easily — and very quickly — we reach our goal. And when we reach our goal, with great joy, great happiness and great peace we discover our life and the secrets of our life. It cannot even be said how great a joy we then experience.

12. In one way or another, everybody is living, some way or another, lugging around their own baggage. In some senses their life has some value, in other senses, it has none; their life is absolutely useless in some senses, and in other senses it is useful, too. And the decision of 'yes' and 'no' here will be taken by the Unknown.

13. O human being! The voice of the mind is not correct. The mind is unstable. Its instability takes you to the edge of the abyss of numerous material indulgences. If you really want to live a sweet life, you should learn to recognize the voice of the soul — and remember, your soul will always give you the right inspiration. It provides light like a candle.

14. By praying to Ma-Guru, beings become indestructible. By contemplating on *atmaram* (the Soul-God) every trouble is destroyed right at its root. One who recognizes the voice of the soul sees even those things that are invisible.

15. That little lamp of ours, that little candle of ours, is always ready to give us ample light. And, on the one hand the arrival of the night, and on the other hand the chirping of the birds with the arrival of the light of the dawn — these two things show us that we should not be disappointed, we should remain very hopeful. Definitely, our real truth will take us to our ultimate goal. Let us not be discouraged at all. Whatever we are doing, whatever we are made to do or whatever we end up doing, it is all by grace of the divine, it is all a kindness of the divine. We do not have even a little bit of an egotistical part in it.

16. This body is a corpse. On this corpse the seeker-soul, relinquishing its weaknesses, with great determination, enhances its power of pure desires. Try that this may be so. Then, when this power becomes strong, whatever you wish shall happen.

17. This soul that is ours — if we try to find something through abandoning the reflection of that soul, then this thing is impossible to find. It is absolutely impossible.

18. It is the commands of the soul that bring meaning to a fruitful life. Not listening to them brings disappointment and failure.

19. The soul is indestructible. Conquer-ability and invincibility have no meaning for the soul. And the soul acquires complete peace through good conduct and a self-absorbed sentiment.

20. Everything is easily available in this world for a pure soul.

21. The primary centre of happiness and peace is the purity of the soul. To achieve purity of the soul is a difficult practice.

22. O children of the spiritual path! The indestructible that is in your soul, this is the light of the path of the cosmic creator Maheshwar. Your entire life should be devoted towards gaining an experience of this light. This light should provide inspiration and strength, it should be all the momentum of your life. This essence of the truth of life and religion provides an experience of the Truth in this ephemeral creation and establishes your place in it.

23. On hearing the words of the soul, tell no one else. Just ponder it within your mind.

24. One whose soul has died is a walking grave.

25. Do not be afraid of those who inflict injury on your body. They can never even touch your soul.

26. An Aughar has a soul-centred intellect. Likewise should you be absorbed in the soul.

27. The soul itself is the guru. The soul itself is the wish-granting tree. Wishes made under this tree are certainly fulfilled. Therefore, you should protect your soul. Protection of the Self is the biggest duty.

28. The voice of the mind is never united. You should listen to the primary voice of the soul.

29. Inspirations come from within a human being from two different directions. The first inspiration comes from the direction of the soul; the second, from that of the mind. There is a great difference between the soul and the mind. The soul gives your heart the right inspiration, while the mind in its turbulence makes the person wander lost in every ephemeral moment. Therefore, listen to the voices of your souls, and listen not to those seekers and ascetics who listen to the voice of their mind.

30. O souls! Accept that which is a complement of your inner light in the cosmos.

31. Knowledge of the Self is the best amongst all kinds of knowledge, for its acquisition destroys the numerous desires of the mind.

32. The being is indestructible, but suffering the fruits of your actions is inevitable. Hence, you should remain involved in good actions.

33. Peace is the biggest fountainhead of the soul; non-peace is the greatest power that lessens it. But, if you find everlasting peace in your soul, then disturbances can never enter therein.

34. There are two categories of beings in this world. One kind of being has life in it, and the other kind of being is a being in itself, but it does not have life in it.

35. Life-force is a kind of air, but Being is just Being. It is to be found in the inactive and non-moving as well as in the active and the conscious.

36. Every being, every type of being in this world — each has a natural process which everyone knows. These natural processes happen every day for everyone, in excreting, eating and numerous other natural acts, which everyone is forced to do every day.

37. Trees, vines and the like are also *jiva*, but they do not have the *pran*. That is why, when you cut them, they immediately become numb. But there are some beings who do not become numb immediately when cut.

38. We have not even realized the soul as yet. We remain merely distracted in the many considerations of beings, life-force and the numerous living entities.

39. Self-control is not just a word. It includes everything like getting up, speaking, talking, walking and moving. If you remain disciplined in a good way and if you get away just a little bit from the natural tendencies of the beings of this world, and get away a little bit from the life-force as well, and go into the world of the soul, then you will get to know in advance from the sky, or from people unknown to you, or through the voice of your children, what is going to happen in the future. You will know what will happen today, what will happen tomorrow, what happened a little while ago, and what happened after that. You will have a very concrete experience of this.

40. Let all the beings of this world acquire a soul-consciousness, and in that soul-consciousness, let them have a vision of the soul.

41. On attaining his goal, a person rises from the state of being an inconsequential tuft of straw to that of becoming the goal itself; the goal which is acceptable to everyone, which is praise-worthy, and which is to be revered by everybody.

42. If you are just sitting there and your time passes away, then this is known as death. You are dying slowly every moment, moment by moment. And you are not even thinking of becoming free from this state.

43. One should not dirty a clean and pure place by either spitting or excreting there, because a good soul might be living there. It is possible that, due to some reason, a great soul may have taken birth there in the form of trees or vines, and may be spending its time there in that form. Many great souls remain in some places for hundreds of years waiting to be rid of their curses, in the same way that many bad souls, falling into desire, wander lost for hundreds of years in the form of tiny little floating particles in the air.

44. This life is slipping away at a very fast pace. Childhood is gone and youth is about go. Slowly, humans progress towards a certain apex, and then they begin to roll downwards. Everyone is going through this process. It is an absolute truth and this will happen to everybody.

45. People say that if you can make your mind listen to you, then this will be very good. But the good comes not by the mind merely listening to you. Yes! if the mind is within itself, if it is not mindless, then it will be useful. But if your mind is not within itself, if it is mindless, then you will have to suffer pain and agony just searching in the wilderness of the mind.

46. Whatever I have said you will understand only if your understanding is within your understanding, but if you are venturing somewhere in a far-off place, then you will not understand what I am saying. If you are wandering somewhere else inside yourself, then what I am saying will not have any effect on you. Actually, it is your ideas that I am expressing. In this way, then, you will remain deprived of your own wealth, of your own inheritance. I hope you will remain here. One who remains with himself, everyone comes and wants to meet him.

47. In the same way that *kama* or carnal desires enter somebody's body and force them towards lascivious acts, so also do bad souls abduct the souls of great people, of good people, and thus overpowering them they sit within them and, influencing their conduct, thoughts and behaviour, make them do unwanted acts. So as well, bad and dirty souls enter our minds and prompt us to believe in all sorts of undesirable things.

48. Without tact, even that [good] soul can run away from you. Devotion without this deliberate intention can be terrifying, in the same way that a parrot that learns to recite "Rama, Rama" forgets it and begins to cry when it is caught by a cat. But, then, it doesn't cry "Rama, Rama".

49. The 'Self' that we have, and the divinity of the earth, of this land where we live — we are at fault for neglecting them both, and our ambition to acquire heaven, or earth or the netherworld also remains unfulfilled. And then again, what will we do with it anyway, even if we do get the kingdom of these lesser divinities [of the senses] who are weak, greedy and unethical? In our history, I have heard that demons had even snatched away their kingdoms many a time, and made them weak.

50. Without liberation from the process of birth, one does not become truly free. We keep wandering lost like tiny particles in the atmosphere. Despite being bodiless, we will still be afflicted by desire and greed. We will see all kinds of tantalizing material things around us but we won't be able to get them. We will keep wandering lost, like tiny particles.

51. You should not think that every soul is good and that you have to behave the same with each one of them. This will not be discriminate; in fact this will be an indiscriminate tactlessness due to which, instead of becoming worthy, you can also become unworthy.

52. This life is like the flame of a candle. The wind is blowing very hard. You must always be careful that it does not blow out in that wind. Life runs towards darkness again and again. But this light is the only thing, and this light itself is life, O seeker.

53. One who becomes liberated never dies. One who is liberated remains ever present, at all times. He remains for all days that are there.

54. Our own Self gives rise to negativities in us, and gets us trodden underfoot. And if it wants, from its own side it can have a harmonious tie with its own Self, that omnipotent consciousness, and thus win a big prize beyond value.

55. [Be aware whether] the breath that is coming out of your nostril is long or short. Does it extend to two inches or four, and what kinds of forms take shape within it? Be aware whether those forms are influencing your mentality adversely. Also, be aware whether it is the form of that dear divinity of yours that you're so eager to see.

56. Yes, what within us is most intimate? If can discover this, then we will understand what we have been until today. Are we what we seem to be or are we something different from that? If we understand this, we will get to know everything about ourselves, we will understand everything, we will know everything.

57. Because of our excessive cleverness, we have stopped respecting that Soul. It is because of this that we have to suffer all sorrows. Let us do just one thing: let us give up our cleverness. Let us be devoted to the service of that Unknown.

58. Happiness, peace and prosperity take birth amidst nice souls. The person in whose home good souls arrive in the form of sons or daughters, or a wife or a friend, they learn every truth.

59. Let us finish everything we have left to do in this life itself, so that we do not have to take birth again, to endure the process of rebirth again.

60. When the soul gets separated [at death] from the body with desires, overwhelmed by desires it then wanders for many days in desolate and dry places without food and water as a ghost in this solar system. This ghost-soul remains deprived of drinking water despite living next to a river. It is unable to satisfy its hunger despite living in a house full of food. Things absolutely do not remain in that soul's sphere of rights any longer. If it wants to steal something, even that it cannot do — in the same way that you desire many things but are not able to achieve them.

61. Friends! As long as we do not become like roasted seeds, we will keep taking rebirth. We will die again and again and we will suffer sorrows again and again.

62. If you are involved in acrimony, then when your soul leaves your body it will have to wander for thousands of years as a ghost-soul, like those tiny motes in the atmosphere.

63. Austere practices are not involved with torturing the body, suppressing your senses, prohibitions on interaction or food and drinks. Neither is it true penance to lose yourself here and there in poems, stories or scriptural things, because such penance and being lost [in stories etc.] keeps us away from getting to know that Unknown, the essence of the scriptures, and ourselves.

64. This life is momentary. We don't know how long it will last.

65. This life itself is a life of dreams. This life and the whole world are made up of dreams. All these dreams about our life that we see, all these dreams that arise in us will all disappear on the arrival of light. As soon as we wake up, all this will end. But right now, because of our minds, we are afflicted by desires and we keep running here and there, like deer.

66. Bad souls live with you folks, amidst you, in the same form as yours. You know very well how much hatred you produce within yourself the day you put your hand into the hand of a bad soul. Self-conceit begins to rise within you. Because of self-conceit, you get involved in many bad actions, and you reach such a low state that your invaluable life becomes cursed; it comes to an end, and then — for thousands of years — our soul wanders as tiny particles in the spaces between the planets, between the earths and the stars.

67. Whatever thoughts we think once we get up from bed in the morning, sitting under the wish-granting tree of our soul,

similar things will we keep getting the whole day long. If we think about evil things, Satan rises before us. If we think about good behaviour, then the whole day is spent in good deeds. The kind of thought-determination that we make, everything begins to happen that way. The person who has pure thought-determination gains everything like fruit dropping into the palm of his hand.

68. When your soul becomes very strong, and once you've relinquished everything your mind tells you, you begin to talk with the soul; whatever arises within you, all that will be fulfilled. Let us keep pure the purity of this pure soul of ours. It is that which will give everything to us.

69. Many people have grown tired, floundering in this ocean of life. We can see that the possibility of our dying within ourselves has increased. If we die within [ourselves], then that consciousness that is within us will be lost for hundreds of thousands of years, and we will wander as tiny motes in the atmosphere for thousands upon thousands of years. Due to our desires we will remain unsatisfied in this atmosphere and we will hear, understand and experience the various kinds of pains that affect us. Although this doesn't really happen, it seems so.

70. From his place in the cremation ground, the divinity of the cremation ground calls to you that your body — which you've taken to be everything, which you're so conceited about, with which your name and prestige and everything else that you call your own is associated, and which you call your own — that this body is for him, now. It is pre-ordained that this body will one day be burnt in the fire of the cremation ground, yet nevertheless you do not strive to find yourself.

71. Chase away bad souls. Social life is growing poisoned; light some lamps.

72. In every house, our own enemies from earlier times get reborn within the family and create all kinds of frustration, all kinds of sorrow, all kinds of pain.

73. We divide things into heaven and hell and then wish for heaven. But heaven is nothing that can be indulged in without the body. What will you do with heaven without your body? Your good actions themselves are the form of heaven. And actions are performed through the medium of the body. When a person performs good actions he rises from the level of a human to the position of a divinity. But if he remains human and spends his life like a little insect from hell, then he will be born like an insect from hell and die like an insect from hell.

74. Whatever wrongful or proper wandering — or eating, or drinking — that you have performed to calm yourself or to be rid of your stress, or which just happened through you in some way, one tones for all this by simply remembering your guru or God. By going to those sacred places where lies the dust of great and pure souls, if even a particle of that dust falls on us then our body of blood, flesh, bones, excrement and urine will find redemption.

75. When I approach you, when I meet you, then I too find many changes taking place in my temperament, that "such-and-such a thing should not be done; it is a low act". It happened, but I will forget it now. If it happens again, then I'll remember my guru. If it happens again, then I will remember my divinity. If it happens again then I'll remember my parents and the glory of my family. Now it will not happen again. But if this thing keeps happening again and again then I will discipline myself to be time and period bound, and then I'll welcome it.

76. I see some people saluting gods and goddesses, the divinities and the great souls by lying fully stretched on their belly, like a stick. Now, a stick is like a cane for the elderly. [And their

feeling is] "Oh God, I fall at your feet like a stick". Whose stick is it? Of an old person. We are old souls. Now, this old soul which has gone through life and death many a times and has reached this point, it should gain liberation. Please pick up this stick. This is the purpose of prostrating ourselves before God. One who falls prostrate before his divinity does not have a short life. He has a very long life, friends.

77. A human's faith is his eyes, a human's good scriptures are his eyes, a human's humanity is his eyes, and that humanity is imbued with the intimacy of his soul. One who has such soul-intimacy with everyone is a very great person. He cannot be evaluated even on the scales of God.

Kapaleshwar

Kapaleshwar is the name given to that rather detached, somewhat formidable form of the God Shiva who is the dear divinity of Aughar ascetics. By performing ascetic practices, even a human being can reach the state of being a kapaleshwar.

1. The person who has devoured time is known as a Kapalik, one who calls home the skull of the sky, one who is the maker of the entire cosmos.

2. That Kapaleshwar cannot be measured either by knowledge or by devotion; he just cannot be measured. Knowing him depends entirely upon his grace.

3. The plants and vegetation, the vines and the leaves of the ashram live in peace and happiness; waving their green petals, they express their immeasurable love for you. Look at this source of sweet joy in the form of God Kapaleshwar.

4. All the devotees, gentle people, seekers who come to the ashram — if you give the dust fallen from their feet to some sick, unhappy or mentally pained person by remembering God Kapaleshwar, then how happy and satisfied that person becomes!

5. The fruits and flowers, the trees and vines, the dirt and dust and everything else of the ashram come within the category of Kapaleshwar, within the category of Shiva. This is what is known as the sacred dust, and the glory of that dust.

6. One who has heard the sweet voice of the Kapaleshwar has not even the smallest desire to hear or know of the music or poetry or sweet words of anyone else.

7. When you get to know yourself, then you can understand the Kapaleshwar from up close, in the same way that nobody can actually see the life-force, but everyone still knows that the life-force is present in the living being. Know him in the same way: he will be there only when you are there.

8. He was. I asked, how were you? [He then replied:] Here in the bowl of the sky, where the Kapaleshwar lives. In this same sky-bowl. I used to live as a subtle soul.

9. The sky and the earth: these two messengers of God Kapalik are everywhere. They watch everyone's good as well as bad actions.

10. O Kapalik! Face the situations that come before you with patience. One who battles the situations that arise in life is the best person. In the same way that exercise improves the body, and the mind improves by solving complex problems, so also facing difficult situations begets us the inner strength of the soul.

11. O Kapalik! Human beings come in this world with some specific purpose in hand. The work that really interests you is your real work. The path of your fate is made by the lines of your behaviour and conduct. If you have found your appropriate place, then devote all your mental and physical strength to make it successful. You will definitely achieve success.

12. O sons of the sacred way! The Indestructible that is within your soul is the sacred light of Maheshwar [Shiva], the Kapalik of the sky. Your whole should be spent seeking an experience of this light.

13. At the boundary of this ashram, next to the meeting hall, sitting atop the palm trees, I watched vultures talking amongst themselves today. Standing there, I listened to their conver-

sation. I do not understand their language very well, but I do understand it a little bit from being close to them. Because they are associated with the cremation ground and dead bodies, and many of my actions are also associated with the dead body, the cremation ground, the creative energy and those vulture friends.

14. One who keeps his mind carefully under control is known as a truly detached person, as Aughar-Aghoreshwar, as Kaul-Kapaleshwar.

The Body

In Indian thought, the body has oft been called a microcosm that represents the macrocosm. Within the microcosm reside hundreds of worlds, the creator of the cosmos and the animating power of the universe. Those who talk about the body being a temple should also treat it so, for herein resides the deity that they worship outside.

1. Seekers! Know that person to be *aghoreshwar* who makes his body a repository of virtues, who worships virtues, who cultivates virtues, and who constantly finds virtues within himself.

2. The purpose of the body is action, but the purpose of action is to find the *atma.*

3. When you get to know yourself then you can understand the Kapaleshwar, in the same way that nobody can actually see the life-force, but everyone still knows that the life-force is within the living being. Know him in the same way: he'll be there only when you're there.

4. How do we know what the eye sees, and what speech says? The eyes have no speech, and speech has no eyes.

5. Oh! Liberation matters to that person who, living in the body, thinks only as a living being with a body. One who lives in the body but is inspired by the sentiment of the eternal Brahm, he needs no liberation, he needs no position. Also, for him, heaven and hell do not exist.

6. Your inner being is very pervasive. It makes someone else say the things you should hear. This inner being is such an instrument that, through what one hears from another's speech,

we hear what we need to hear. We do not know what kinds of instruments exist in this body.

7. The excrement and urine, the muck that we have in our body — it's because of this muck that our body is clean and healthy. It has strength. It has power. We derive strength from it. A human being without this muck becomes very pitiable.

8. Your own body is like a corpse and on your body many lowly desires have realized their fulfilment. You also can keep it very fulfilling by thinking nice thoughts.

9. Everything can be achieved through this body.

10. Divine rays are inseparably associated with our body. However, they only stay near those people who are worthy of them.

11. Let us focus our attention on the instrument that Kapaleshwar has put into our own skulls. In this instrument, all the knowledge and all the sciences are indicating the right path and direction.

12. Speech is an instrument in which arises every truth. Speech is the only instrument of its kind which pervades and comes to light everywhere at the same time.

13. The conscience is purified through action. First comes action, then comes knowledge; each is a complement of the other. Without one, the other remains incomplete. When the conscience is purified through action, knowledge arises.

14. Purification of the body is known as *tap* (austere practice). These practices should be undertaken early, in one's youth.

15. If you have affection and love for the glory of the body, then be kind to it. My kindness is not so important, as your own kindness can help you be free.

16. O Kapalik! The human body has a great purpose: remember, you can find a home again and again, you can gain the earth again and again, you can find friends again and again, and you can find a wife again and again, but you will not get a human body again and again. Hence, having received this human body, you should do that which will make your life very clean.

17. On getting the human body one should definitely do some respectable deeds to be of benefit to this world, as well as to the other.

18. The source of energy is within our body itself.

19. The strongest element present in the body both produces and nurtures life. The body cannot withstand its misuse.

20. To increase the glory of your country, to increase the glory of your culture, and as an inheritance from your ancestors, you have found this body. For the happiness and peace of others, learn about the many different [mysterious] things that happen in this body.

21. The body — for which we fall to a very pitiable state, or which we put through every kind of distortion — this same body, if we walk the right path in our speech, will let us achieve progress in possessing our innate knowledge.

22. Vibrations emanate from every person's body. Some people give off very polluted vibrations, dirty vibrations, foolish vibrations. And from some people, if they have a pure body and a high and proper understanding, very nice vibrations emanate.

23. These senses of ours, these are the very same demigods that produce all kinds of obstacles. As long as they're being fed, they'll be greedy for more.

24. There are nine senses, and then there is one mind. As soon as they see any fodder for their indulgence, they open every door and say "Welcome, welcome!"

25. The head is known as the king; the belly is known as the *vaishya* (trader, merchant). The two together are also known as *vaishwanar*. We constantly put oblations into this *vaishwanar*. If we don't feed this *vaishwanar*, our body won't be able to function. It will become very frail, fall to the earth, and break.

26. It is as gold mixed with poison:
A beautiful body, with bad actions.

27. Even if we close all these ten doors, a pile of garbage accumulates in this house [of the body]. We have to constantly keep sweeping and mopping it. Then only can we experience cleanliness. Cleanliness is very pleasing. It is, of course, beneficial for us, but it's also beneficial for others.

28. While cremating a dead body, the skull is broken open because the life-force known as *dhananjaya-pran* remains in the skull. *Dhananjaya-pran* never goes away. Through the medium of that *dhananjaya-pran*, many beings can be brought under control, and beings can also be moved from one place to another. It happens, and it happens all the time on this earth. This is known as Tantra.

29. With good thoughts along with contemplation, keep doing good acts with your hands and feet and your body so that they remain straight and healthy, and keep functioning well.

30. We are all worried about making a name for ourselves. And what should the name be? That's really not so important. Today, we're born in this house and so we have this name. Tomorrow we'll be born in a different house and then we'll have a different name. The day after that, we'll have yet another

name. The form that our body has now, this form has never remained constant — not throughout childhood, nor through youth, nor through old age. It is rapidly moving towards frailty and decay.

31. O conqueror of the senses! After conquering them, always remain very vigilant about your victory. And keep secure the fortress of your body, in which resides a weak mind that produces fear. Otherwise, this fortress of glass can easily break with the slightest blow, O seeker.

32. As long as you stayed in the eternal form (*safal yoni*) you lived in joy, you lived in peace and your life was very happy. But the day you disregarded that achievement and came into this condition, that day everything that had been yours was snatched away from you. All your happiness, peace and joy have been snatched away from you. Now, what remains? Only a body of flesh and bones! And that body experiences diseases, it experiences sorrow, it experiences troubles, it experiences decay, and it experiences many ups and downs. You cannot escape this.

33. Vibrations give us inspirations. If our mind and heart are in a proper state, then we will certainly find happiness and peace. In this sacred place of the *siddhas* [spiritually realized persons, with special reference to Krin Kund in Varanasi], the sky and the directions all around are imbued with the light of their souls. If we are worthy enough, and if our heart and mind are attuned, then — despite being hundreds of thousands of miles away — we can get good inspirations [from here]. But if our heart and mind are not attuned, then despite being nearby, we remain deprived of that light and those vibrations.

34. At every moment we are beset by the three maladies of phlegm, bile and gastric troubles. But we want respite from these three maladies because their disorder means certain death. That is

why we need to understand our energy flowing in these veins. The day we understand the process of these veins, we can take appropriate measures to be free of these three maladies.

35. Every part of our body — hands, feet, heart, mind etc. — is our friend. If even a fly alights upon our body, the hand swats it away. If the body hurts, the hand holds it. But our own blood is our enemy. When a deer is wounded by the hunter's arrow and flees, it is the blood dripping from the deer's body which tells the hunter the path that the deer has taken and where it hides! In the same way, the sun is a friend of the lotus, but if there is a scarcity of water, the same sun burns the lotus and destroys it.

36. One who sits in solitude, or — if he is concentrated — even in a crowd, then by watching the length, force and shapes of his exhalation, he can easily determine his tasks for the day. It's very good if the length of the breath is short. If it's long, this means that there will be sorrow. It can pull one towards material indulgence. The shorter the length of the breath the better it is. If the breath stops within, this is even more joyful. If the breath is flowing regularly, then what forms take shape within in it? Is that form like a cartoon, as it exists in our minds, or is it like what our guru had said it would be like, that our divinity will be such-and-such, and its form will be like so? Is that form [in our breath] wearing white clothes, or red or green or blue, or is it some auspicious deity in yellow colours?

37. Sitting in solitude, sitting in ashrams, we try to concentrate inside ourselves the vibrations that have come out of the bodies of great saints, which are scattered all over the sky and the atmosphere — [this concentration] depends upon the physical posture of our bodies. This *tap* (austere practice) bears fruit and takes the person to that divinity which he needs in his life, and which he has been unable to understand.

38. In a sense, our whole body is full of excrement and muck, yet we say it is very pure. And everyone acts very pure, too. Despite being wrapped in bad actions, they pretend to be very pure.

39. Prodded by the mind, we heat our body and we cool our body, and we throw it in the fire of many indulgences which burns it, and burns it, and turns it to ashes. Then, after a definite period, a time will come when even our breath — the God-connection in us — will also stop, and from this point of view, creation will disappear for us. In our sight, this creation will remain no more.

40. After only the ten digits of mathematics, the eleventh is said to be the mind. Actually, the digits are nine only, and then comes zero; after this, this 'eleven' is an illusion. In the scriptures, after ten senses, the eleventh has been called the mind.

41. One who has a long neck [that is, intrusively curious people] might have a longer distance between his mind and his heart. Such a person can have a greater capacity for war, for generating wars, or for putting people into worthless trouble.

42. By living in the company of ill-perceiving people, your aura, your lustre, your glory and the rays emitted by your body — all these become subdued. Again and again you will be seen as an egotistical person, and within that egotism will be hidden that terrible anger which is actually not yours, but which has come to you. Until it departs, you will not find peace, You will not find happiness.

43. After That [everlasting truth] comes into your body, the good vibrations emitted by your body will provide happiness to others as well. The bad and wrong vibrations emitted by your body will make both you and others unhappy. Whether it troubles others or not, that bad vibration will definitely burn you up. This is why the company of undesirable beings is prohibited.

Mental States

What is happiness? What is sorrow? They are both nothing but a mental state. If a person keeps his or her mental state in equilibrium, the world appears to be a harmonious place. However, if his mental state is discombobulated, then the world appears unsavoury.

1. If our mentality remains correct, we will learn every mystery [of the world] in the same way that a stage manager or an actor knows everything about a play but doesn't get attached to it.

2. Afflicted by attachments and growing weak, we produce all kinds of troubles. We can't sleep well. We can't think straight, and we're even afraid of our own shadows. Our own shadow has become a scary ghost for us. All this will improve only when we abandon egotistical people and welcome saints and seekers.

3. If you bow before the undesirable demands of your mind, you will lose your unique personality. If your personality does not remain, neither shall you. In such a state, you'll be pretty far from getting anywhere or doing anything.

4. The first thing you should do is to isolate yourself from both praise and criticism. Never hanker after praise. Praise even those things that are criticized, and that which is praiseworthy is to be praised appropriately. It is not to be criticized.

5. Regarding good and bad deeds — if we pay due attention to the inspiration we get from our guru and from our conscience, this can be very good for us.

6. A non-jealous person begins to witness every happening of life without getting attached, as would like a third person. In

this way [you too will] stand and watch everything, like an actor or an acrobat, but instead of getting attached to it, you'll laugh. You won't be surprised by the daily happenings of the village, the home, the city, the country or the society. All your confusion will vanish.

7. O Sudharma! The truth is that if we become anything which we really are not, then our being undone is also natural — and in this process of becoming, and of becoming undone, we must keep burning. On becoming something it is absolutely necessary to become undone, this is certain.

8. Only once we stand in the presence of a saint, or in front of a holy temple, or before a divinity or sacred rivers like the Ganga or the Yamuna, only then does the other [the divine] arrive there as well.

9. Our divinity passes right by us and we don't realize it. Who praises excrement or muck, garbage, dirty clothes or dirty things? It is only a true saint who can praise even those.

10. You are very stable. Whoever might pass before you — a king, a pauper, an emperor, a beautiful woman — it doesn't matter to you at all. No waves arise in you. When the speeding turbulence of your mind begins to experience this, know, then, that you are in the company of God.

11. When you have no pride in your knowledge but have the feeling that you are absolutely poor, that you know only that you do not know, and when you have stability in thoughts with humility in your behaviour, then only will you be worthy of that reverence.

12. Instead of making friends with ourselves, we remain our own enemy. By going to the places of saints and Mahatmas, all that we learn is how to be a friend to our own selves.

13. If you are experiencing some kind of pain or sorrow, if your mind is giving rise to undesirable thoughts, then try to go to the very root of it and seek the truth. This too you should learn.

14. In every place in this universe, humans have their own faith in themselves, and with that faith they try to involve themselves in very respectable and praiseworthy acts. Those who know its value do so, but those who are ignorant and wander lost, they have a separate character of their own. Those who are young have an enthusiasm of a different kind.

15. Where you find the feeling of service to others, and of learning and teaching, there you will have to accept everything in the same way that the river Ganga takes unto herself both the dirty drains of the towns and cities as well as the sacred rivers coming from the mountains. They all merge together and flow with the flow of Ganga which redeems others; she provides service to others. If she were alone, Ganga couldn't have done so. Exactly the same is Aghor.

16. Without the right determination, you will remain deprived of any benefit from your knowledge or from whatever prayers and worship you perform. Not having faith in yourself also leads to great loss and much damage to you. You cannot have faith in yourself as long as the effects of bad company stay with you.

17. Despite the waning of the light, your conscience has not been stolen. In the same way, effortlessly, a person of calm and stable mind achieves that Supreme Joy.

18. It is because of faith that we become respectable in our home, among friends and relatives. When that faith breaks, we lose all that is ours. Faith is not merely a word. It has a very deep relationship to the good actions of a person, as well as to the ideal behaviour and conduct towards one's mother and father,

friends and relatives, acquaintances, wife and children. It is also associated with our behaviour towards nature, from which vibrations constantly radiate.

19. A human being sees things according to his mentality and temperament.

20. *Bhagwan*, *Bhagawati*, God or demigod — whatever there is — these are a gift of the mind. Due to mental troubles, diverse forms arise in our consciousness and we end up spending a lot of time in our life lost in them. This mind, together with being a symbol of man's weakness, is also a vehicle of his capabilities and efficacy. God, *Bhagwan*, *Bhagawati*, disciplined practice, meditation, concentration, or worship — all these are done only through the mind.

21. This, the illusion of the world — this system, this legality, this policy, these rules which are known as 'religious' — if you fault it, even if only a little, your own mind begins to condemn you; society also condemns you, and you yourself feel as if you have strayed from the path. There you see no God, no Goddess, nor do you see anyone who is your own, or anyone who is not.

22. Because of mental weaknesses, we are not able to understand what the truth is, exactly. This mind becomes the biggest obstacle in every disciplined practice of ours, on the path of every one of our successes — because of this obstacle, we cannot see that reality; we don't recognize that reality. It is because of this mind that we neither understand the essence of the sacred books, nor do we ever meet the knowledgeable people who know those sacred books. We are unable to learn about the entity to be revered, and we also never get to know the respectable people who know about it. As long as you're easily lured by the illusions of the mind, you will never find peace and happiness.

23. The desire and determination that we make in the morning and in the evening should be a very pure resolve. If we let no other desire join with that pure determination, then we can get to know the hidden entity behind that disciplined practice — confronted with whom, even demigods [i.e. Brahma, Vishnu, Mahesh] have been known to bow. But if your determination is not pure, if you listen to your mind, many kinds of conflicting thoughts arise in your mind, saying this is not so, that is not so, and so forth; then, all your happiness and respite turns into uncertainty and sorrow. The mentality of jealousy and animosity then begins to destroy your home and your family.

24. These disciplined practices (*tapasya*) are not associated with torturing or destroying your body. These are actually mental disciplines. You really don't have to do these practices with your body too much. It is to be done through your mentality, through your consciousness, where you have to fill your senses with good character.

25. The advice and friendship of people with bad conduct is a cause of great sorrow. From listening to their advice we remain deprived of becoming virtuous ourselves.

26. Those people who consider themselves as having a big family and circle of friends, who consider themselves to be very rich, very scholarly and better than others in many ways — these are actually very limited people. Few people are more limited than them. They are very parochial. It is this way of their thinking and understanding which, due to attachments, prompts them to act in wrong ways.

27. More than being insulted by others, we get insulted by ourselves. Because of flaws in our disciplined practice and good conduct, and because of our parochial mentality, we become deprived of happiness and joy, and are overlooked by others.

28. Living under a roof, we also live with cacophony.

29. If you are going to provide a good foundation to your family, if you are going to start something good, then for that you will have to consider the appropriate time, your right determination, your resolute desire; also, you will have to encompass the mentality of the people who you support, for you will have to determine whether their minds are flawed. You will have to decide whether their breath is heated up [in anger], or if, instead of a beautiful vision arising in their thoughts, an ugly vision emerges. Furthermore, shall they eventually be destructive to the whole endeavour?

30. The crow, the lion and the donkey, the elephant and the horse and so forth — different animals and birds have been depicted as vehicles of the various demigods, but that doesn't mean you should think their actual vehicles are such. It is we who — despite our tailless human form — acquire beastly tendencies and then are assaulted or ridden by those demigods; due to this, we remain under their power forever. They pull us where they want; they take us wherever they want. As they wish, so do we speak; as they want, so do we see. This is what is thereby taught to us through the form of those animals.

31. We are unable to have faith in ourselves. That produces doubts regarding the success of our undertakings. When doubts arise in a project, it becomes difficult to complete it properly. All this depends upon our own mentality. If we doubt the knowledge, mantra or sacred words of our guru — even just a little — the hard labour of years disappears in a moment.

32. We people fight constantly, and because of jealousy and envy, we create perpetuating feuds. It is not as if we fight in one given moment and forget it the next, as water-spots on white clothes disappear once they dry. Rather, we perpetuate these

animosities for months or years, and sometimes until the last breath of our life. Because of those tendencies, our form changes, our character, virtues and temperament change, and we begin to attack our own friends and relatives. The result of all this is self-destructive in every way.

33. When a person acquires the ecstatic consciousness (*samadhi*) and he wakes up, then he becomes capable of doing many things. His nights are not spent in dreams like those of people who are always moving and never stable, due to their own innocence and to bad company.

34. Let there be no scarcity; let there be nice sentiments everywhere. One whose mentality and way of thinking and understanding begins to be like this, he shall find a skilful boatman knowledgeable about the coastlines — as well as about the deep waters of the streams, rivers and tortuous valleys of home and family and society — who will easily take him across the ocean of life. It has also been said: "Step only in that person's boat who has a deep knowledge of both the shore as well as of the midstream".

35. This life is very valuable, and is full of unfathomable energy. We should banish hatred from our life because where there is hatred there is acrimony, and where there is acrimony, wisdom does not prevail. Then imprudence takes birth, and as a result, the passage of time — which beats no one with a stick — takes away the person's intellect, prudence and good thoughts, and prompts him towards hateful actions. In this way, involved in wrong actions, the person smoulders like grain husk, burns up and destroys himself.

36. A stable consciousness is what the yogis have described as '*samadhi*'. Great saints have called it a 'desire-free consciousness'. Aughar saints have called it '*mahavibhuti*' (the great glory).

37. Even while living at home with a family and fulfilling every daily duty, we can acquire that state of change. In this way, being content with whatever is available due to past deeds, the person remains very calm from within and spends his life on the earth in this way. On leaving this earth he goes to a different solar system and stays there as a witness for eternal time. He does not get affected by ups and downs, the storms and hurricanes of the earth.

38. By nature, every person wants to get away from instability and become stable, and wants to avoid wrong company and feelings of guilt. The day you have a stable mind, that day you will acquire forbearance, you will have no anger, you will have no tendencies towards unnecessary arguments — you will become a saintly person. Your life will be spent in great purity. This is what purity really is. When we acquire that purity, our ill-acting mind will become virtuous and self-disciplined. And when we become virtuous and self-disciplined, we will be able to sculpt other forms in this way as well. Our children and grandchildren, and our disciples, will have ideals, virtues, traits, temperament and conduct similar to ours. They will be flawless.

39. We just say we are in your refuge, O Ma Sarweshwari! I am in your sanctuary. If I am in your refuge then my burden, my weight, the conduct of my life is now no longer in my hands. Now she is the one who directs everything. If she directs it then it will be miserable for me to create obstacles in there, to argue with my intellect, or to create disharmonious feelings. It's because of such sorrows that we do not achieve those supreme successes. When we fail to achieve the supreme success we become afflicted by illusions, we become sorrowful, we have to face troubles and our improper actions appear threatening before us, O friends.

40. There are many people who bring alien winds and alien thoughts in here and regurgitate them here, speak them here,

hear them here. They don't know what they're doing. Why are they polluting someone else's mind so much by saying all this? Why are they polluting another person's mind, why are they polluting another's intellect? They don't know it, but they say it, and the ill-effects of saying it are instantaneous for the other.

41. First we ask for fearlessness: Make me fearless, O Mother. From whom should you make me fearless? From those activities that are excessive; may I be unable to do them. Those tendencies and activities should never come to me: neither should I ever invite them, nor should I ever meet people who indulge in them. Neither should I see them, nor should they see me. Wouldn't you like such a life? If you'd like such a life then you'll be a very good sculptor. You can sculpt your coming generation very well.

42. I was sitting in the evening, looking at things, and I was also thinking about how this deep thought-stream has been continuously flowing. Despite being so close, the seekers experience distant things, and how close and concentrated do they seem [to themselves]. They have no desires, no wishes, no hankerings.

43. I feel great joy when I see you progressing towards that concentration and contemplation, when your mind is absolutely empty and you are sitting with a relaxed body in solitude. I also see that all around you radiates a circle of very nice vibrations, and that all around you scatters beautiful rays — beautiful not only to you, but to everyone who sees without anger, envy, hate, or jealousy; also, that peace [in which you repose] must be again and again begging you to become quiet and still. Become as quiet as we become in a procession of people carrying a corpse to the cremation ground; how humble and non-violent we become at that time, friends. Will you give away such joy in life?

44. Becoming internally still, you should definitely search for that quest for which you seek. The day you grow satisfied, nothing will happen in your awareness; nothing will arise therein, from that day on you will have a very calm heart and mind. Thereafter you will never live an undisciplined life. With the advent of self-discipline, you won't do any wrongdoings. You won't have any accidents. But, as soon as indiscipline returns, this whole argument will resume. Then, aggravation, restlessness, troubles and obstacles will re-emerge.

45. In prayers, in worship and in this faith is hidden the great strength of faith which every day we see, but overlook. The day we pay attention to it, give due importance to it, we will automatically come into the category of 'great souls'. Our thoughts will change, our sentiments will change, our clothes and behaviour will change, our walking and moving and believing will change. Our old polluted thoughts will not come to us as they once did. Everything will change. It is that mental state of change that we look for, friends.

46. The person who remains aloof from all attachment of pride or prestige towards this ephemeral body, he is known as a saint. Someone in whom respect and disrespect, caste, lineage and religion and the like all do not exist — that is to say, someone who shuns such social institutions — that liberated saint can be tied to no one.

47. I pray to that Unknown that he provide peace, happiness and prosperity to everyone, and that we might avoid all our bitterness and remain hate-free. If we have to hate, let us hate ourselves. If we have to spit, let us spit upon ourselves. What will we gain by spitting at the Sun, since that spit will just fall right back onto our own face?

48. Failure gives rise to anger.

49. It is not good to live like a loquacious spirit. Such a life is very rough and fearful. Fear arises due to ill-advised actions.

50. Those people who want to live a happy and prosperous life, like kings, and who want their senses to live as their subjects, and who want all their well-wishers to remain with them as friends — these people avoid infighting, attachments and illusions. In front of this difficult mental discipline of theirs, even Brahma, Vishnu and Mahesh bow down. They live unperturbed lives. In their consciousness arise not those things that produce sorrow.

51. You should be patient. You should use your courage. Do not be afraid of circumstances, and give importance to prayer, for in prayer there lies a great strength. It is on the strength of their prayer that our foes can attack us. So let us be united as well. If we sit and act together, we will have no retrogression within us and nobody will be able to destroy us. We will be victorious. We will achieve what we desire.

53. That Mother is an epitome of faith and love, but she also can come before us in a very distorted form if our mentality itself is distorted. You do not know how that Mother will appear before you, because it depends upon your good thoughts and sentiments, friends.

54. *Upasana* (worship) also means 'a close place' (*up* + *asan*), i.e. let our place be next to where our dear divinity is, and let us mould our nature according to its nature. In such a situation, your mental state should be very bright and holy. You should not become sad, disappointed or sick if somebody says something [unseemly] to you. On hearing the worthless talk of various people, doubts of your faith and devotion might arise. If you have doubts about the actions you have performed, then you will lose the fruits of those actions. Therefore, pay no attention to the bitter words that even I

might say to you. I will request you only to keep working with diligence in your own field of work, and with that, to also be attentive towards those signs and indication which — once we recognize what the stars are foretelling — tell us about the immanence of the day of the arrival of our dear divinity, our union with it, our ecstasy in it. That the vibrations of that divinity are coming to us, and this is actually going to happen! We get to know of this sometime before it actually happens. When you receive this symbolic message you should become very alert. Then you will be able to properly recognize that entity, to properly see and hear it. If you ignore this message, then I suppose you could even miss this experience.

55. We see demigods and demigoddesses, God and the Goddess in the form of idols every day, but it does not profit us in any way. The reason is that our process of thinking and looking at things is faulty. Our sight itself is faulty. If, while folding our hands to them, or during our prayer and worship, when approaching them we perceive how great we have become, how humble we have become, and how the feelings of peace and happiness arise in us, only then can it be said that we gained something from prayers and worship. If we look at it from this point of view, and if we mould ourselves in this way, then everything will be easy for us.

56. With the arrival of the 21st century everyone will be happy, prosperous and able to carry a little cash in their pockets. But at that time their mentality will be so tormented that they will go out to seek those same things that the yogis, the *mahatmas*, the *rishis* and the *munis* would look for centuries ago, lighting their sacred fires. But then, it will be very difficult to find. Then, they will need to go to such tiny huts. They will then look for such ashrams and huts where they can go and cleanse their mentalities.

57. We have anger within us, we have a hesitation within us, and we have many worthless ideas within us that do not allow us to stay with ourselves. We want to be with ourselves in silence, but our own subjugation does not allow us to do that. That is why when we are without any refuge; we cry for mercy and remember that great Unknown entity again and again. Then our own silence, our quiet makes us reach that place without wind or light or any other medium. But we are unable to remain silent; cannot stay alone.

58. We are tormented by fear. Even while watching, listening and recognizing the meaninglessness of life, we are like that owl for whom the daytime sunlight is useless. The owl can't see at all during the day — despite that, in fact, sunlight exists for anyone with two eyes.

59. I hope that, slowly, as your intellect becomes mature and concentrated, and once dualities do not arise in it — that is to say, when your intellect will not create any more doubts for you — then you will achieve that state of joy. Whenever you have any doubts about anything, that thing will fail.

60. Uncultivated intellect can give rise to weapons instead of social welfare and sacred texts. In such a situation, destruction becomes imminent.

Mantra

In Hindu meditation, repeating the mantra given by the guru to the disciple is very important. Usually, the mantra is a syllable or word that the guru deems beneficial for the disciple's spiritual growth. The disciple then repeats the mantra in his mind, and slowly his own body begins to resonate with the vibrations of the mantra. That is a state of deep meditation, and it has many positive effects on the disciple.

1. Only when the deity of your mantra manifests itself within you do you begin to turn towards many kinds of good deeds.

2. Friends! We hold a strange misunderstanding about mantra, deity and rituals, because of which our divine friend comes right before us, looks for us, and goes away. We are not able to either see or recognize it. That is why we should keep progressing through life with right thought, living a simple and sublime life so that, when the time comes, we disembark at the designated station.

3. Mantra is potent and already charged — its power depends upon our simplicity and ability to harness it. This mantra that you have received is that friend who is always with you, and is like the earth orbiting around the sun, receiving light from it. It is that friend, this mantra, which shows you the way at every step of your life. If it is mistreated, it can also lead to great destruction. Then, it will slip away from your hands. If it slips away from your hands, everything slips away from you.

4. No names are mentioned in mantra. The *rishi*s have seen those mantras, and in those visions, they heard those sounds which carry attraction within them. It makes our divine friend responsive to us, making it take interest in the great soul calling

it; taking interest, it fills us with unfathomable power, divinity, strength and ability. It releases divine rays into our body — those supercharged, divine rays that give us everything.

5. Similar is the mantra which is not chanted by voice. It is kept quietly in your heart. It keeps calling in every vibration of your heart. Your attention is fixed on it, quietly. Once you silence your mind you will see that every pore of your body, from the tip of your toe to the top of your head, is resonating with '*krim*'. And it harbours such joy, such happiness, such peace, such tranquillity, which requires patience to be enjoyed.

6. Mantras are written in many books. But mantras of books cannot be beneficial unless they are heard spoken from the mouth of a knowledgeable person.

7. If you have faith in your guru's mantra then never recite it out loud, even absentmindedly. If you have faith in repeating the beads of rosary as he has taught you, then take care that the rosary does not make any sound. It should not go click, click... If you have faith in those mantras, then your tongue should not vibrate while saying them. Say "*Ra*" as you go to sleep and "*Ma*" when you wake up.

8. If we repeat a harsh mantra, we will feel harsh and angry. If we chant a sweet mantra, we will feel very good from the inside.

9. The mantra that guru gives you denotes friendship. Mantra is not a material thing that a Baba-ji gives you, neither does it represent those surreptitious meetings that ministers have. He gives you a friend in the form of a mantra, a friend who is always ready to help you in times of strife, trouble and pain. It provides support when our life becomes sorrowful and seems to be disintegrating. This is the meaning of the mantra of the guru. You feel great joy, inner happiness in meeting a true friend, and great pain on separating from him.

10. The mantra that guru gives as a friend is a word. It's merely a word, merely a sentence. One who receives it should be righteous, determined, and of stable mind. He is never frightened in the face of the hurricanes of trouble; he remains stable like the Himalayas. He does not rise and fall like shallow waters. He is like an unfathomable ocean.

11. We should be careful that we are not repeating the mantra of an excitable deity, nor are we giving it to others. We succeed when we recite the very cool, peaceful, auspicious mantra given to us by our all-caring guru. Reciting the mantras of to angry deities makes us very unsettled and restless. Many difficulties then arise before us. Repeating a harsh, hard mantra also makes our own temperament very hard, and makes us intolerant towards others. We begin to burn in the fire of our own anger, and experience physical pain as well.

12. When we sit to meditate on the mantra, when we sit in our designated seat (*asana*), then this body acquires the shape of a triangle. At that time we should make our mind and heart very simple and at ease.

13. Whether you recite "*Om Sacchidekam Brahma*" mantra or some other favourable mantra that your guru has given to you, you may open your lips while saying it, but it is supremely beautiful if you do not open your lips, and you achieve great internal intimacy and peace. When you concentrate on the vibrations of your heart, or become focused from your toes to your head, you experience that mantra resounding in every pore of your body. You do not need to exercise either your lips or your tongue. This experience happens by itself.

14. When you express that mantra through your voice it gets infused in all of the cosmos, my friends, even before you have closed your lips.

15. When meditating, we add '*Namah*' to the end of a mantra; in fire rituals we add '*Swaha*', and so on. In using it for another certain specific purpose, we add '*Phat*' at the end of the mantra. These three (*Namah, Swaha and Phat*) lead to different results. One should be very careful about which is to be used where.

16. To achieve instant success in a given task we add '*Phat*' to the end of the mantra while reciting it. Thus, one should very intimately learn the power and gravity associated with this 'word', and knowing it well, learning it well, should teach it to those who come in contact with him. In his life he should teach it to at least ten people.

17. A mantra obtained by cunning and deceit is not effective.

18. When you recite your mantra, you should touch the earth with your left hand and perform *japa* (meditating on the mantra with the help of a rosary) with your right.

19. While performing *japa*, when you reach the head-bead of the rosary, turn back from there. *Japa* is not performed in the same direction after reaching the apex. You learn this by practice. Whenever such a person closes his lips this process begins within him automatically. For the whole of his life, whenever he becomes stable, this process of *japa* is always happening inside him.

20. By performing *mantra-japa*, many dirty and vicious inclinations in our veins and blood are dissipated. A new, wholesome temperament develops within us which is beautiful and joyful not only for us, but also for others. It is for the welfare of others, and our own temperament turns towards the welfare of others.

21. Regarding initiation into a mantra, it is necessary to keep in mind through whose lips we gain this knowledge. Who will

be auspicious and beneficial for us? To learn it from a person who himself does not know the path, who has not walked on it, this can never be beneficial.

22. The mantra given by the guru should be kept proper and safe. Instead of saying it with your voice, it is most beneficial if recited in the vibrations of your heart. This will provide us with great equanimity and stability, and this stability will save us from any kind of wilful actions.

23. The atomic power of the mantra is such that, as it is recited, it attracts a multitude of minuscule power-particles — bringing them into our speech with profound consequences. From that time you should be very careful not to use unseemly words even with your children, wife or relatives, for these words can have an instantaneous effect on them.

24. *Aghormantra* is neither agitating nor difficult. It is a very cool, peaceful and simple mantra. It is by nature *aghor*, that is, very simple. *Aghor* is another name for being without hate. It isn't at all difficult. It is not harsh or bitter. Even the *brahmamantra* is not like this.

25. Amongst *aghor* mantras, those who repeat the seed mantra of the fire, or the seed mantra of the earth, they become a very forgiving person. Alcohol, meat, fish and the like, food both edible and inedible: everything gets incinerated as if in a furnace, in his belly. Other mantras do not have the power to burn away such toxins. They are afraid of even garlic and onions. And as far as turning things like alcohol, meat or fish to ashes is concerned, they just don't have the capacity to do this.

26. An Aghor guru blesses the mantra with the capacity to be beneficial for everybody; he fills it with the capacity to attract any power, and gives it to the disciple on the right day, and in

the right condition, with the [moon in the best] constellation, at the most opportune moment. Such a mantra is for the benefit of all. After that, it depends upon you: upon how much feeling and faith with which you accepted it, and upon how much feeling and faith with which you recite it during *japa*.

27. It is the performance of *japa* which endows spiritual power. Persist in doing *japa* and success will be yours.

28. If you have no faith or trust in your mantra, then it remains ineffectual. You never achieve the desired success. There are many uneffective mantras. To expect any effect from them would be like expecting a barren woman's baby to win a battle.

29. The power of mantras remains great so long as they are not traded, bought or sold. In such a situation, whatever mantra you recite, you can use it as an instrument by adding '*Phat*' to the end of it.

30. As far as your question about the mantra of the Divine Mother is concerned: mantra is always self-realized. You do not have to charge it. What is important is to make oneself conducive to that mantra. One should follow the vow he has undertaken, and remain simple and straight. This is the simple answer. One should remain straight with oneself. For, when you recite your mantra, perform worship or undertake spiritual practices, that divine shadow begins hovering around you. If you remain steadfast to your vow, if you follow your word, then you will achieve success.

31. During *japa*, when your mind becomes fully focused, you will be able to see with open eyes the forms emitted from your body through your breath. You will be able to see very clearly how very small rays come out and take different forms. Then, when your hearing begins to hear every sound, you will know everything, effortlessly. You will know that this is that.

32. The way the poison of a snake bite or scorpion sting can be cured through mantra, friends, it is possible only because of our vow to ourselves. We give our word to the snake, that O Being in the Form of the Cobra! O, bearer of venom. I will not harm you, your family, or anyone associated with you. So please help me. This person who is dying from poison, please take his poison away.

33. It has been said, "Guru's mantra is a sharp sword". This sword in the form of the mantra chops away the enemies residing within your own body, and provides a happy, healthy and peaceful life to human beings.

34. If you practice the mantra your guru gave you unceasingly, you will fully understand the five elements and have complete knowledge of their characteristics.

35. *Mantra japa* cleanses our veins. It purifies the mind. It destroys the three ills. Of its own accord our mind begins to feel good, our heart begins to feel good, and we begin to do nice things.

36. Misuse or faulty use of the mantra given by the guru can also have adverse results. Therefore, one should be very careful.

37. We recite a mantra. What is that mantra? We recite that one letter that does not embody any name. The one that has the names of gods and goddesses attached to it is not a mantra, friends. It is not a mantra. It is a bait, to invite somebody in, or to see them off. It is like a hook thrown in water. If the fish is caught, well and good; if not, no problems, the fish swims away. But the real mantra, friends, is what you desire it to be. It provides you with very pure fruits. It does not have anybody's name in it, or anybody's form. Nor is there a prayer to anybody in it. It keeps happening by itself.

38. Whose *japa* should be performed? Do that of the *Brahm*-knowledge. What is this *Brahm*-knowledge? It is that one letter. What is the effect of that one letter? I, or you, cannot express that. If we have truly learned it from our guru, and know it well, and if he hasn't taught us hurriedly, if we have really learned by being close to him, then none of our knowledge will fail. It must be effective.

39. During your worship and meditations, during your spiritual practices, when that one-lettered mantra begins to emanate through you, then, in your speech, a multitude minuscule particles gather which you can use to make many things favourable to you. Furthermore, if you say something to someone while in a distorted frame of mind, then those others have to bear its effects, friends. That is known as a curse, when a person who both meditates and knows this mantra has cursed someone with it.

40. My friends, you are all sculptors. When you become bored and tired performing *japa* and doing your practices, at that time make your mind absolutely empty. Make your body very loose. Become concentrated. Sit absolutely peacefully. Your mantra will not emanate out of your tongue or speech, but from each of your hair follicles. It will appear that all the pores of your body, from head to toe, are resonating with that essence. Then you will see that the divinity of that mantra will begin to enter your body, reside in your body, operate through your body, this divinity whose mantra you have in your heart.

41. Many people perform *japa* in similar ways. Many people also do *japa* in different ways. Many people perform *japa* of the one-lettered mantra, and many people have a name-word attached to their *mantrajapa*. When you express these through the medium of your speech, you are not merely expressing yourself. The swarm of minuscule particles that covered your

speech and voice radiate outwards to collect great, pure particles which you can use to create new sculptures; meet that divinity face to face and from that shall emanate those words that will be favourable to you. It is that word that you refer to as 'finding the Divine Mother' or 'finding a divinity' who has given their word to me. Now that I have their word, my work will certainly be accomplished.

42. If you aren't excited and impatient all the time, and if you keep straight with yourself, then that mantra remains self-charged. You do not even need to charge it. Your success demonstrates how straight you remain with yourself.

43. You know that the mantra does not incorporate a name. Name and mantra are two different things. Mantra is one lettered, while the name, has a name and a form to which you remain tied, as a form of bondage. This is known as Sat (truth). It appears that so-and-so is your name, and that your form is such-and-such.

44. The mantra is our friend, and it is one-lettered. It can appear with a name, and it can exist without a name too, such as first truth (*sat*), then peace (*cit*) and after that, joy (*anand*).

45. The potency of a mantra is such that people even counter snakebite venom with it. The bad characters in our fate and life, drawing us towards negative habits, acts and inspirations our whole life, prevent us from being a positive person and keep us subservient to the standards that other people have set for us. By performing *mantrajapa* even the most evil fate is expunged from our life.

46. This is meditation. Sitting silently, remain with your friend, your mantra. Seek advice from it. It will lead you on those paths of life which you must tread, and will take you to that place which is yours. There, nobody exists but you.

47. [The effect of *mantrajapa*]: You cannot understand how great is the effect of *mantrajapa* on you. It is our protector and the source of our inspiration. It is the guide on our path that inspires us to go among good people, saints and great souls.

48. Have not a critical view of worldly acts. Instead, have a positive view. When you come together with yourself in your heart, that mantra of yours — that letter which is vibrating in a poetic rhythm within you — begins to flow from every pore of your body, by itself.

Women

India is a largely patriarchal society. In a patriarchal society, women can be relegated to a secondary position to men. Baba insisted that women be given their due position in society because they, themselves, are a form of the mother goddess.

1. The woman who, knowing that she is right yet still asking for forgiveness, she is a great soul.

2. In many villages and cities, because of their mistakes or misdeeds, women are forced to leave their homes and live on the streets. If they stay at home they have to endure beatings and violence; out on the road, then they have to bear with hardships. It is the duty of any saint or Mahatma to show kindness to such beings and free them from their frustrations. They should also protect them from those bad souls and bad people who lure away young women and make them do base acts. They should inspire all those weak human beings who come to them, who otherwise might be caught in a spider's web. There is no generosity or kindness greater than this. They should be kind to them and say nice things to them so that those people can give up their weaknesses and be freed from their difficulties. They should inspire novice seekers, egotistical and shameless people towards higher acts. There is no worship greater than this. This is the greatest worship.

3. Why do women get old? Because of the cruelty of men.

4. I know I look like a prostitute. The man who still keeps staring at me should die [of shame].

5. To chastise again an already tormented woman is unbearable.

6. O Sudharma! Look! Because of mere suspicion how many helpless women find their lives in danger.

7. Mother's love is associated with the nectar of immortality [that is, her milk] right from the beginning. In that milk, water is not mixed. It is pure milk. There is life there, and that life itself is like her worship, her readings, her meditation, her contemplation, her prayer, and only that can free us from innumerable lives [rebirths].

8. Be the women of one's own family or of another's, from one's neighbourhood or from the fields, people always fight over them. That is why one should not be too talkative with them. They are respectable; we respect them. We give them a position of reverence. Friends, respect them.

9. We have unfathomable respect and reverence for the whole of womankind. Our organization has always made efforts towards their upliftment. Right from its inception, many projects for the upliftment of women's were started among the programmes of Sri Sarveshwari Samooh. Against the demon of dowry, on whose sacrificial altar hundreds of thousands of women have been sacrificed, and because of which women have had to suffer through disharmonious marriages and suffer through them even today, since the very beginning have we wages our struggle, and in this we've met more success than we expected. In addition, widow remarriage and many other programmes are supported by our organization. Our will towards women's welfare and the respect and reverence we feel towards them is evident from the name of this organization ('Sri Sarveshwari Samooh') which is in the very form of a woman's name. We hold them in a position of reverence. I am very proud to be the chairperson of such an organization.

10. For a family to develop and stay united, the most important role is played by women. But it is sad that, due to the narrow

thinking produced by the pressures of material values and desires, mothers today are not effective in properly fulfilling this role. When I see them neglecting the harmonious values of Indian culture, and blindly copying the misleading, superficial, grotesque and glitzy aspects of western civilization, my mind becomes full of sorrow and due to deep agony, against my own wishes, I become forced to criticize their behaviour. Even behind my criticism lies the sentiment of their welfare and progress because I want to see them revered, which is not possible without good behaviour and conduct.

11. The unique joint family system is breaking up very quickly today because of the narrow-mindedness of women. The menfolk, faced with their stubborn mentality, find themselves helpless and are compelled to merely watch and bemoan the sad and painful sight of the diminution of the family.

12. *Nari* ['woman, vein, artery, water-channel'] is the one responsible for everything, be it of the neighbourhood or of the home. Be it of the field or of the residential street. Be it of the urinary tract or of the highest part of the body. Be it of the *Ramayana* or of the *Mahabharata*. It is because of *nari* that everything ever happened, and happens even today. To cleanse this *nari* [i.e., the vein] is also known as *tapasya* (disciplined, austere practice), the practice before which even the trinity of Brahma, Vishnu and Shiva bow down and are forced to give their blessings. But, having received these blessings, people would force them to leave the earth and return to the heavens.

13. Women should have due affection, respect and a friendly demeanour towards all elder and younger members of the family lest those people begin to harbour bad feelings and chastise them. To the best of their ability, women should give them milk if they ask for water, because a mother always gives milk. The woman who does not do this gets into a [social] situation as bad as any hell.

14. Gurus have said to their disciples that all are to be revered, but you should also surely revere you mother — be she your earthly mother, or your mother of the sky and space. She from whom you expect milk, food and water, you can address as your mother.

15. A woman should look at her husband's younger brother as her father if he is elder to her, or as her husband's friend, if he is younger. Looking at them with other sentiments creates misleading ideas, and an uncertain condition is produced which can lead to a negative result.

16. A husband should also treat his wife as his mother once their children cross the age of ten. Behaving with her as a mere wife can lead to an imbalance in behaviour and conduct.

17. It should be explained to women that they have not discharged their duties simply by feeding their children or by giving them milk. It is their great duty to fill their children with sentiments of friendship, to give them good ideas, to make them capable of doing things, and to inspire them to keep the company of good and wise people and to avoid negative people. If, due to circumstance, the parents are sitting with a negative person, they should be careful not to call their children there at that time. To disregard this gives rise to great sorrows.

18. During the period of their pregnancy women should not read negative and hostile literature. They should not wear dirty clothes, and they should not roam around the marketplace too much. They should not keep the company of negative people, nor should they discuss their actions. All these can have a bad effect on the baby in the womb. Their diet should be balanced and regular. Keeping the company of peaceful, accomplished and polite women, they should cultivate a feeling of friendliness towards everyone. In that condition, they should not worship the icons of demigods like Kali, Durga or Vishnu

who are depicted as carrying weapons. They should also not look at those pictures of demigods that encourage the tendency towards violence. If pregnant women look at pictures of friendliness, or at pictures that inspire friendliness, then it will have a good effect on the baby in the womb and it will have the capability to bring friendliness to everyone.

19. The five elements and their 25 tendencies are also represented in the form of women. When we elevate ourselves over these elements, our mind will find itself. That is why these representations are worthy of respect and we regard them so in our worship. They always remain a source of attraction for every being.

20. Women who use vermilion are a symbol of strength. After sunset, vermilion is never given outside the household. Wise shopkeepers also don't sell it after sunset because it also represents Lakshmi (the goddess of wealth). While the sun is setting, even then it isn't shared from one house to another. Doing so means that now I am about to lose my loved one, my respected one, my husband or my deity.

21. Before their husband, or in front of anyone else, a woman should not stand with her hair open or without putting on vermilion, because it weakens their strength, their aura, their everything. Then their mind gets befuddled, they become angry, and because of this mentality of theirs, they destroy their family.

22. Men whose wives' have a good conduct — who use vermilion, who wear the sacred wedding thread, who cover their head and who wear bangles before their husbands — they are very fortunate. They receive respect everywhere. They have good friends and well-wishers. They are invited everywhere and they gain every position and much prestige. Their children, and whole family, everybody stays happy.

23. The mentality of the respected women of our house has a deep influence on our life and our way of acting; thus, we should definitely try to observe them, to contemplate them and to understand them. We should certainly consider whether their mentality is destroying us, or putting us on such a negative path that the next generations will absolutely forget us. We must judge whether, blunted by their blows, in a state of social unconsciousness, we are about to give the hand of our precious daughter — like a goddess, and replete with potential — into the hands of some wicked, tailless beast-man, tinted by so-called modernity, believing in every kind of destruction. We must definitely consider whether, influenced by their narrow mentalities, we are neglecting our duties and responsibilities towards our aged parents, to the widows in the family, or to helpless women in the neighbourhood, thereby generating agonized minds which burn down and destroy homes, families, and block after block of communities.

24. More important than your prayers and worship, meditation and contemplation in your life is your sense of responsibility and duty towards women, and its skilful performance. If you pay no attention to it, you will slowly destroy yourself. Your mind will stay contaminated. You will stay frightened and, having neglected them [women], your vision will become weak; your mind, intellect and physical health will also deteriorate, for their agonies will also influence you. You will lose all your happiness and peace and, despite having all luxuries, you will not be able to use them in peace.

25. Friends! You will have to learn to respect and revere the women in your own home. Because these women expect security, welfare and proper guidance from you men-folk, your responsibilities towards them grow even greater. There is no pilgrimage or divine vision greater than your sense of responsibility and fulfilment of your duties towards them.

26. In many families and homes, the neglect of their old women and widows engenders household misery, and their thoughts then begin to destroy that home. Their weeping and speech then grows frightening in the family, like the sound of a bird of prey at night. Many inauspicious signs and symbols of destruction begin to appear in the home from which only the guru's idol, the remembrance of great souls, and one's own stability gives protection. Our agitation can take us on a very wrong path.

27. There are many villages and communities whose women stray very far away from good thoughts and good sentiments. Their life is so cursed that it is hard to say what lies behind it.

28. Because of being deprived of the amenities of toilets or protected places for such purposes, women who have to go in the fields or by the roadside to relieve themselves often become sick from shame, fear, hesitation and the undesirable sentiments and malevolent eyes of negative people, for then they cannot relieve themselves in a timely manner. Their temperament also becomes irritable and their mentality becomes acrimonious.

29. There are deadly consequences to women letting their hair loose. Keeping their hair loose before their husbands over the course of a few days is equivalent to putting them to sleep forever. Sometimes they are forced to urinate in the cowshed, and that too has deadly and inauspicious consequences for their husbands. Such unnatural actions of women can be very negative for their husbands, sons and dear ones. People of the family begin to lose face. Food becomes distasteful in that family.

30. Many of the problems that arise in front of you might be caused by the influence of the mentality of women. If their mentality is not pure then guru can protect you personally,

but he will not be able to protect your family and friends. Even your divinity will not be able to protect your family then. Therefore you must keep your women happy, and in that happiness, inspire them towards God.

31. It is necessary for men-folk to maintain a balance with the temperament of women. If their balance is maintained then, wherever they be, their breath and the vibrations of their body will protect you like an electrical field. As opposed to this, the bodily vibrations that arise from polluted minds, thoughts and sentiments will not save you from any evil fate.

32. Our country is addressed as a mother [Mother-India]. Not every country in the world is addressed as the mother. Those geographical areas are unique. In the same way, our home is addressed in the name of the mother. Home and family are that lap of the mother in which we find great rest, happiness and peace.

33. The word *nari* is a word full of controversy. Whether it concern the Sita of the *Ramayana*, or Draupadi of the *Mahabharata*, or Belwa, or any other woman, controversies arise because of them. These women aside, brothers quickly rise to fight with each other because of the women in the house. Leave those women aside, too: people become ready to behead each other because of the women who live in their street and neighbourhood. Because of the women in the fields people become ready to kill each other. Whoever dies like this has no value.

34. There are many women in our prayers and worship as well.

35. If we do not have pure feelings towards women then this mentality can destroy us. But if pure feelings towards them arise in us, then understand that even the most difficult of our tasks will be successful. If you strive to see them on the road to happiness, with their heads covered, with all their

make-up, and if they look at you even once as if you were their son, all your work is done.

36. If the mentalities of a husband and wife are negative, this will have a bad effect on their children, and this mentality will destroy them. They will not succeed in their tasks.

37. I can gauge how united are the women by looking at the vermilion on their forehead. Those women of our homes wearing vermilion show that they are united. Joining one and one they are not two but become eleven. This is how you can recognize them. Those who do not have vermilion on their head appear available for everyone. They are dear to everyone. Those who wear vermilion are the bride of the lineage, and on looking at them you feel as if they are the revered divinity of the lineage. Salute them, express respect to them within; all this amounts to a worship and prayer of the Mother Goddess. This is also one way to progress on the path of your practice.

Nature

The nature that we see all around us — trees, plants, rivers, mountains, plains — they are but an external manifestation of the true or super nature. Nature is actually the element that animates all things in the perceivable world. Everyone is under its influence.

1. Nature plays with beings.

2. Super-nature in the form of sleep made even Vishnu unconscious and left him in the ocean of milk.

3. Your night, which gives birth to the lamp [of light] should be well spent, while you search behind all your deeds from dawn to dusk.

4. After night comes the dawn. This is the dawn in which you become active to perform pure deeds with a renewed eagerness, a renewed pace, and a renewed enthusiasm. The dawn gives you activity, while the night gives you this lamp so that you should not stay in darkness. Sitting in my light, solve all the mysteries of your life. Even dawn will come. Right after this night shall the dawn arrive. In that dawn we will become so active, we will become so active that we will even turn towards happiness and prosperity.

5. Be aware of time. Super-nature is not easy to find, but it is simple.

6. However hard may you try to have your own way, Super-nature spoils it in no more than two or three days. Oh, right after having them trimmed, don't your hair and nails grow back in two or three days!

7. The person who keeps his eyes, his ears, his nose and his speech under his control gives that enchantress of the universe, Super-nature, an immense joy. You should mould yourself into your Self. Those who are not moulded cannot be sculpted.

8. Those whose intellect becomes spirit-centred become the 'self-arisen ones' [emergent] from the Super-nature.

9. The welfare of the world and its beings lies in worshipping the creative energy. This worship should begin with the creative energy that exists within you. Over time, to merge your worship into the worship of Sarveshwari, the prime creative energy behind all creation, is beneficial for yourself and for the world.

10. The Kali, Durga, and Chandi whom we worship are not only limited to the temple. If they were, then how could they reach us when we remember them in our happiness or sorrow? They help us, and on praying they pull us out of all sorrows. Everywhere there are temples to them; everywhere you find their icons. Everywhere lies their lustre and their aura. One who sees so sees them everywhere. One who sees them only in the temple thinks that they are limited to the temple, and sees them only within a narrow limit.

11. The one whom we address as Sarveshwari is actually a single form of three Goddesses. She never gives birth to wars, nor does she produce sons who wage wars. Her weapons are merely the imaginations [of various people].

12. Durga — she is that Goddess living in a house or home who kills the buffalo of beastly instinct. That is why Durga has been called the buffalo-killer. That Goddess rings her bell so loudly that the buffalo-demon loses his hearing, and then she pierces him with her spear. Who does she pierce? She pierces

that bad soul that overpowers us repeatedly and disturbs us, the one who shows us a little greed and glitter and tricks us in every way. With her bright lustre, the Goddess takes away his lustre and ends him.

13. Listen. To be right to others is known as godliness. The day you gain the knowledge of the left and the right, you will learn the secrets of dear *Vagishwari* (the goddess of learning and speech). The right is frightening. It has no sweetness in it. It is prescribed to inhale the life-force through the left nostril. The right nostril is for exhalation. Women are a complement of the heart; they are a joy. Oh pandit. You are foolish! It is a simple mystery. *Prakriti* (nature) is a complement of the *purush* [the creator, or God]. It is the *prakriti* that reveals the innumerable mysteries lying within us; She gives them to us. She is the one who has been addressed as *apara*, *parameshwari*, *sarveshwari*, *uddhareshwari*. She is the auspicious one, She does good for all.

14. That creative energy is the Goddess, whose prayer and worship every human always does, in one form or another. They do it in the form of food and drinks, they do it in the form of their happiness and conveniences, and they do it by indulging in many right or wrong acts and thereby producing sorrows for themselves. In one form or another they all worship her. Now it is important to ask, What in that worship would be appropriate for us? What will be good for us? We cannot decide about that. That decision [which is Her's] will be the right decision, it will be appropriate, and it will be true.

15. If we remember Her even once in twenty-four hours, while performing all our other actions, then it gives us unfathomable creativity and unlimited organization. And it is that same creative energy that in every way, in every field, makes us meet good people.

16. She, who is the great creative energy — Ramā, Umā, Shivā —

these, the great creative energies, when they enjoy our company and focus their grace upon us, then everyone will shower their grace on us.

17. If they have no interaction amongst themselves, even birds produce animosity. What is this animosity? When that *mahamaya* (Goddess) takes her graceful eyes away from us, when She lifts away her tender arms from us, this gives us unbearable agony.

18. [Her] inspiration is such that [it indicates] She is in everyone and everything like the air, like the rays of the Sun, like the earth extending everywhere; She just can't be collected together into one place. That is why her touch, her smell or the prayer and worship of her every limb can be accomplished anywhere and everywhere.

19. Knowingly or unknowingly, whatever good actions you end up performing, you definitely reap its fruits. And be it action performed knowingly or unknowingly, if it is a bad action, then of course its result is bad. Whether the act be with your knowledge, then too, and whether the act be without your knowledge, then too. There, you do not receive forgiveness or kindness. For, both forgiveness and kindness have been counted in the category of crimes.

20. Morning happens, evening happens, and the life keeps passing by. It keeps ending. Not even by a moment does it become prolonged. It keeps dissipating. The day you are born, that very day is the time of your death also fixed.

21. Friends, this is how it happens on the earth. You speak here in this room. Now look! If your word can go so far through the medium of a tool, then can't your inner thought reach that divinity? It definitely does. Furthermore, it finds its designated place.

22. We have never paid our attention towards the sounds of nature. We thought She would speak in the same language as we do. So, even if She comes before us and speaks in this language, we wouldn't believe her. Because of this disbelief it is possible we insult her, or even strike her.

23. We are all the children of that one God; we've all been produced by the same instrument. All our lives have a common source of emergence. And that is the vulva.

24. Trees, vines and the like are of various categories, forms, and colours. Mother Nature, father nature, the sun, the moon, the rain, the sky and the earth all look after them in the same way for each type. Besides the five elements, the Unknown present within us also gives us accurate directions, and in doing so it is not at all mindful of sin and virtue, big or small, rich or poor, scholarly or stupid. With these true elements and with the five elements everything remains within the periphery of this solar system under the rules of Mother Nature, and performs its own actions. If you overlook this then neither will you be able to save yourself from the suffocation of [the natural processes of] that eternal truth, the five elements, and the Super-nature, nor will you be able to save any other being in the solar system.

25. You will see, very hard times can come even into your life. To acquire the capability to face them, to pray to the divinity Super-nature present within you with an unvocalized speech — which is in effect a very powerful communication — will not remain unheard.

26. The nature that you want to learn about to then gain the knowledge of tantra and mantra —that is with you, too. In fact, you do it more than me, and you do it every day.

27. Your divinity passes by right in front of you many times a day. Lord Shiva, the ever-pleasant Aghor-Bhairava — he passes

by you every day, Shiva and Parvati pass in front of you every day. Every morning and every evening you get these signs from your own children, from your family and friends, or from other beings in your home or from the people you happen to meet. But you do not even have the time to hear or recognize these signs. By not keeping yourself empty you've accumulated so much garbage within yourself, there's so much dust and dirt in your mind, you just can't understand it.

28. Everywhere today, good sentiments are scarce. In the absence of good sentiments, nature cannot forgive any planned action to pluck and destroy these, the delicate blossoms and flowers of innumerable mothers, who had a desire, who had a will to do something with their lives.

29. In the cremation ground lie the ashes. Ashes contain grandeur and a good aura. Good persons arrive at such a place.

30. What is Her style, what is Her desire, is very important. Let us pray to Her thus: "O Mother! In ignorance the effects of bad actions which have surrounded us and made us so greedy, sever these effects from us and fill us with good actions for the service of society and the nation. Fill us again with those pure sacraments which were there in the beginning of the creation when our soul arose, and cut away all our polluted traditions, O Mother!" That is why we try to achieve that condition within us by saying "*Om Hari, Om Tatsat. Namo Devyam, Bhairavam, Akshobhya, Aghoreshwaraya*, peace to the sky, peace to the earth, peace to all directions".

31. Before your birth and with your birth the promise you had made to yourself not to indulge in unnatural acts; forgetting this under the bad influence of family members and relatives, you have become forced to live in an unnatural way, and you are suffering from all kinds of troubles.

32. Learn from these ants and their group, which is very united. The ants have a unique discipline. They move in one line, single file. They are never particularly eager. They have only their self-confidence. They never act in a way so as to need laws or regulations or religion. Religion is actually a social organization. Ants do not oppose each other in vain like we humans do. They do not insult each other.

33. One who sees his divinity's nature in his own nature, he is a divinity. One who sees his own nature in his guru's nature, he is a guru.

34. The creative energy has passed by you many a times, it has even touched you; you too must have touched it, but you were not able to keep it. You are actually bent upon losing what you have, and are bent upon looking for that which is absolutely lost, which does not even have an existence. These two strange things are in your mind, because of which you are not able to keep it.

35. What will we do by worshipping a deity that gives rise to absolute immortality? There are many deities that give rise to immortality. And there are many that give birth to ideals. And there are many who are so cruel they actually destroy their own worshipper. They bother him in many ways. They strip him of everything, including his underwear.

36. [Regarding the worship of the Mother]: We people worship Mahakali, Mahalakshmi, and Mahasaraswati. It is said that these deities are mentioned in the scriptures, and that of these, that Lakshmi (the Goddess of wealth) is a very nice deity, that she is a very good deity because when she stays with us, we will live in great happiness and peace. But, tell me yourself: what is the behaviour of those people who own a home, a house, wealth, a car? Their conduct is in shambles. They do not have anything in the name of virtue. They do not have

shame in their eyes. The vehicle of Lakshmi is the owl. And like the owl, these people think that they are the best in the world. They think that they know everything. This is their condition. Therefore, if, you worship this deity then — due to a little greed — you will be saddled with a great negativity.

37. You may think, "Alright, I'll worship Saraswati (the Goddess of knowledge and learning)". The condition of Saraswati is so poor that you will not find even any token ideals arising in any college, university or in any scholar in this country. Only animosity, jealousy, envy, hatred and debauchery arise in them.

38. Now, the question of Kali. She is a deity who looks very black. She actually is very black. But that blackness is not a black spot [of soot]. She devours the blackness of time. She laughs openly in the cremation grounds. She lights a lamp in this inert, corpse-like body of yours. She beautifies this inert body. In fact, she sends a hundred people even to accompany a corpse. If not hundred, then she definitely does send at least ten or fifteen with the corpse [to the cremation ground] on that day. That is certain.

39. Amongst Mahakali, Mahalakshmi, and Mahasaraswati, whichever deity you worship, her unique grace will be on you, and it will be on you not only all through your life, but also upon your children and grandchildren, your wife, your family, and everyone else.

40. We have to worship only that which is within us. She is the Mother. She is the creative energy that gives us good inspirations, and which gives us the indications to progress towards our dear divinity.

41. People who do not have the grace of the creative energy, and to whom the creative energy does accords no respect, these people are listless. They must face defeat everywhere.

42. It is the creative energy that has mesmerized all of us in various forms. Children, wife, grandchildren, friends and relatives, rituals and mantra and so on — are all her forms. She brings attachments in these forms, as well. One person has one particular illusion, another person has a different attachment. Afflicted by illusions, we are unable to cut away Her net. As a result, we get afflicted by diseases and spend an inactive life. Such a life has no value.

43. I hope that your imminent dawn will be highly beneficial for you, and that this night doesn't bother you. May you achieve stability this night, and may the coming dawn fully inspire you with the enthusiasm of the new day. May it influence you towards good actions. Being involved in these actions will make all your senses very conscious and alert, you will dispel all the darkness from your mind and consciousness, and you'll be able to know the real form of that Unknown Great Mother.

44. All beings are attracted to the vulva (bhag), the goddess (Bhagavati). There is no being not pulled towards Her. Insects and moths, frogs, fishes, birds, animals: She attracts every being. This is what her illusion and attachment is, and the person who knows the reality of these illusions does not get into trouble. That person doesn't get into any trouble at all.

45. From the dawn of creation, everyone who has practiced cleverness has done so in vain. Take Vishnu, as an example. Even in India there are proportionally very few people who are his devotees. That is because he tricked many people. Even Krishna [an incarnation of Vishnu], who declared himself to be God, had to suffer negative consequences.

46. Friends! What you see as very clean and nice and attractive is actually something that takes you towards your death. "Don't neglect what's yours" — this is what you're told in the places of saints and Mahatmas. This is very important.

47. [Have faith] in your own faith; don't have faith in everybody's faith. You have a faith of your own. In your faith itself lies the faith of Mother Sarveshwari. It is the faith of that saint, that seeker, that guru, which has come up to you in the form of a message.

48. In the clean and pure sky you will begin to venture like that bird which flies across every country, every state, and every region. It has no boundaries or limits. It knows no barricades. Everything is hers, and everyone is hers. Such people belong to the family of Sarveshwari.

49. The vulva towards which all beings show such eagerness, such attraction, is said to be a very profound and confidential [subject]. Neither is it something to be bandied about on the road or in the market nor is it to be treated with indiscipline.

50. You know that the entity that is addressed as Narayan Vishnu has the form of the vagina, and it is said to be joyful, if alone. It is like humans. If it has four hands then it is in the form of that joy and happiness that everyone desires. But his worship has not been prescribed in the scriptures under this form. It has been prescribed in a different way. In this way, the deity is described as having 18 arms; those arms belong to the nine sisters we call the Nav-Durgas, or the 64 Yoginis, and worship them as such. They are not a temple idol. Such things happen in our thoughts and behaviour, in our everyday conduct, like the passing of morning, noon and evening.

51. When we will have confidence in ourselves then everything will be easy. You will easily gain all knowledge and you will be able to gauge the impending effects and happenings by recognizing various signs and forms, and the auspicious or inauspicious scenes of various animals and birds.

52. The daily growth of hair, beard and nails demonstrates that nature wants to turn us into the form of an animal while, in opposition to this, we trim our hair, beard and nails and want to be imbued with human traits. However, our effort seems to be limited to the aesthetics of our bodies.

53. What is the desire of the Super-nature; how can our nature be assimilated into Hers? If we become assimilated to that nature then there will be no increase or decrease within us, no rise or fall, nor will we be unbalanced by either happiness or sorrow. Whatever will come before us, will be so. O my Mother! Please give us such inspiration that we may become faultless. May we become free from deceit — if not for anyone else, then at least for ourselves. May our nature be assimilated into yours. We will learn of your arrival once you enter our body. When you enter our body, our mind and heart will become very calm, and in this peace we will begin to live amongst those humans who are divine souls, pure souls, beautiful souls. There all our deceit and wickedness will flee from us; then, in the same way, peace arrives when anger goes away, peace arrives when illusions go away, friends.

54. If you properly sculpt the coming generation, sculpting them in keeping with the [realities of the present] time and period, in keeping with the course that everything has to take, and keeping in mind the natural rules by which things operate, then — assuming auspicious astrological configurations — that arriving person will be even more talented than you, my friends.

55. Friends, how we will find happiness, how we will find peace, how our mind will become stable — these depend upon our nature. That means that, when our nature finds us, we will have happiness, peace and stability. If our nature is not at a similar level to the nature of those around us, and if we nevertheless remain with them, then we will be insulted, chastized and will suffer mental pains. We will be sad.

56. The teaching that we have received from our gurus — to keep quiet — this quiet is something that destroys a thousand animosities. Sitting in this quiet state, in this stable state, a person beholds that supreme consciousness and perceives that the whole earth belongs to it. [He perceives that] there is a belly [of the Mother], and in that belly is a hall in which we people exist. This garden [of the world] belongs to it and here grow the multicoloured flowers, our individual and diversely-featured faces. In this [quiet state], whatever is good, as well as whatever one is attracted to, to that extent are they filled by that sweetness, do they achieve that joy and happiness, do they achieve that peace.

THE LIFE-FORCE

We are alive because within us we have the life-force. The life-force is but an energy which is maintained by the incessant process of the breath, inward and outward. By investigating the nature of breath and the life-force, a seeker can understand the deepest mysteries of life and death.

1. The fire in the belly which maintains the life-force in beings, this always burns. To give oblations to it is equivalent to giving food, affection, respect, and virtue to the life-force. To give oblations to it is equivalent to worshipping the cosmic God.

2. In the body, the life-force is the animating factor of the living being. Cosmologically, it is known as air.

3. The life-breath is the one we worship. Our own worship is our worship.

4. The guru in the form of the life-force can be seen and found in all times, everywhere, very easily, through practice, and many fruits can be gained from him. Guru is not a body, he is the life-force.

5. Faith in our own life-force seems to be decreasing. If your faith goes and adheres to an invisible God whose voice can't be heard, this will inevitably have disastrous results.

6. One who hides and nurtures attachments deep within himself — the life-force is very far away from him, and he remains unacquainted with it.

7. Remain respectful to the life-force until the very final moment — because the only thing to be destroyed is this perishable

body. In this cosmic bowl, the *pran* will always maintain our memories of our many practices, activities, and so on. Whenever you desire you will enter a beautiful body, and recalling the past incarnations of your life-force, you will be able to do anything.

8. Having neglected their life-force, overwhelmed by attachments and fear, beings seem aflame in the pyre of worries.

9. [Giving] respect and honour to the life-force is like worshipping the knowable God.

10. The life-force is the lustre of glory itself.

11. The life-force is one with the infinite. That which has neither beginning nor end, such an infinity is known as the life-force. The life-force is not knowable through external eyes or touch. It is identical to the vibrations within us. Knowledge and experience of this can only be given to us by saints.

12. The life-force is the one known as the unborn, the infallible, which can always be found, in all times and in all places.

13. This Mother in the form of the life-force is very easy to know through our actions.

14. The day this Mother in the form of the life-force leaves us, people will cremate this body like a tuft of straw.

15. The day this Mother in the form of life-force takes this life-force and merges it into Herself, that day the whole world will turn into darkness. In my eyes this will be the absolute end of all existence, even if it be otherwise in the eyes of another. In my eyes, just as at the end of existence, everything will disappear.

16. Resting within every being, the eternal consciousness produces vibrations in the form of air. However clean the being may be, if he is not stable, he cannot see himself, or me, in the swing of the life-breath air.

17. One who gathers and saves the life-breath achieves the state of ecstasy and omniscient consciousness very simply and easily.

18. Air, without vibration, provides complete stability to this life-breath.

19. One who does not see earth as earth, one who does not see air as air, one who does not see the lustre as lustre, one who does not see water as water, but who rather sees them all as a refuge for his life-breath, he is the one who sees in the right way, O Sudharma.

20. The divinity concocted by the human mind is like lightning in the clouds. It is momentary. One who holds the religion of the life-force can never have such thoughts.

21. He who knows himself, he who knows the life-force within himself, he who can recognize the life-force in others: only he has the right to provide happiness and convenience to the whole world, and only he does so. One who believes so is a place of refuge for all beings.

22. Real seekers worship the living beings in whom God himself has established the life-force.

23. Sitting within us is the life-force who cannot be prayed to. You will find it, away from eagerness, aggravation, desire, ambition, or considerations of us and them.

24. This golden body is not meant to search for anyone else. One who seems to be looking and searching like this is actually

looking for someone else and has no idea about himself — he has no clue of it. You should understand the one who bows to his life-force. Every pore of his body resonates with the sound of *pranav* (the resonance of Om). From his body blossom a pure shadow and a cool aura. Nothing rises in him, nothing sets in him.

25. Through the discipline of the life-force does the omniscient consciousness arise, and the body is the spring from which arises the life-force. Absorption into the life-force is an achievement of great glory.

26. Action is the source from which the life-force sprouts forth.

27. Becoming free from the desires of being either awake or asleep, and practicing to stop the life-breath wherever it is: these give rise to a new inventive creation within the body which is both real and directly evident.

28. In just an instant, the sight of the form [of a thing or person or entity] can make the body tremble. Rishis have said, "Do not look at the form, do not enjoy its charm". Only the enjoyment-free essence can be helpful in knowing the life-force.

29. When the life-force departs, the body becomes flaccid and merges back into the five elements. Regard the life-force as an indicator of all perception. Without the life-force, the being is unble to perceive either the world or the creator of the world. Only through the medium of the life-force residing in the body can the world or its creator be known.

30. When does the life-force go away, when does it return, when does it expand itself: these cannot be asked. When the body is bereft of the life-force, people call it a corpse, an illusion, as clay, as the dead, as worthless straw.

31. When the life-force becomes separated from you, there are absolutely no vibrations within you, nor can anybody know, hear or see.

32. God is self-created. He does not reside in the sky, or in the Himalayas, or at the North Pole. He is right amidst us. He is in the form of the life-force.

33. The valour of the Mother in the form of the life-force is not limited to interesting lines of poetry. The energy hidden within us is the first sign of her valour.

34. The sacred discipline of a householder is to provide oblations of food-grains into the life-force of living beings.

35. The life-force is an energy. The beings are living forms of this energy. The actions of this energy can be understood only by beings with this form. In getting a body, the being is trying to keep a minuscule particle of this energy within bounds. The being, actually, is ever liberated. How can he have fetters? When the body is abandoned, the being-particle goes to its centre-point. It merges with the life-force through yoga. This is the kind of union that a yogi desires.

36. Being in the refuge of the society of Mahabhairavamalini has brought our life close to the life-force. In response to someone's insult, even if it be from an enemy, it is our fearlessness that brings us to victory. The act that has far-reaching consequences has sweet, delicious fruits.

37. The scriptures and the oral traditions have divided the body into four categories, and the feet are accorded more importance than the head. You must have seen that we salute the feet of gurus and other respected people. Even then, O Darshi! According to this categorization, the feet are considered to be the Shudras (the lowest caste of people in India), but how

important are these Shudras! The day you know and understand this, and establish yourself within the feet, that day will you know, in a real sense, the life-force which is found in all beings.

38. It is the same life-force which is reflected in the same way in the Brahmins, the Kshatriyas, the Vaishyas and the Shudras. But, neglecting the life-force residing in the feet in the form of the Shudras, by admonishing them, by insulting them, we are bent upon destroying ourselves.

39. One who provides oblations with all his five fingers to the life-force residing within him and within all other beings, without discriminating between them according to their being big or small, in an equal way and at the same time, he is a true Kshatriya.

40. The life-force itself is the Aghoreshwar, the Aughar, the Sarveshwari, the observer of equality, the one free from hate, from contrast, from category-distinctions.

41. All the four kinds of edible substances [solid, liquid, jelly-like and gummy] exist only for the preservation of the life-force. Without them, this Ishwar (God) of ours, this *I-swar* [*I-* followed by *-swar*, the continuous breath process] will end. When the breath stops, creation will disappear from sight. Everyone knows of this mortality.

Worship

What is worship? Is it offering fruits and flowers to a deity at a certain appointed time, or is it listening to the deity and following the inspiration it gives to the seeker? Human beings need to decide what the nature of their worship is, and then communicate with their deity in the best possible manner.

1. The day you make an effort to look at yourself, that day all your thoughts bound by your desires and by your past deeds will disappear. As long as you keep trying to look at the other, you will find yourself to be without shelter, and very far away from yourself.

2. In the form of the sacred festival of Navaratri we have this time available to us which can give us great strength and intellect and wisdom, and great knowledge. If during this period within ourselves we become free from deceit, wickedness and flaws, and if perform our *japa* and so on, then we will definitely achieve success.

3. [On Navaratri]: This festival is called Navaratri by those people who have their secure monopoly in the reading of *Saptachandi* or in some rituals or worship. We think that the name of this festival is 'New Day'. The newest day of our life is about to arrive. We should beg that creative energy that our torpor might be broken, and that those numerous dreams of sorrow that we see might all be destroyed right by their roots. This is why this festival is celebrated. Where people should have talked about 'the new day', instead they named it 'the nine nights'. Who doesn't know that the night is made up of dreams? At night many bad dreams take place, and what dirty deeds do we do in our dreams! Only the robber roams at night. A saint does not roam about at night.

4. Your hunger, your desire, and your greed bother you and they all begin to assault you together. In that condition, if you perform a fast then it is good from the point of view of your health. But in this *Kaliyuga* even this is not required. If you fast on the first day of the lunar fortnight (*pratipada*), and then on the eighth day (*ashtami*), then even that is enough.

5. Friends! This New Day is an occasion for making a vow. If you make a vow, you will be able to carry out the newest tasks of your life. The rest of your life will progress very well on its path. Otherwise this life will end as a curse. On the occasion of this sacred festival of the New Day, may you relinquish your night full of dark dreams, and may you move towards the newest that is yours, and may you make a vow for it.

6. On the occasion of this sacred festival of Navaratri, whatever you learn, teach it to worthy people who come to you who want to progress on the path of truth. Never tell it to undeserving people. This will weaken your own strength as well as theirs.

7. [On the worship of the seven goddesses]: In the villages, the seven-headed edifice that you see represents the lineage deities of the seven main backward castes in the villages. They represent the worship of their lineage-daughters. With them the eighth icon that exists is that of Aghor-Bhairava, also known as Akshobhya-Bhairava. Village folk worship the seven goddesses to chase away evil souls from the sky, for peace, to maintain a good and pure atmosphere in the village and at home, and to protect their homes, family, friends and the village from the attack of evil souls. We derive everything by worshipping them. Even demigods bow down and are forced to give us the fruit we desire. These seven icons represent the lineage-brides of the seven backward castes in the villages which, respectively, are the gardener, the barber, the washerman, the janitor, the sweeper and the cowherd. They are

ritually established and worshipped by the Kshatriyas or by *kshatriya*-like people of the village.

8. You should know the ideal of your worship, its various aspects and mysteries. [You should know] in which form should we worship her so that the ideals of our family, friends and society are maintained, while also keeping her character intact.

9. Destroying our bad deeds, we worship to achieve our dear divinity.

10. You perform a fast where potatoes, jackfruit, bananas, egg-plants and various other fruits are prescribed. This is not a fast, friends! This is a scheme by traders to cheat innocent village folks. All these rules that have been made for prayer and worship — that you should eat only these things, and that you will only find Her if you eat these things, otherwise not — is nothing but an absolute lie. However might you remain, if She is to find you, then She will find you. Oh, you should at least stay there. However, you aren't even prepared even to be present there, friends.

11. We relinquish absurd things, absurd thoughts and absurd ravings. That is what we call worship, friends.

12. You should worship the creative energy. I will not ask you to worship things.

13. Tomorrow is the festival of Janmashtami. Due to goalless-ness, there will be a lot of singing and dancing and ostentation. That very day is the birthday of the Mother. Poets and historians have linked this day with the Mother's birthday so that the priests who worship the Mother's birthday may be able to join in these festive celebrations. The same sentiment is hidden in the festival of Navaratri during the month of Chaitra (March-April). In Dashahra, Vijayadashmi and the others

are the creative energy that is worshipped, rather than being a particular person who is worshipped.

14. We are not able to understand: Why did this particular bird come into this garden today? Why did we see this particular animal here today? What will be the result of seeing these symbols over the course of a week? If such-and-such forms or such-and-such tendencies become visible to us, then what does that mean? If we saw such-and-such a thing in the morning, what does it portend? That is why, on getting up in the morning, we pray to our own Self, O, my morning! May you be very good. O my afternoon and my night! May you be very nice, very peaceful and very auspicious. May you give us good sleep. Let us not be assaulted by any inauspicious asterism, or robber or marauder or anyone else. Let not sleeplessness attack us, let not any thing whatsoever attack us, let not any sorrow or pain attack us. We want peace. We like to live in peace.

15. [Elaborating on the importance of Ananya Diwas]: Today is not my birthday. On this day, I received the grace of food from the hands of an old woman. I used to roam about begging and I had not eaten in many days. Wherever I went to beg, all would insult me. If I would go amongst spiritual seekers, they would chase me away too. Everywhere was I only welcomed with insulting words. I was very neglected. On today's date, on the 14th of the dark half of the moon in the month of Magh, that woman, who was eating some grains, she gave me a handful of her own food. From that day onwards I received clothes, I received water also, and I received so much that I began to give it to others.

16. The inspiration that comes to you from deep within when you sit down to perform your *japa*, your worship — which is known as worship with offerings of flowers, incense, lamps, food and everything else — that is a mere formality. That

worship has already happened. As soon as a pure thought arises in your heart that "I have to do this act", that act gets done right there and then. Then you sit down to fulfil the formality of its performance, and a unique vibration emanates from your body. That vibration is such that it begets for you even the company of that divinity.

17. Regarding worship, *japa*, and meditation, and with the divinities and their icons, the cleverness that we have turns into stupidity. That stupidity [socially accepted cleverness] gives birth to many faults within us.

18. The extended time that we take to perform the various actions during worship is engendered by the sentiment that most of our time ought to be spent in doing good actions. Otherwise, if someone we know can hear us just by our calling them once, won't that divinity be able to hear the noise of our many prayers? It hears everything.

19. Nothing else happens with prayers and worship. What happens with prayers and worship is this: our free time — in which we get tricked, engrossed in playing cards, or gambling or fruitless debates, or gossiping — that time we use well, and we begin to live in happiness. That is why the Munis and the Rishis established this tradition of prayers and worship, meditation and contemplation, so that we may be able to fully use our free time which we otherwise squander uselessly.

20. The icon that people addressed as Mother Durga and worshipped for nine days, today on the eleventh day they are saying goodbye to her. They are taking her to set her afloat on the water. Who made this rule? What kind of a formality is it to give birth and then to kill it? Why establish life, and then take that life away? This is what is known as sin-mixed virtue. This has more sin and little virtue. This is a crime that is knowingly performed and which is not forgiven.

21. The process of worship that is delineated in the Aghor treatises is not very different [from others]. Here they prescribe the performance of *vrat* (fasting) while there [in the Aghor way] they prescribe the undertaking of *vrat* (making a vow or resolve). For Aghor it is not prescribed to fast. Keeping prescriptions and proscriptions and assets and faults in mind, they make a vow to do a particular thing or not to do a particular thing.

22. Within the procedure about making a vow in the 21st chapter of the Aghor treatise is found a sentence which says that all those we think to be bad, or those who are very bad, this is merely an adverse public opinion, for even they can become someone of great value someday. Therefore, do not throw them away, nor should you accept them completely. In its own time, even poison can act as *amrit.* It has a unique character of its own. Let it remain where it is.

23. In the same 21st chapter there is another sentence which says we will eat fish but we will not cast the net, for who knows how many more beings may have to be killed because of that. We will make only one our food, one whose life has now come to an end. That is why they throw the hook, so that only one approaches.

24. Also in the same [book] is that passage called the *Treatise on Shakti*, wherein it is said that the creative energy is variously identified as Devi or as deities of many different kinds, and that we try to understand her by dividing her into so many categories, but that this is a way for us to understand her, and is not her way. There's only one style in her style, and there is no other style in it. From that creative energy described in the *Treatise on Shakti* you can perform *tantra-mantra*, magic and things like that, and you can also get to know God or the nature of the Aghor, as well as fulfil the great vow that you have taken in your life, for it is said there that after these performances we should also move towards our pure livelihood.

25. In the morning, when you people are involved in prayer, worship, meditation and contemplation, many small birds perched on these trees and vines make sounds with their very sweet voices. If you've been paying attention you might have heard them, too. Even Hanuman once said this sermon in the form of a parrot:

> "On the ghats of Chitrakut saints have gathered.
> Tulsidas makes sandalwood paste, and anoints Raghubir's forehead."

In the same way, at Kedar-ji (Kedarnath in the Himalayas) above Gupt Kashi is a temple to the Mother. There, the Munis saw the Mother in the form of tiny birds. In our culture and in our worship these birds are very important to us, whose songs are so sweet, and who sing alone as well as in groups.

26. "Ring the gong to rid the ills." That is, I am ringing that gong which will make all my worldly, other-worldly, physical and divine enemies lose their hearing, and their gaze will not fall onto us. Then the Mother, lance in hand, should destroy them. With this sentiment should that sound emanate, and from the *damaru* (a hand-held, hourglass-shaped, two-sided drum) as well similar sweet sounds should ring. If the *damaru* is played then it should be in the hands of a very well-trained person so that the sound of the instruments has some meaning, that it has some symbolic language. If this is not possible then it is better not to play it at all. Like the temple priests who don't know much, ignorance does not suit you people.

27. When you perform worship then, if you ignore the sounds of those birds, it's possible you may remain deprived of the right way to know [the truth]. It's possible the voice of our dear divinity be in that form. In this form, our saints, Mahatmas and *mahapurushas* have found their dear divinity.

28. When we worship we sit in an *asana* (posture); we meditate sitting in a triangular *yantra* form. These postures have a great importance. Looking at their physical postures, one can assess a human , and ask, what kind of thoughts would this person have? What was he thinking ten minutes ago, what was he affected by an hour ago, and what was his mental state on coming here? You will find this vision if you worship with an alert eye.

29. Dear friends! In prayer and contemplation we keep our backbone straight and we make some postures with our arms. Sitting in these postures, the lustre, the aura, the vibration that emanates from our body [is so very beneficial that] you cannot yourself gauge what kind of a mental state you're in. How stable a person you become; you also get to know whether you are fickle or not. Whether you be performing your prayers and worship or if rather you are involved in earning your livelihood, it makes no difference in your stable condition. If someone comes to you out of the blue and rudely asks you about such-and-such a person or such-and-such a work, even then you'll behave politely with him; because of its effect, he'll even become polite himself.

30. Eating, drinking and putting things in the sacred fire is not *yagya* (ritual oblations into a sacred fire). That is why we should be very alert to each one of our acts.

31. If your way of thinking and your mentality remains good, then you will be dutiful. All the *tantra*s (bodies of knowledge; organizations) that you have — the *ashram-tantra*, the home-*tantra*, or *tantra* of prayer and worship — these *tantra*s will give you knowledge of the mantra. Knowing the mantra, you will achieve that sight in which you will see only friends everywhere. You will have no enemies. You will achieve great joy.

32. With your valour, strength, intellect and prudence, you can progress. If a human wants, he can progress even farther than that if he has faith in *tantra*. I am not talking here about *rajatantra* (monarchy), *prajatantra* (republic), *lokatantra* (democracy), or *samajtantra* (socialism). This is also a *tantra*. *Tantra* means any organization which is very correct and mature and which takes us towards an equal vision and behaviour for all. Humans have great valour; relinquishing any other hope, walking the path shown by their guru, and with their difficult discipline, they can achieve that.

33. When the worldly mother has unfathomable love, then what to say about the Other-worldly mother? You will have a right to that when you live within the *tantra*. When you live in the *tantra* in the right way, and when you know well what this *tantra* is, in the end, after all. This is also a *tantra* like *rajatantra*, *prajatantra*, and the other *tantras* which have been made to give direction to society. [These are principles] which unify society, hold it together, and give it a good organization. In the same way, whenever you get skilled in *tantra*, your mind, heart and all the senses — which normally all sing their own songs separately — will unite together and help you.

34. That which is the Truth, we have been involved until today in investigating it, that our mind should get involved in that Truth, it should turn towards that Truth. But our mind just can't do it. The day you get to fully know that Truth, that *tantra*, that worship, that thing, on that day your heart and mind will become completely free. They will go even beyond the state of ecstatic consciousness.

35. Until the day of your death, with even but a moment of that time you can achieve that supreme essence which is addressed as Parameshwari, Bhagawati, Bhawani, and Sarveshwari. Then, the *tantra* that we have will continue for many days in

the traditional way. Followers of *yagatantra* (a body of knowledge concerned with giving ritual oblations to the fire), *gyantantra* (the body of knowledge concerned with achieving Supreme Knowledge), *sadhanatantra* (the body of knowledge of austere practices) and their worshippers will keep coming here.

36. [The effects of *tantra*]: It creates a lustre. That aura is very efficacious. If you say something to someone, if you give something to someone, if you think nicely about someone, then all those things happen. And more than that, the biggest *tantra* is that all the veins and channels that are in our body, we thread each one of those into this *tantra* (tapestry). In the same way that people move their rosary in their hands, someone else will move us, this threaded garland, in their hands. He will move us again and again and, in doing so, he will bring into us that charm and joy.

37. [After my leaving]: New people will arrive. There will be a new organization. A new *tantra* will arrive and that *tantra* will continue so long as that next *tantric* remains. If that *tantric* is a good knower of mantra, then he too can change the lines of fate. In the Bharat region of Jambu Island, and especially on Ganga's banks, this knowledge known as *Brahm*-knowledge can be achieved in the shortest time possible.

38. Peace is not just a word. Just screaming peace-peace is not peace. It does not happen like this, actually. When in solitude you are alone and you are concentrated then you achieve peace, and you feel good. You stay away from any thought that would fling your heart and mind into illusion and take you towards ill-virtue. This is disciplined practice, and paying attention [to subtle things] is nothing more than such a disciplined practice. Sitting calmly in peace, as an instrument you maintain attention on all that happens within you.

39. On this sacred occasion of Navaratri we try to bind that Unthinkable into our thoughts so that She stays in our thoughts so we can make this life of ours fruitful, so that we might be able to cleanse the filth of social disapproval, which make a human a target of adverse notions. Although to think about that Unthinkable is not within the realm of our mind itself, nevertheless, prayer and worship performed with affection and care, meditation, *japa* and contemplation — all this does not go to waste. This is the only way to bring that Unthinkable into our thoughts. There is no other way.

40. The festival, for whose celebration you all came today, is a very tender, sweet, charming, and profound one. It teaches us to fold our hands, to be polite to each other, to give garlands to each other. With that it also teaches us to sit, to sit and remain silent, and remaining silent, it gives us that gravity which is very important for human beings. It asks us to leave all fickleness.

41. Friends! What we call prayer and worship, what we call religious acts, what we know under numerous names and forms — all this is effective only when we give up our excessive cleverness. Excessive cleverness makes a person weak and opens the way for ignorance to enter. With that, excessive cleverness forces us to worship demons instead of gods.

42. Prayer and worship, meditation and contemplation, silence and calmness take away all animosity, all sorrow and every trouble. However may you be, you will surely transform. You will evaluate your change yourself. The other person who sees you will also think that you are a very sweet person, a very humble person, who keeps his hands folded day and night. Who keeps his knees on the earth. Who never becomes unrestrained. Who is never ever seen as being verbose.

Time

Baba was always very particular about time. It was, he said, a good friend and a great resource. It can mould our lives beneficially, or destroy them, if neglected. Therefore, one should always be aware of time, and use it well.

1. Our extremely valuable time is rapidly running away in a continuous succession of morning, afternoon and evening and today and tomorrow. Today goes away every day and tomorrow stays tomorrow: it will never arrive. Tomorrow, something else will come.

2. If we keep overlooking time, if we keep misusing and cursing it, then we will not be able to make any history of our own, and there will be no justification for our taking birth.

3. The bad habits that we have, instead of attending them in a timely manner, we invite many kinds of uncalled-for diseases into our lives. Having done so, we are forced to pray to and to beseech God, and so we try to snatch away His time as well.

4. You have come into this world alone and, like the morning, the afternoon and the evening, you will depart with this day and this time.

5. Although it is not good to fixate on the past, neither it is good to completely forget it. Nor is it wise to understand the present only as the present, because the present is very different from what you now understand it to be. It's *so* different, we just can't know. It is the Unknown who knows this, that Unknown whom we call God. It is He who gives us the inspiration to say something, to hear something, and to come up to this point of understanding.

6. Everyone wants to gamble away their valuable time on a bet, and destroy it. Not only do they not realize its value, along with their valuable time they also devour their feelings of [self] respect. Then they exude terrible darkness into their environment and destroy their lives.

7. Whenever a good day or a good time begins, obstacles definitely arise therein. Many obstacles begin to arise.

8. When you become as time-bound as are the birds and the other animals, then you will be victorious over your senses, and even over that faulty life of yours shall you have some victory. Then your daily routine will become a source of inspiration to others. Your livelihood will also make others happy with you, and nobody will give it the evil eye or try to destroy it. Be they rulers or thieves, nobody will attack it.

9. Do not destroy time. Time will destroy you.

10. This life is not designed for doing just one thing for your whole life, or for the whole year, or for the whole month. It is time-bound: for such a time shall I perform such an act. After that I will also make an effort towards my livelihood through which I will be able to nurture and provide for my dependents, my friends and relatives, my children and grandchildren, my family and my aged parents. If we have an insulting attitude, that we are the only one [i.e. the best], then our quest will be absolutely incomplete. The result of this incompleteness may lead to our disciplined practice, our contemplation, our meditation and everything else to go to waste.

Glossary

Abhayadhar	An Aughar adept who is totally fearless.
Abhinavagupta	Abhinavagupta is one of the greatest exponents of non-dual Kashmir Shaivism, and adherents of this faith consider him to be an incarnation of Shiva. Abhinavagupta was a prolific writer. His literary works probably date from 990 to 1014 C.E. (http://www.digiserve.com/mystic/Hindu/Abhinavagupta/)
Achamani	An act of drawing water with an instrument in the left hand, putting that water on the palm of the right hand, and then drinking that water from the palm of the hand.
Achyut	*Meenakṣhi Hindi Angrezi Kosh* (Meenakshi Prakashan, India, 1990) defines the word *achyut* as '1. Not fallen, not deviating. 2. Infallible'. In yogic terms, however, the word signifies the state wherein no worldly illusion affects the person; in essence, his seed does not fall.
Agahan	Skt. Agrahayan Name of the month corresponding to November-December in the Gregorian calendar
Aghor	The word *aghor* literally means 'that which is not difficult or terrible'. Aghor is a simple and natural state of consciousness. There is no place for feelings of fear, hatred, disgust or discrimination in the eyes of an Aughar. A person who practices these virtues may be designated as an Aughar or an Aghori. With constant practice, when the soul is established in that state, such a person becomes an Awadhut, regardless of his path.
Aghorachal	An aughar who is absolutely stable and steadfast in his mind. A mountain of *aghor* stability.
Aghorbhairavacharya	King Harshavardhan's father's Guru.
Aghoreshwar	An Aghoreshwar is an Awadhut who has gone through all the various stages of Aghor and then has returned to society for the benefit of others. Even though an Aghoreshwar remains above and beyond all social and material illusions, distinctions, and categories, he can bring many social reforms into effect. Realizing his divine nature, retaining the carefree, unattached Aghor state of being, he may have at the same time the appearance of one observing the contemporary social norm rather than of a recluse.

Aghor-Ganga	The stream of spiritual thought that subsumes people of all castes, classes and religions.
Aghori	A practitioner of the path of Aghor.
Aghorpeeth	The seat of Aghor.
Ahuti	Oblations that are offered to the sacred fire in a fire sacrifice ritual.
Amla	Indian Gooseberry. Amla is used extensively in India both for its medicinal value as well as for cosmetic purposes. Amla contains pretty much all the tastes. It is sour, sweet, bitter, pungent etc. It is praised as a miracle ingredient for curing any problem in the alimentary canal. Amla oil helps decelerate premature graying, baldness, etc. Amla is also used in making pickles. (http://polimetla.tripod.com/forus/spices.htm#3)
Amrit	The sap of immortality.
Asana	The place where one sits, or a yogic posture.
Ashram	A hermitage or dwelling place dedicated to spiritual pursuits.
Ashtabhuja	The eight-armed goddess. The goddess is the personification of Power, or *shakti*. She is known by many names: Kali, Lakshmi, Saraswati, Chandika, Durga, Bhawani, Ambika. (http://www.indiaa2z.com/festivals/Navratra.htm)
Atma	Soul; the presence of Brahman as the deepest essence of the self in all entities; the Divine Self, a synonym of Brahman.
Aughar	A practitioner of the path of Aghor, or one who has achieved the Aghor state of the mind.
Aughar Bhabbar	An Aughar who has become angry. He then has the ability to even move creation.
Auliya	Friends, protectors, helpers; a realized Muslim saint.
Avadhoot/Awadhut	A traditional Indian term for one who has 'shaken off' or 'passed beyond' all worldly attachments and cares, including any motive of detachment (or conventional and other-worldly renunciation), all conventional notions of life and religion, and all seeking for 'answers' or 'solutions' in the form of conditional experience or conditional knowledge.
Ayoni-janma	Born without a womb, materialized by one's own self.
Bali	Brother of Sugriv in the epic *Ramayana*.
Banyan	The Banyan tree grows in India and Bangladesh and is held sacred in both places. The mature Banyan's canopy may cover an area more than 1,000 feet in diameter. The stems below the canopy form a kind of columned room. (http://www.banyantree.org/)

Bhag	Vulva, as the doorway of creation and a focus of worldly attraction.
Bhagawati	The Goddess.
Bhagwan	God. Also, an adept who is in absolute unity with his female counterpart.
Bhakti	Devotion; ecstatic loving-devotion to the Almighty.
Bharat	Brother of Rama, the hero of the epic *Ramayana.*
Bhawani	The Infinite Energy, which streams forth from the Eternal and sets the wheel to work, who looms up in man's vision in various aspects and infinite forms. Sometimes She is Love, sometimes She is Knowledge, sometimes She is Renunciation, sometimes She is Pity. This Infinite Energy is Bhawani.
Bhutashuddhi	Purification of the past. It also means purification of the various elements of the body.
Brahm/Brahman	In the Upanishads, Brahman is the name for the ultimate, unchanging reality, composed of pure being and consciousness. Brahman lies behind the apparent multiplicity of the phenomenal world, and is ultimately identical to the *atman* or inner essence of the human being (see *vedanta*). (http://www.encyclopedia.com/articles/01794.html)
Brahma	The Creator-god in the trinity of Brahma, Vishnu and Mahesh.
Brahmin	Brahmin-a member of the highest, or priestly, Hindu caste. Brahmins alone may interpret the Vedas and perform Vedic sacrifice. The vast majority of modern Brahmins are in occupations unrelated to religion, but they have retained their social prestige and many caste conventions. The Brahmins of India are divided into ten territorial subcastes, five in the north and five in the south. (http://www.encyclopedia.com/articles/01794.html)
Brahmarandhra	The highest point within the body, before the *bindu*, to which the Kundalini rises in the course of its ultimate union with the infinite.
Brihaspati	Vedic God of ritual; the planet Jupiter (*guru*).
Buddha	Lord Buddha; a self enlightened person of the Buddhist tradition; the ninth incarnation of Vishnu according to the Vaishnav tradition.
Caste	The pattern of social classes in Hinduism is called the 'caste system'.
Chandika	In the Devi-Mahatmya there is a description of Durga's appearance: The gods saw a stupendously big fiery mass, like a

flaming mountain, filling the firmament with flames. That matchless splendour, born from the bodies of all the gods, came together in a single place, pervading all the worlds with its lustre, and it became a woman... Devi bellowed aloud with laughter over and over again. The whole atmosphere was filled with her terrible noise, and from that deafening, ear-shattering noise a great echo arose. All the worlds quaked, and the oceans shook. The earth trembled, and the mountains tottered. The gods, utterly delighted, cried, "Victory!" to the one who rides on a lion.

And so the Great Goddess is born, ready to fight the enemies of the gods. In her battle with the demons, she easily wins, and must finally confront the general, Mahisha himself. For this battle she is called Chandika, 'The Violent and Impetuous One', in part because Mahisha so infuriates her by changing form every time she attempts to kill him.
(http://www.maabatakali.org/raudra.htm)

Chethariya Vir Baba — The figure of a realized saint in Baba Aghoreshwar Bhagwan Ram's book, *Aghor Guru Guh*.

Dattatreya — Dattatreya's Brahmanical portrayal, as well as his even more archaic characterization as a Tantric antinomian figure, combines both Vaishnava and Shaiva motifs. Over the course of time, Dattatreya has come to embody the roles of the immortal guru, yogi and *avatar* in a paradigmatic manner. From the sixteenth century, Dattatreya's glorious characterization emerged as the incarnation of the *trimurti* of Brahma, Vishnu, and Siva. Although Maharashtra is the heartland of Dattatreya devotion, his presence is attested to throughout India and extends beyond the boundaries of Hinduism, being met with in Sufi circles and even in Buddhism and Jainism via Nathism.

The scarce attention which most Western scholars of Indian religions have paid to this deity contrasts with its ubiquitousness and social permeability. Devotion to Dattatreya cuts through all social and religious strata of Indian society: among his adepts we find yogis, Brahmans, fakirs, Devi worshippers, untouchables, thieves, and prostitutes.
(http://www.sunypress.edu/sunyp/backads/html/rigopoda.html)

Devi — Any female deity.

Dhut — A short form of the word Avadhoot.

Dhrim, Dhrim, Dhrim — The mantra resonated by Mahabhairavi at the end of creation.

Dhyana	Meditation.
Digbandhan	Tying the directions. Essentially, this action builds barricades in every direction around the seeker against unwanted forces.
Doob grass	Known as Bermuda Grass, Giant Bermuda Grass, Bahama Grass, Devil's Grass, Couch Grass, Indian Doab, Grama, Balama grass. Used in Hindu rituals
Durga	The Goddess as the destroyer of demons; one of the energy forms of Siva.
Durvasa	A realized saint in the ancient Indian tradition, known to become very angry and curse on impulse.
Fakir	A wandering mendicant in the South Asian Islamic tradition.
Ganesha	Shiva's son; The Lord of Obstacles; Lord (*isha*) of the Host (*gana*) of Shiva. He has the head of an elephant and a very large pot belly.
Ganga	The river Ganges.
Gangotri	The place in the Himalayas considered to be the source of the river Ganga.
Ghats	Riverbanks that are used for domestic purposes.
Ghee	Clarified butter.
Gita/Geeta	The renowned *Bhagavad-Gita* has its origin at the battlefield of Kurukshetra, where the warring armies of the Kaurawas and Pandavas faced each other. A chapter in the *Mahabharata*.
Govind	A name of Krishna. This story is very popular: an elephant went to the river for a drink of water. A crocodile got hold of his foot in the river and began to drag him in. They fought for many hours but the crocodile was about to pull the elephant under. At that moment, in abject helplessness, the elephant remembers the name of Krishna, Govind, and says Govind. As the story goes, he could utter only 'Go', but nevertheless Krishna came and killed the crocodile, thus freeing the elephant from the throes of death.
Grihastha	Person at the second of the four stages of life, the stage of the householder.
Guna	The three *gunas*; see *the three humours*.
Gur	Molasses.
Guru	Enlightened spiritual teacher.
Guru-mantra	The mantra given to the disciple by the Guru.
Hawan	An offering of fire in Hindu worship.
Hrim, Hrim, Hrim	Mantra resonated by the Goddess Mahabhairavi at the dissolution of the creation.

Isht/Ishta	An individual's chosen deity.
Ishwar/Ishvara	God.
Jambudweep	Jambudweep is a name given to India in the ancient texts.
Janak	Father; also father of Sita, the heroine of the epic *Ramayana*.
Japa	The chanting of the mantras.
Jati	Birth; the caste system.
Kali	The divine Shakti, representing the creative and destructive aspects of nature, a transcendental symbol of human abilities.
Kaliyuga	Dark or iron age.
Kaluram	The preceptor of the modern lineage of Aughar ascetics in Banaras.
Kamechha, Kamakhya	The Goddess Kamakhya, who grants the wishes of her devotees.
Kapaleshwar	A form of Shiva.
Karttik	The name of a month in the Hindu astrological calendar.
Karttikeya	Shiva's son named Kartikeya has six heads. Hence he is also called Sharanan, which means exactly that, six-headed.
Kauravas	One of the warring lineages in the epic *Mahabharata*.
Ketaki	A frog.
Kinaram	A sixteenth century saint in the Aghor tradition of Baba Kaluram.
King Harshavardhan	After the downfall of the Gupta Empire in the middle of the 6th century AD, North India was again split into several independent kingdoms. The Huns established their supremacy over the Punjab. It was after this period that one of the greatest King of ancient India, Harshavardhan began his rule. He became the King of Thanesar (Kurukshetra) in 606 AD and later went on to become the ruler of most of North India. (http://www.haryana-online.com/history.htm)
Kshatriya	People of political values, belonging to the second of the four Hindu classes of society, traditionally a warrior, ruler or administrator.
Ksheer	A Sanskrit word meaning nurturing milk.
Kundalini	Power of the subtle body, the coil of energy at the base of the spine, visualized as a serpent.
Lakshmi	Goddess of prosperity, fortune and beauty; consort of Vishnu, sometimes called Shri.

Lalita	The Goddess of bliss.
Ma	The Mother.
Mahabhairava	A form of Shiva recognized in the Tantras.
Mahabhairavamalini	A name of Parvati, as a consort to Shiva in the form of Mahabhairava.
Mahabhairavi	The female consort of Shiva in the form of Mahabhairava.
Mahadevi	'Great Goddess', the Mother Goddess of Hinduism.
Mahakali	A form of Goddess Durga in the text Durga Saptashati.
Mahakapalik	Ancient precursors to the modern Aughar ascetics.
Mahalakshmi	The Goddess of abundance.
Mahamaya	It is believed that during the battle between the Gods on the one side and the demons or Asuras on the other, the king of Gods, Lord Indra fought against the mighty Mahishasur. In this great battle, the demon king overwhelmed Lord Indra, because of which the other gods decided to take cover and went straight to Lord Vishnu and Lord Shiva for protection. Both Lord Vishnu and Lord Shiva got angry at this cowardly act, and so they combined their powers to create 'Mahamaya', a goddess with all their good qualities. She was later called Durga or Mahamaya or Jagdambe or Jagatdhari and was responsible for the destruction of all the demons, including the powerful Mahishasur. (http://www.shubhyatra.com/htm/chattisgarh/mahamaya.htm)
Mahapurush	Great soul, great person.
Mahasaraswati	The *tantrashastra* which concerns itself with the subject of *parashakti* is called *saktatantra* and the same *parasakti* is known as Tripurasundari in the Tantra Shastras. All that was regulated in the world in three different manifestations was called Tripura and the collective energy of Brahma, Vishnu and Mahesh was known as Tripura or Shri Tripurasundari which is also known as Mahasaraswati. (http://www.koausa.org/Glimpses/Tantricism.html)
Mahatma	A great soul.
Mahesh	Shiva.
Maheshwar	Shiva.
Malang	A wandering seeker from Afghanistan.
Mantra	Sacred formula based on the principle that sound has a spiritual significance and power; incantation.

Mount Kailash	A mountain peak described in the ancient texts, believed, geographically to be in present day western Tibet. Mount Kailash is supposed to be the place where Shiva resides. And God Shiva is also supposed to be rather fond of intoxicants. Mount Kailash and Lake Manasarovar are sacred to both Hindus and Buddhists.
Mudra	Posture, gesture.
Muni	A saint or seeker in ancient India; a seeker in the Jain tradition.
Nanak	The first guru of the Sikh tradition, in the fifteenth century.
Narayan	Another name for Vishnu.
Navaratri	A nine-day Hindu festival devoted to the goddess Durga. The word Navaratri can be translated in two ways: a) Nine Nights, and b) New Nights. The proper noun 'Navaratri' denotes a festival where the Mother as creative energy is worshipped for nine days and nine nights.
Nirvana	Liberation, the state of absolute freedom or salvation.
Nisha	The night.
Om	The mantra '*aum*'; The sacred sound and symbol which represents Brahman in its unmanifest and manifest aspects.
Pandit	A person who is an expert in a subject. Sometimes, a priest in India.
Parameshwari	Another name for the Mother Goddess.
Paramahansa	An enlightened person, pure as a swan.
Paras	The philosopher's stone.
Parvati	The Goddess, the consort of God Shiva.
Pind-dan	Four balls of rice prepared on the twelfth day after someone has died to symbolize the union of the deceased with his or her forebears.
Piyush	Skt: nectar
Pran/prana	Breath or life-force.
Pranamayi	Mother or Shakti in the form of life-force within a living being.
Pranav	The vibrations produced by chanting Om.
Pranayama	Yogic control of the breath.
Pran-vayu	The life-breath.
Puja	Ritual worship, Hindu honour, respect or worship of a deity, flower offerings.

Punya-dan	Offering of good deeds in charity.
Puranas	Hindu texts.
Purashcharan	The act of wrapping up *japa* or other rituals.
Quran	Holy book of the Muslim faith.
Rajput	A person of the Rajput caste from Rajasthan, a Kshatriya.
Rama	Considered the seventh incarnation of God Vishnu, in the household of king Dasaratha, as the prince of the kingdom of Ayodhya in North India, as the hero of the epic *Ramayana*.
Ramayana	Hindu epic scripture dealing with the heroic exploits of Lord Rama.
Ravana	The demon villain of the epic *Ramayana*.
Rishi	An enlightened seer or sage, usually pertaining to ancient times.
Rudra	Terrible and wrathful form of Shiva.
Sadguru	An enlightened Guru.
Safal-Yoni	A book about how to worship the mother, published by Shri Sarveshwari Samooh, Varanasi.
Samadhi	A state of sensory non-consciousness, but of acute, all encompassing awareness. This is a state where the mind has been stilled, but awareness has become super-heightened. A person in *samadhi* experiences non-sensory divine bliss.
Samadhi-chitta	A state of being in absorption, bliss, trance.
Samooh	A society, a gathering.
Saptachandi	A scripture read during Navaratri.
Saraswati	The goddess of knowledge.
Sarveshwari	The mother of all beings.
Satsang	The act of spending time in good company, usually with realized saints.
Shaiva Avadhoot	An *awadhut* whose principle devotion is to God Shiva.
Shakta Avadhoot	An *awadhut* whose principle devotion is to the Goddess in her various forms.
Shakti	Power; the secret force permeating all creation. The female, form- giving, energy of creation and the leading transcendental symbol of Tantra and tantric rituals.
Shastra	A scripture in the Indian tradition.
Shiva	One of the Hindu trinity governing destruction and transcendence.
Shivaa, Shivâ	Feminine form of Shiva.

Shivaratri	Night of ritually worshipping Shiva and Parvati.
Shudra	The fourth of the Hindu four classes, traditionally the servant class.
Siddha	A person who has attained enlightenment, and with that all the magical spiritual powers ascribed to yogis.
Siddhi	Magical spiritual powers.
So'ham	A naturally occurring mantra that, with each breath, means "That I am". It is phrase that identifies one's own essential nature.
Sugriv	The monkey king in the epic *Ramayana*.
Swaha	Wife of the fire God, Agni. During *hawan* and *tarpan*, each oblation offered is accompanied at the end with the word, *swaha*.
Tandava	The dance of destruction that Shiva dances at the dissolution of the universe.
Tantra	One of a series of scriptures that emphasize practical ways of self- enlightenment, especially relating to the power of Shakti. A method of attainment of higher powers and spiritual flowering through the use of the physical powers endowed from sexual polarity. An organization; a system; a tapestry; a thread.
Tantric	A practitioner of tantra.
Tara	The Goddess in her role as saviour.
Tarpan	The act of performing oblations into water, instead of in fire, which is known as *havan*.
Tatsat	A mantra recited at the beginning of all auspicious tasks, especially rituals.
Ten senses	Five perception senses and five action senses. The perception senses are the eyes, the ears, the tongue, the skin and the nose. The action senses are the hands, the feet, the anus, the penis/vagina, and the mouth. And then the eleventh element in the body is consciousness. This consciousness, too, has four parts, namely, mind, intellect, conscience and ego.
Thir	Stable. In Buddhist tradition, a 'Thir' is a person of extreme stability and absolute enlightenment.
The three humours	The three *gunas*. Phlegm, bile, and wind are regarded as the three humours which are at the root of all physical maladies.
Tonsure	Ritual shaving of the head.
Tripurabhairavi	Tripurabhairavi is one of the ten tantric Mahavidyas. In another text, the English translation of the five limbs, or

panchanga, of the aspect of Goddess known as Bala Tripura; Bala means 'girl'. This aspect of the Red Goddess is the most highly erotic of Her three aspects. Bala is an adolescent girl, Tripurasundari a mother, and Tripurabhairavi a woman in whom menstruation has ceased. (http://www.hubcom.com/tantric/bala.htm)

Turiya — It is a state of spiritual enlightenment where the seeker gets detached from all his faculties. It is also the name given to god Brahma, as specified in the *Vayu Purana.*

twameva mata, cha pita twameva... A prayer to God, eulogizing God as mother, father, brother, friend, relative, knowledge, wealth, everything.

Uma, Uma Gauri — Consort of the male deity Shiva.

Urdhvagami — The words *urdhvareta* and *urdhvagami*, again, in yogic terminology refer to the rise of energy from the base of one's spine towards the crown of the head, rather than flowing down, as happens naturally.

Urdhvareta — A state of meditative practice where the polarity in the body is converted into vital energy, giving it an upward direction and opening higher powers of spirituality.

Vagishwari — Another name for the Goddess Saraswati.

Vaishnava Avadhoot — An Awadhut whose principal devotion is to Vishnu.

Vaishwanar — It is the fire that burns in the belly, and that accepts all oblations in the form of food put into this fire sacrifice. Vaishwanar is also a name for the cosmic God.

Vaishya — A person of the trader or merchant caste.

Vama — The left-handed path of Tantra.

Vamachar — Practices of the left handed path.

Varna system/ Varnashram The fourfold system of dividing the population into Brahmin, Kshatriya, Vaishya and Shudras.

Veda — Ancient sacred texts of the Hindus.

Vermilion — A red powder, derived from the sap of the vermilion tree, used to put red dot marks on the forehead after rituals, and by married Hindu women every day.

Vibhishana — Brother of the villain Ravana of the epic *Ramayana*. Vibhishana had parted company with his brother to aid Rama in his fight against his brother.

Vibhuti — Ritual ashes, applied to the forehead.

Visarjan — The act of dissolution at the completion of a ritual.

Vishnu	God or form of the Hindu trinity governing preservation. Often, Vishnu is depicted with four arms.
Vrat	1) to perform ritual fast. 2) To make a strong willed determination or resolve to complete a task.
Yamraj/Yama	God of Death; ruler of the realm of the dead.
Yantra	Geometrical aids for meditation.
Yoga	techniques of developing and integrating energy; discipline or 'yoking' of the senses and the ego.
Yogi	Practitioner of Yoga.
Yogini	A female seeker with great spiritual powers.

A Few Prominent Places Associated with Aghoreshwar Mahaprabhu Baba Bhagwan Ram

Aghor Peeth Shri Sarveshwari Samooh Sansthan Devasthanam
Parao, P.O. Kusht Sewa Ashram
Varanasi — 221102
Uttar Pradesh, India

Aghoracharya Baba Kinaram Aghor Shodh Evam Sewa Sansthan
Baba Kinaram Sthal, Krin Kund
Shivala
Varanasi — 221105
Uttar Pradesh, India

Brahmanishthalaya
Sogra (Jashpur Nagar)
District Raigarh
Madhya Pradesh, India

Aghor Gurupeeth Trust, Banora
Village & Post Office Banora
Raigarh
Madhya Pradesh, India

Sri Sarveshwari Samooh
P.O. Box 950
Sonoma, Ca 95476
USA

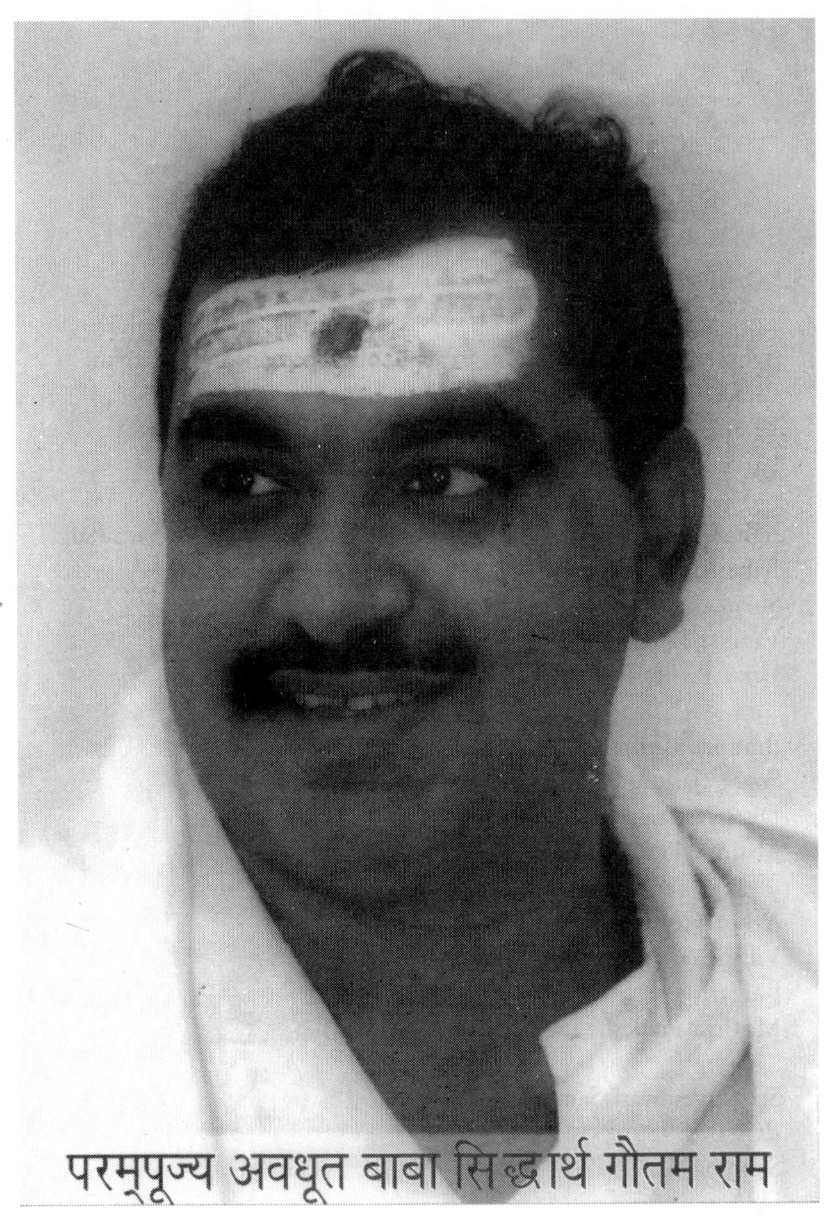

Pujya Avadhut Baba Siddharta Gautam Ram,
11th Peethadishwar, Aghoracharya, Baba Kinaram Sthal

Other books of related interest
published by **Indica Books**:

- **A Journey in the World of the Tantras**
  by Mark S.G. Dyczkowski

- **The Goddess and the Slave**
  The Fakir, the Mother and Maldevelopment
  by Rudrani Fakir

- **My Days with Sri Ma Anandamayi**
  by Bithika Mukerji

- **Death Must Die**
  by Ram Alexander

- **श्री रमण महर्षि का उपदेश : अपनी सहज अवस्था में रहिये**
  (*"Be As You Are. The Teachings of Sri Ramana Maharshi"*)
  सम्पादक *डेविड गॉडमेन*

Distributed by **Indica Books**:

- **Fundamentals of the Philosophy of Tantra**
  by Manoranjan Basu

- **Anandamayi. Her Life and Wisdom**
  photographic book by Richard Lannoy